B.P.R.D. HELL ON EARTH:
THE DEVIL'S WINGS

created by MIKE MIGNOLA

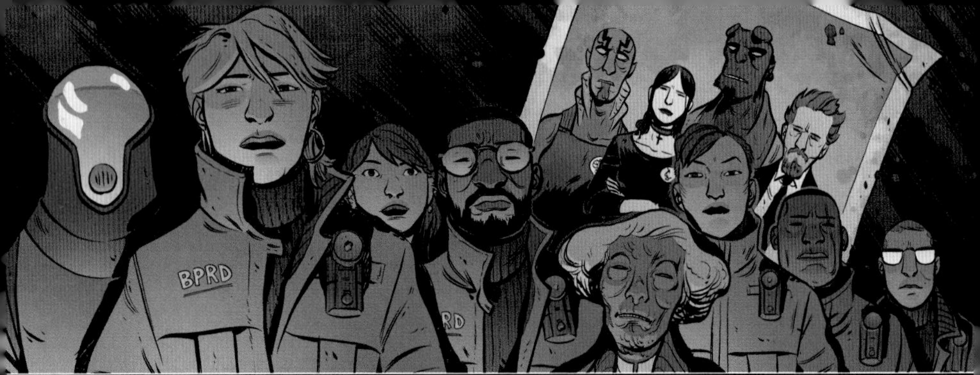
BPRD

When the Black Flame attempted to raise a new race of man, Liz Sherman lit a fire that nearly cracked the world in two in order to destroy him. With Zinco's resurrection of a new and even more powerful Black Flame, Kate Corrigan finds herself in charge of a Bureau facing a worldwide crisis and the new threats that continue to crawl out of the earth, while Agent Abe Sapien remains AWOL

MIKE MIGNOLA'S

B.P.R.D. HELL ON EARTH

THE DEVIL'S WINGS

story by **MIKE MIGNOLA** and **JOHN ARCUDI**

The Devil's Wings art by **LAURENCE CAMPBELL**

The Broken Equation art by **JOE QUERIO**

Grind art by **TYLER CROOK**

colors by **DAVE STEWART**

letters by **CLEM ROBINS**

cover art by **RYAN SOOK**

series cover art by **LAURENCE CAMPBELL**
with **DAVE STEWART**

editor **SCOTT ALLIE**   associate editor **DANIEL CHABON**

assistant editor **SHANTEL LAROCQUE**   collection designer **AMY ARENDTS**

publisher **MIKE RICHARDSON**

DARK HORSE BOOKS

Mike Richardson PRESIDENT AND PUBLISHER · Neil Hankerson EXECUTIVE VICE PRESIDENT
Tom Weddle CHIEF FINANCIAL OFFICER · Randy Stradley VICE PRESIDENT OF PUBLISHING
Michael Martens VICE PRESIDENT OF BOOK TRADE SALES · Scott Allie EDITOR IN CHIEF
Matt Parkinson VICE PRESIDENT OF MARKETING · David Scroggy VICE PRESIDENT
OF PRODUCT DEVELOPMENT · Dale LaFountain VICE PRESIDENT OF INFORMATION
TECHNOLOGY · Darlene Vogel SENIOR DIRECTOR OF PRINT, DESIGN, AND PRODUCTION
Ken Lizzi GENERAL COUNSEL · Davey Estrada EDITORIAL DIRECTOR · Chris Warner SENIOR
BOOKS EDITOR · Diana Schutz EXECUTIVE EDITOR · Cary Grazzini DIRECTOR OF PRINT AND
DEVELOPMENT · Lia Ribacchi ART DIRECTOR · Cara Niece DIRECTOR OF SCHEDULING
Mark Bernardi DIRECTOR OF DIGITAL PUBLISHING

DarkHorse.com   Hellboy.com

B.P.R.D.™ Hell on Earth Volume 10: The Devil's Wings

This book collects B.P.R.D. Hell on Earth #120–#124.

Published by Dark Horse Books
A division of Dark Horse Comics, Inc.
10956 SE Main Street
Milwaukie, OR 97222

International Licensing: (503) 905-2377

First edition: February 2015
ISBN 978-1-61655-617-4

10 9 8 7 6 5 4 3 2 1
Printed in China

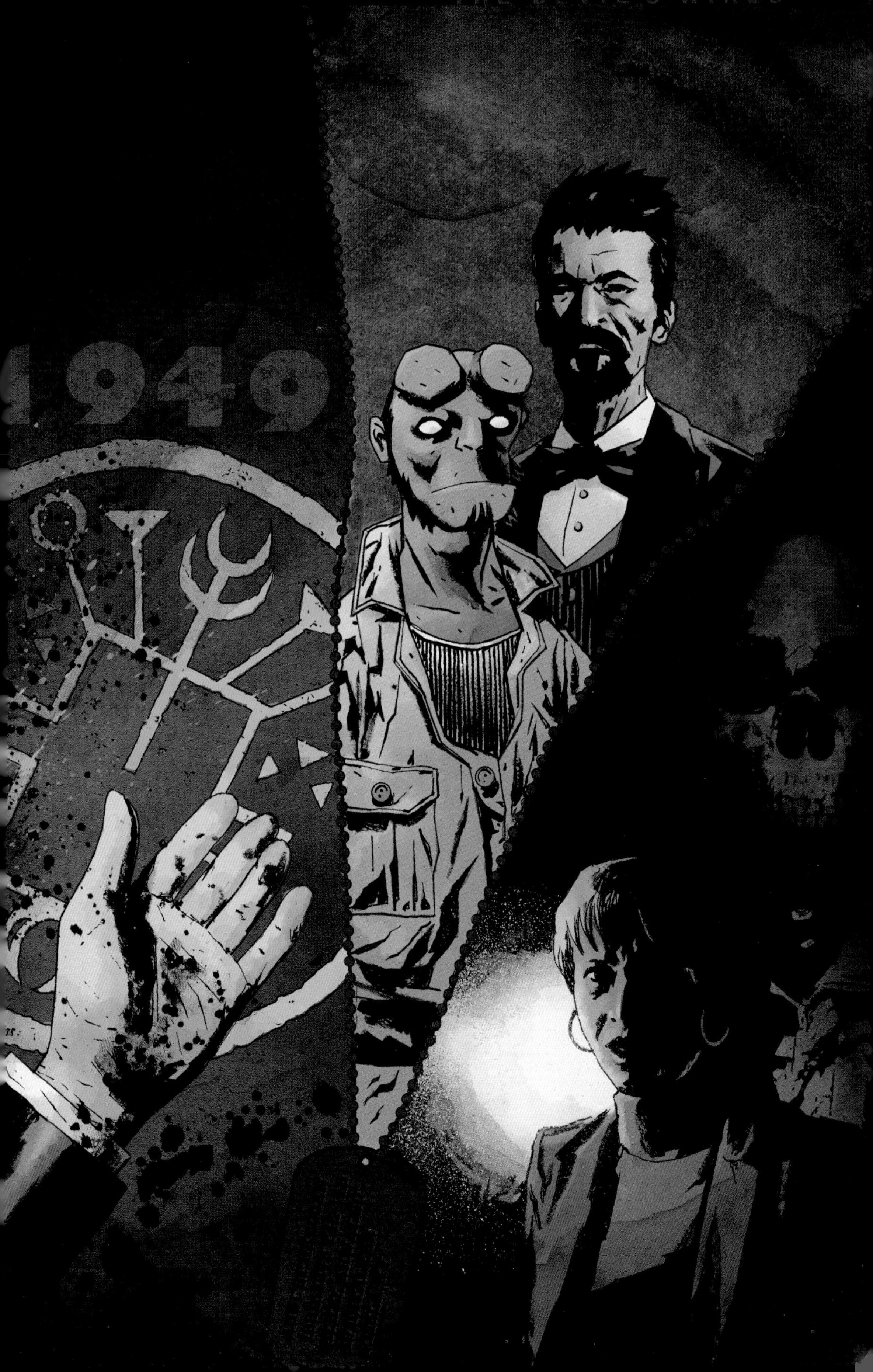
1949

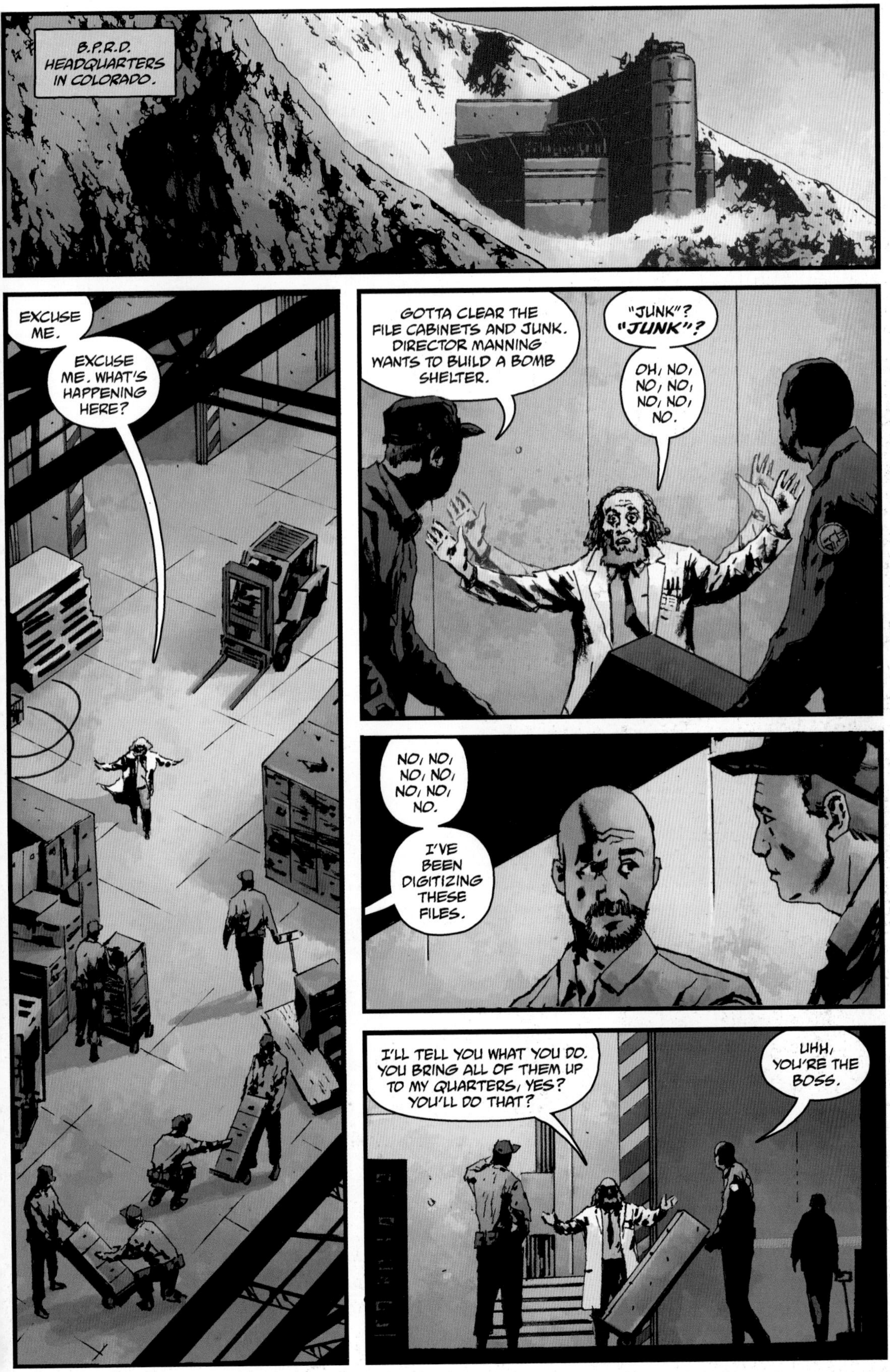
B.P.R.D. HEADQUARTERS IN COLORADO.
EXCUSE ME.
EXCUSE ME. WHAT'S HAPPENING HERE?
GOTTA CLEAR THE FILE CABINETS AND JUNK. DIRECTOR MANNING WANTS TO BUILD A BOMB SHELTER.
"JUNK"? "JUNK"?
OH, NO, NO, NO, NO, NO, NO.
NO, NO, NO, NO, NO, NO, NO.
I'VE BEEN DIGITIZING THESE FILES.
I'LL TELL YOU WHAT YOU DO. YOU BRING ALL OF THEM UP TO MY QUARTERS, YES? YOU'LL DO THAT?
UHH, YOU'RE THE BOSS.

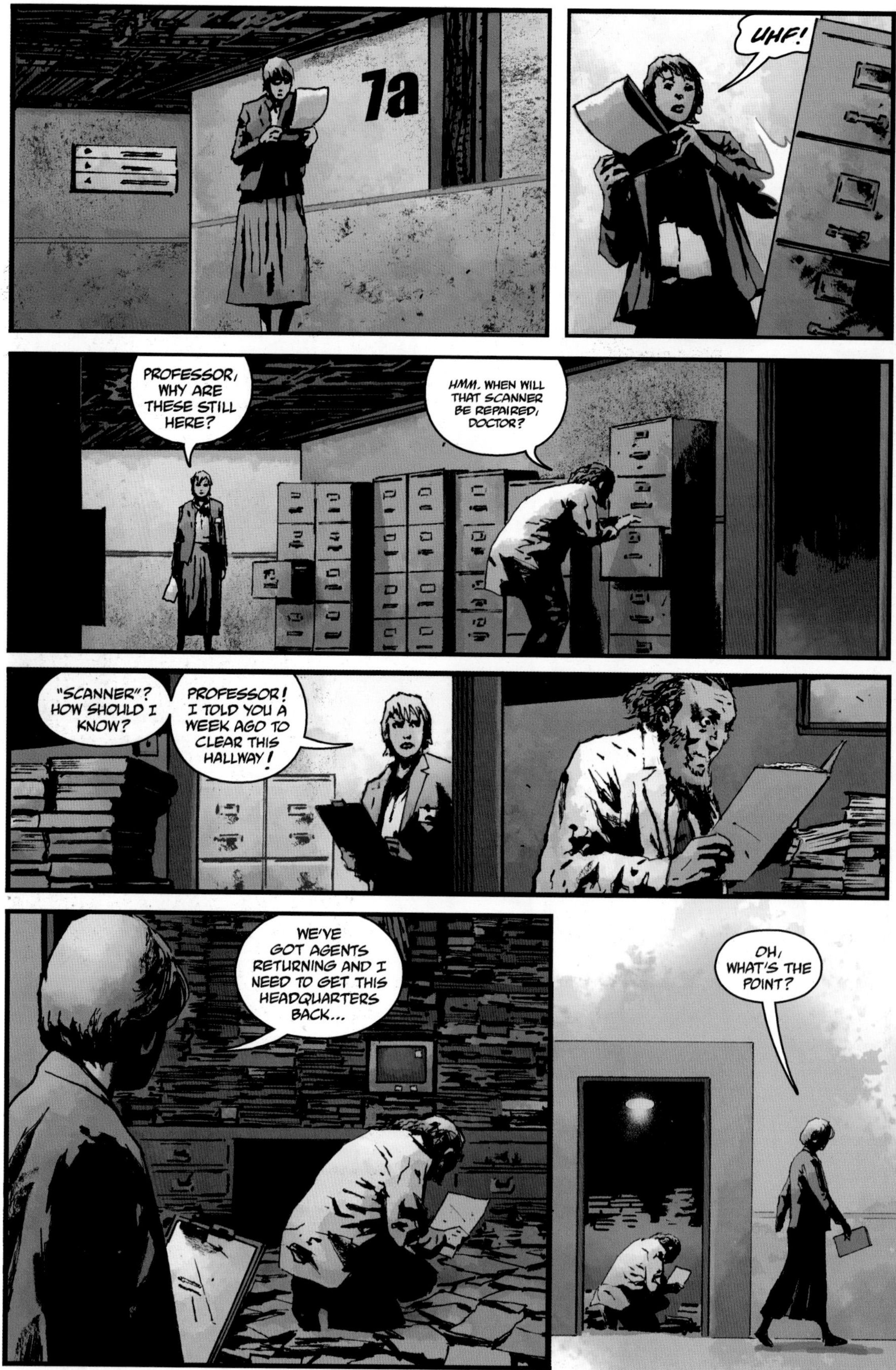
UHF!
PROFESSOR, WHY ARE THESE STILL HERE?
HMM. WHEN WILL THAT SCANNER BE REPAIRED, DOCTOR?
"SCANNER"? HOW SHOULD I KNOW?
PROFESSOR! I TOLD YOU A WEEK AGO TO CLEAR THIS HALLWAY!
WE'VE GOT AGENTS RETURNING AND I NEED TO GET THIS HEADQUARTERS BACK...
OH, WHAT'S THE POINT?

AH, GOOD DAY, KATHERINE. ELIZABETH, CARLA, AND FENIX AREN'T IN YET, IF THAT'S WHY YOU'RE HERE.

I JUST HOPE LIZ ISN'T IN A WHEELCHAIR ANYMORE. SHE'LL NEVER GET THROUGH THOSE HALLS.

WHAT'S THIS? DOESN'T LOOK LIKE A NEWS FEED.

JOHANN HAS ENLISTED A NEWS TEAM IN JAPAN TO TRANSMIT DIRECTLY TO US.

I DON'T EVEN WANT TO KNOW HOW ALL THAT WAS MANAGED.

TO BE FAIR, IT'S A GENUINELY GOOD IDEA-- IN THEORY, ANY-WAY. SO FAR, IT HASN'T QUITE--

HELLO? I THINK THEY'VE SAID YOU SHOULD BE RECEIVING ME.

OH!

YES, JOHANN. WE ARE. WE HAVE VIDEO, ALSO.

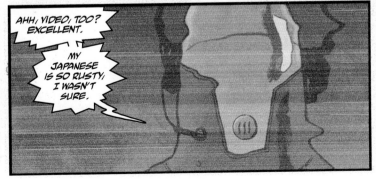

AHH, VIDEO, TOO? EXCELLENT.

MY JAPANESE IS SO RUSTY, I WASN'T SURE.

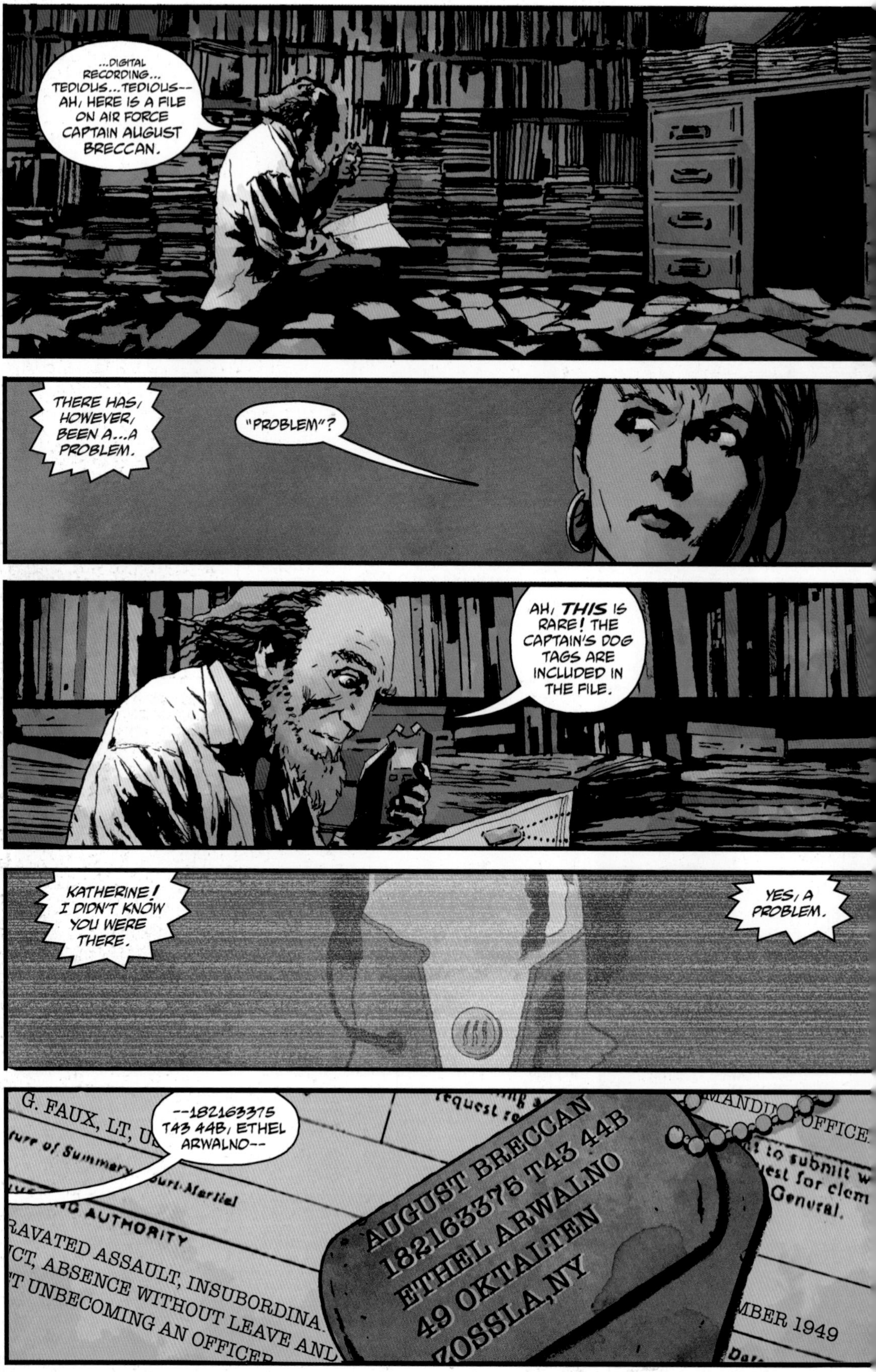
...DIGITAL RECORDING... TEDIOUS...TEDIOUS--AH, HERE IS A FILE ON AIR FORCE CAPTAIN AUGUST BRECCAN.
THERE HAS, HOWEVER, BEEN A...A PROBLEM.
"PROBLEM"?
AH, THIS IS RARE! THE CAPTAIN'S DOG TAGS ARE INCLUDED IN THE FILE.
KATHERINE! I DIDN'T KNOW YOU WERE THERE.
YES, A PROBLEM.
--182163375 T43 44B, ETHEL ARWALNO--
AUGUST BRECCAN
182163375 T43 44B
ETHEL ARWALNO
49 OKTALTEN
ZOSSLA, NY
G. FAUX, LT, U
AUTHORITY
RAVATED ASSAULT, INSUBORDINA
CT, ABSENCE WITHOUT LEAVE AND
T UNBECOMING AN OFFICER
MBER 1949

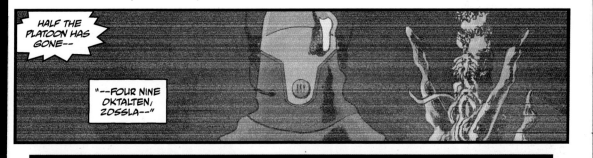

HALF THE PLATOON HAS GONE--

"--FOUR NINE OKTALTEN, ZOSSLA--"

ZEENK

SON OF A...

ANOTHER DAMN POWER OUTAGE?! REALLY?

PANYA, DO WE STILL HAVE RADIO CONTACT WITH MAINTENANCE?

PANYA?

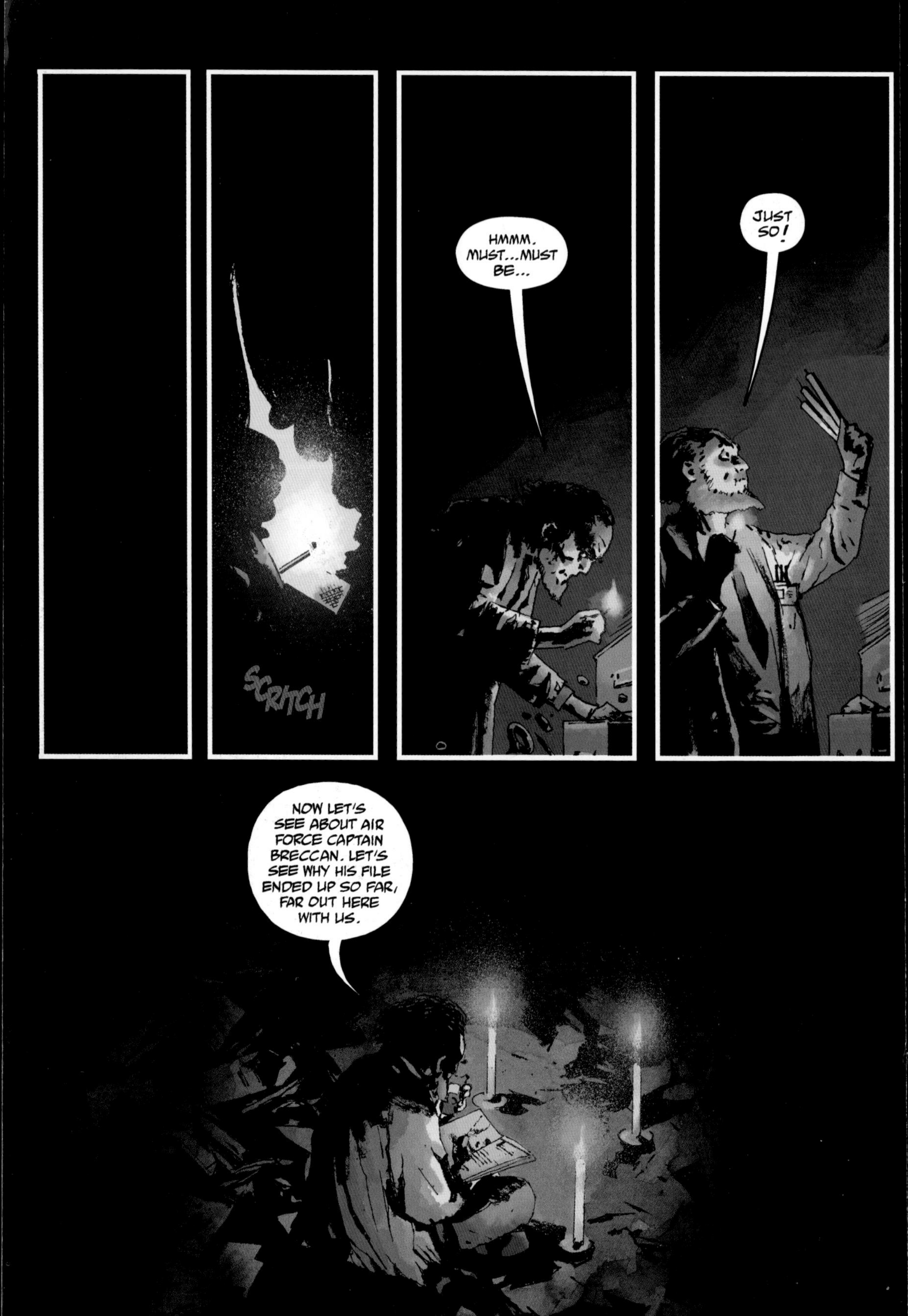
SCRITCH
HMMM. MUST...MUST BE...
JUST SO!
NOW LET'S SEE ABOUT AIR FORCE CAPTAIN BRECCAN. LET'S SEE WHY HIS FILE ENDED UP SO FAR, FAR OUT HERE WITH US.

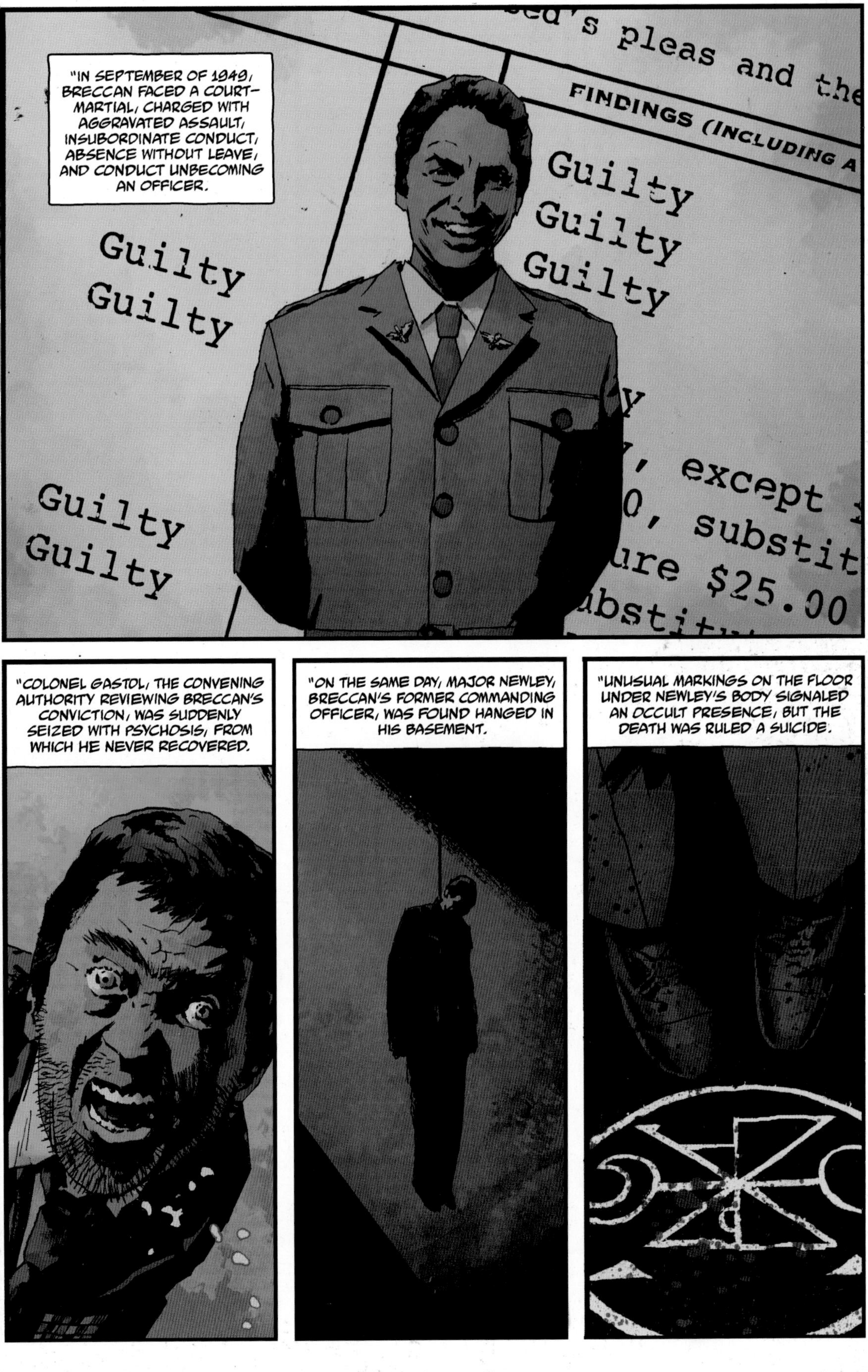
"IN SEPTEMBER OF 1949, BRECCAN FACED A COURT-MARTIAL, CHARGED WITH AGGRAVATED ASSAULT, INSUBORDINATE CONDUCT, ABSENCE WITHOUT LEAVE, AND CONDUCT UNBECOMING AN OFFICER.
pleas and the
FINDINGS
Guilty
Guilty
Guilty
Guilty
Guilty
Guilty
Guilty
except
substit
$25.00
"COLONEL GASTOL, THE CONVENING AUTHORITY REVIEWING BRECCAN'S CONVICTION, WAS SUDDENLY SEIZED WITH PSYCHOSIS, FROM WHICH HE NEVER RECOVERED.
"ON THE SAME DAY, MAJOR NEWLEY, BRECCAN'S FORMER COMMANDING OFFICER, WAS FOUND HANGED IN HIS BASEMENT.
"UNUSUAL MARKINGS ON THE FLOOR UNDER NEWLEY'S BODY SIGNALED AN OCCULT PRESENCE, BUT THE DEATH WAS RULED A SUICIDE.

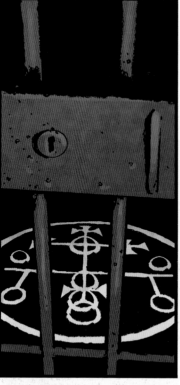

"CAPTAIN BRECCAN'S MIRACULOUS ESCAPE, HOWEVER, RAISED CONCERNS AIR FORCE OFFICIALS COULD NOT IGNORE.

"SECRETARY OF DEFENSE JOHNSON SUGGESTED A CONSULTATION WITH THE BUREAU FOR PARANORMAL RESEARCH AND DEFENSE.

"THE AIR FORCE'S SKEPTICISM WAS BRUSHED ASIDE BY JOHNSON, WHO, DURING THE WAR, HAD BEFRIENDED THE BUREAU'S DIRECTOR--

"--PROFESSOR TREVOR BRUTTENHOLM."

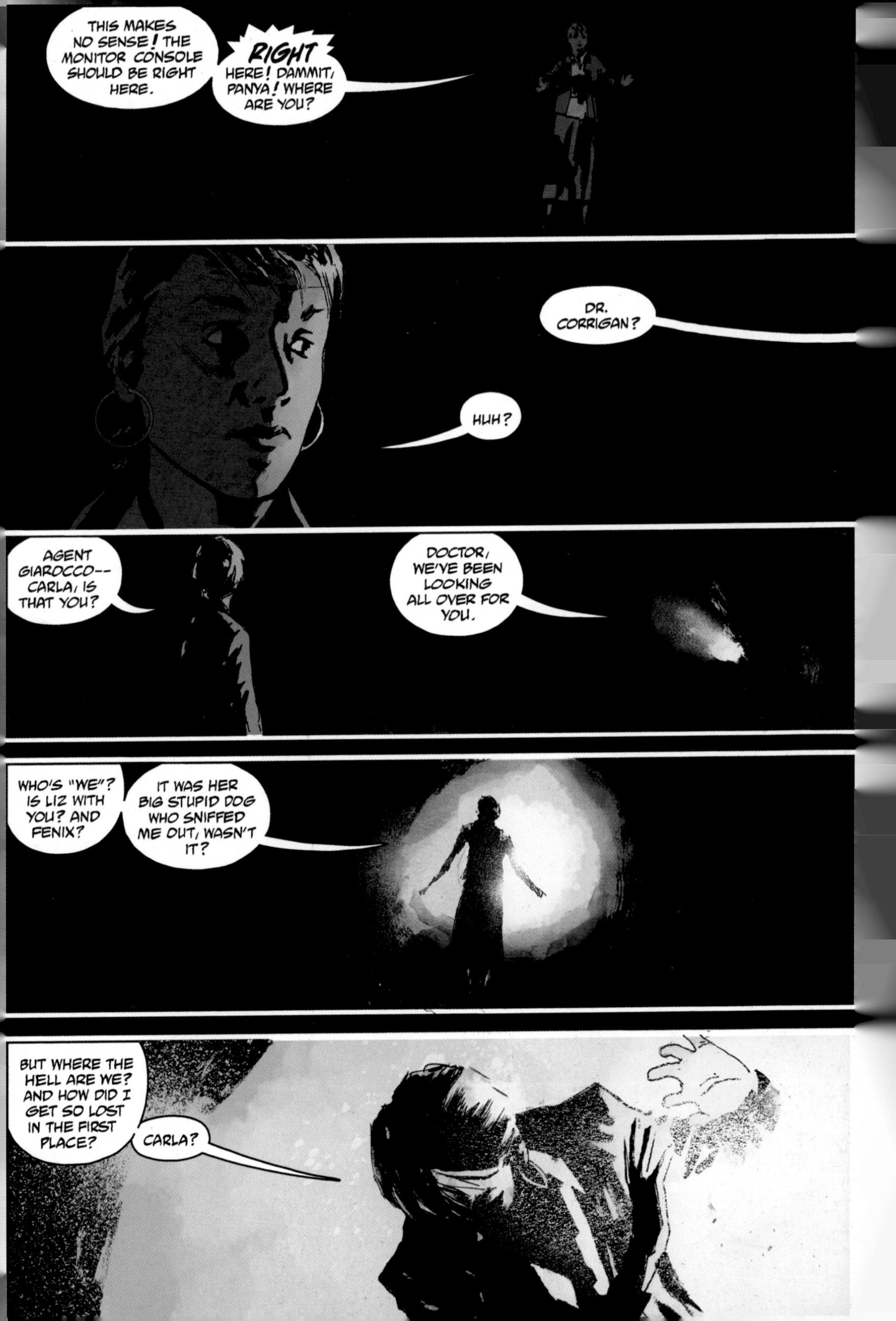
THIS MAKES NO SENSE! THE MONITOR CONSOLE SHOULD BE RIGHT HERE.
RIGHT HERE! DAMMIT, PANYA! WHERE ARE YOU?
DR. CORRIGAN?
HUH?
AGENT GIAROCCO--CARLA, IS THAT YOU?
DOCTOR, WE'VE BEEN LOOKING ALL OVER FOR YOU.
WHO'S "WE"? IS LIZ WITH YOU? AND FENIX?
IT WAS HER BIG STUPID DOG WHO SNIFFED ME OUT, WASN'T IT?
BUT WHERE THE HELL ARE WE? AND HOW DID I GET SO LOST IN THE FIRST PLACE?
CARLA?

GAH!

WHAT...

WHAT THE HELL...?

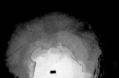

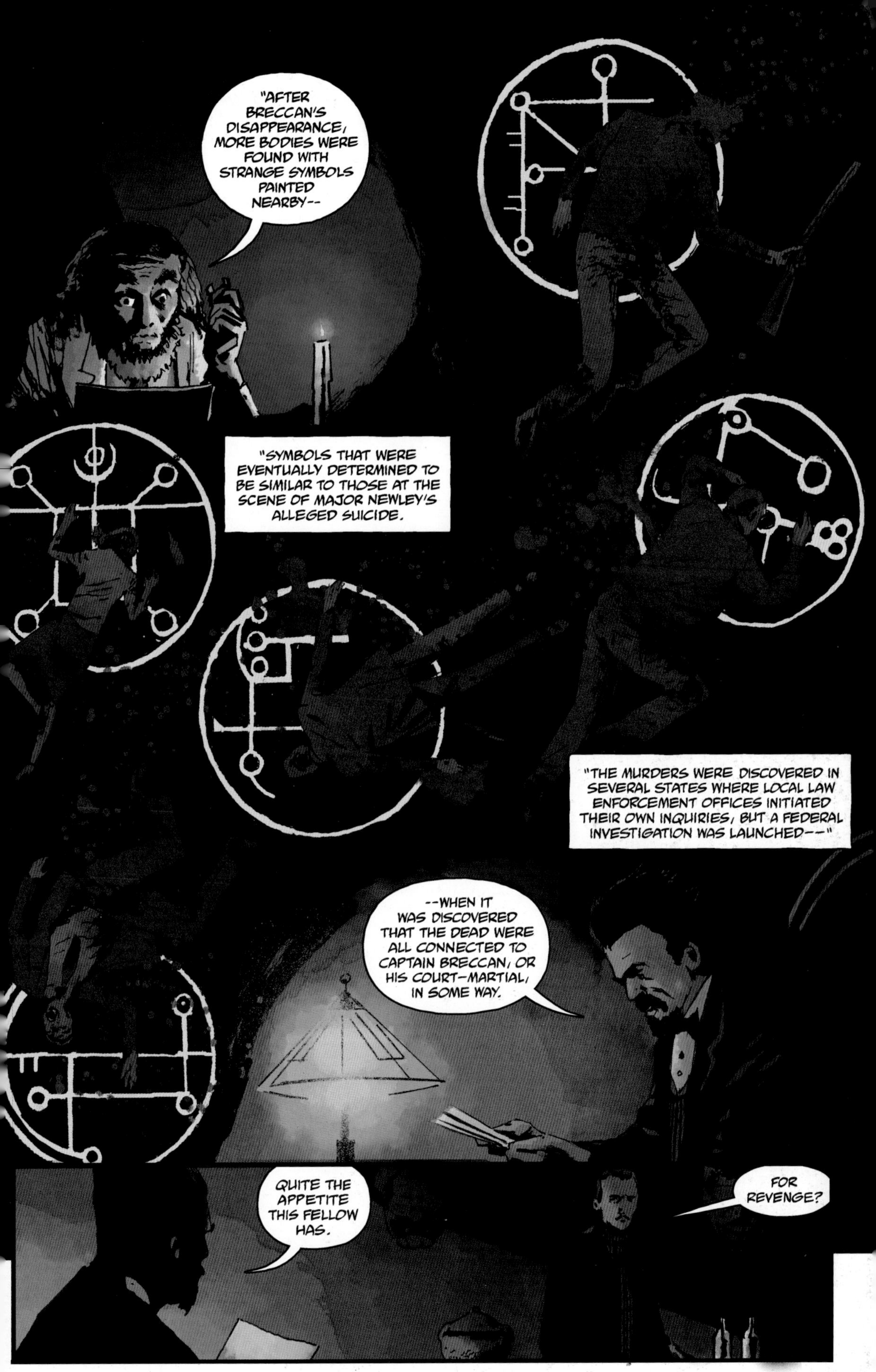
"AFTER BRECCAN'S DISAPPEARANCE, MORE BODIES WERE FOUND WITH STRANGE SYMBOLS PAINTED NEARBY--
"SYMBOLS THAT WERE EVENTUALLY DETERMINED TO BE SIMILAR TO THOSE AT THE SCENE OF MAJOR NEWLEY'S ALLEGED SUICIDE.
"THE MURDERS WERE DISCOVERED IN SEVERAL STATES WHERE LOCAL LAW ENFORCEMENT OFFICES INITIATED THEIR OWN INQUIRIES, BUT A FEDERAL INVESTIGATION WAS LAUNCHED--"
--WHEN IT WAS DISCOVERED THAT THE DEAD WERE ALL CONNECTED TO CAPTAIN BRECCAN, OR HIS COURT-MARTIAL, IN SOME WAY.
QUITE THE APPETITE THIS FELLOW HAS.
FOR REVENGE?

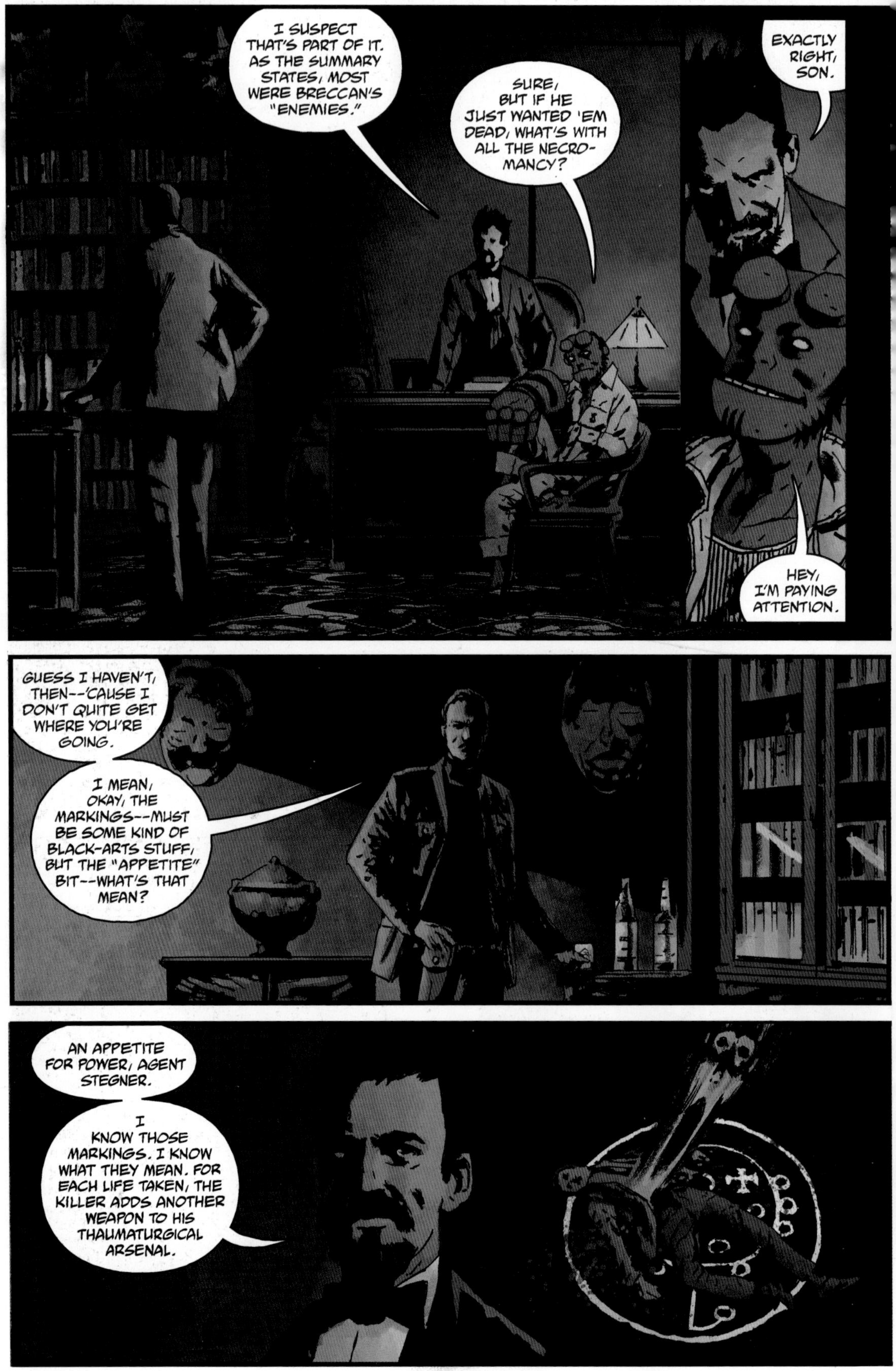
I SUSPECT THAT'S PART OF IT. AS THE SUMMARY STATES, MOST WERE BRECCAN'S "ENEMIES."
SURE, BUT IF HE JUST WANTED 'EM DEAD, WHAT'S WITH ALL THE NECRO-MANCY?
EXACTLY RIGHT, SON.
HEY, I'M PAYING ATTENTION.
GUESS I HAVEN'T, THEN--'CAUSE I DON'T QUITE GET WHERE YOU'RE GOING.
I MEAN, OKAY, THE MARKINGS--MUST BE SOME KIND OF BLACK-ARTS STUFF, BUT THE "APPETITE" BIT--WHAT'S THAT MEAN?
AN APPETITE FOR POWER, AGENT STEGNER.
I KNOW THOSE MARKINGS. I KNOW WHAT THEY MEAN. FOR EACH LIFE TAKEN, THE KILLER ADDS ANOTHER WEAPON TO HIS THAUMATURGICAL ARSENAL.

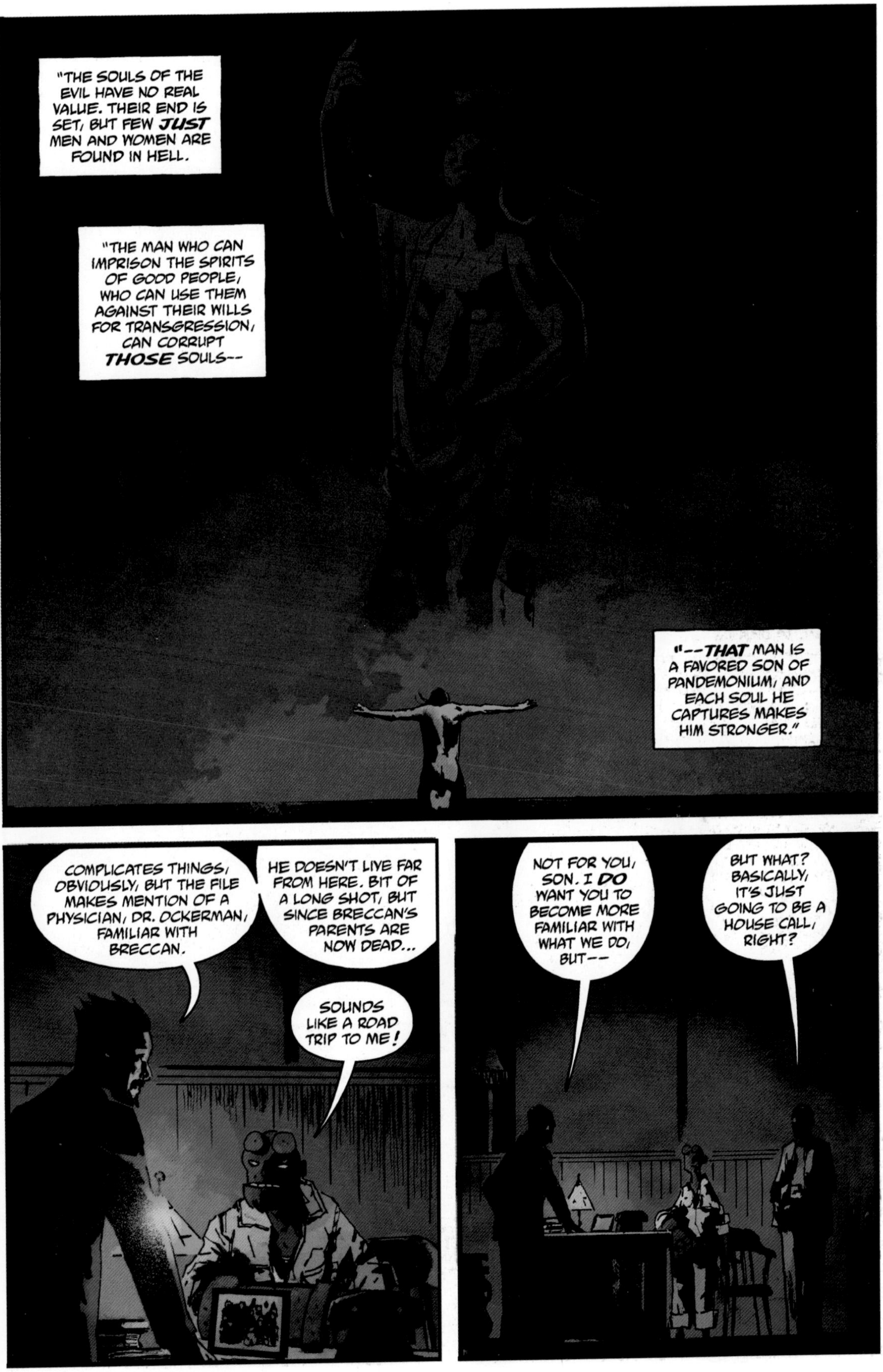
"THE SOULS OF THE EVIL HAVE NO REAL VALUE. THEIR END IS SET, BUT FEW JUST MEN AND WOMEN ARE FOUND IN HELL.
"THE MAN WHO CAN IMPRISON THE SPIRITS OF GOOD PEOPLE, WHO CAN USE THEM AGAINST THEIR WILLS FOR TRANSGRESSION, CAN CORRUPT THOSE SOULS--
"--THAT MAN IS A FAVORED SON OF PANDEMONIUM, AND EACH SOUL HE CAPTURES MAKES HIM STRONGER."
COMPLICATES THINGS, OBVIOUSLY, BUT THE FILE MAKES MENTION OF A PHYSICIAN, DR. OCKERMAN, FAMILIAR WITH BRECCAN.
HE DOESN'T LIVE FAR FROM HERE. BIT OF A LONG SHOT, BUT SINCE BRECCAN'S PARENTS ARE NOW DEAD...
SOUNDS LIKE A ROAD TRIP TO ME!
NOT FOR YOU, SON. I DO WANT YOU TO BECOME MORE FAMILIAR WITH WHAT WE DO, BUT--
BUT WHAT? BASICALLY, IT'S JUST GOING TO BE A HOUSE CALL, RIGHT?

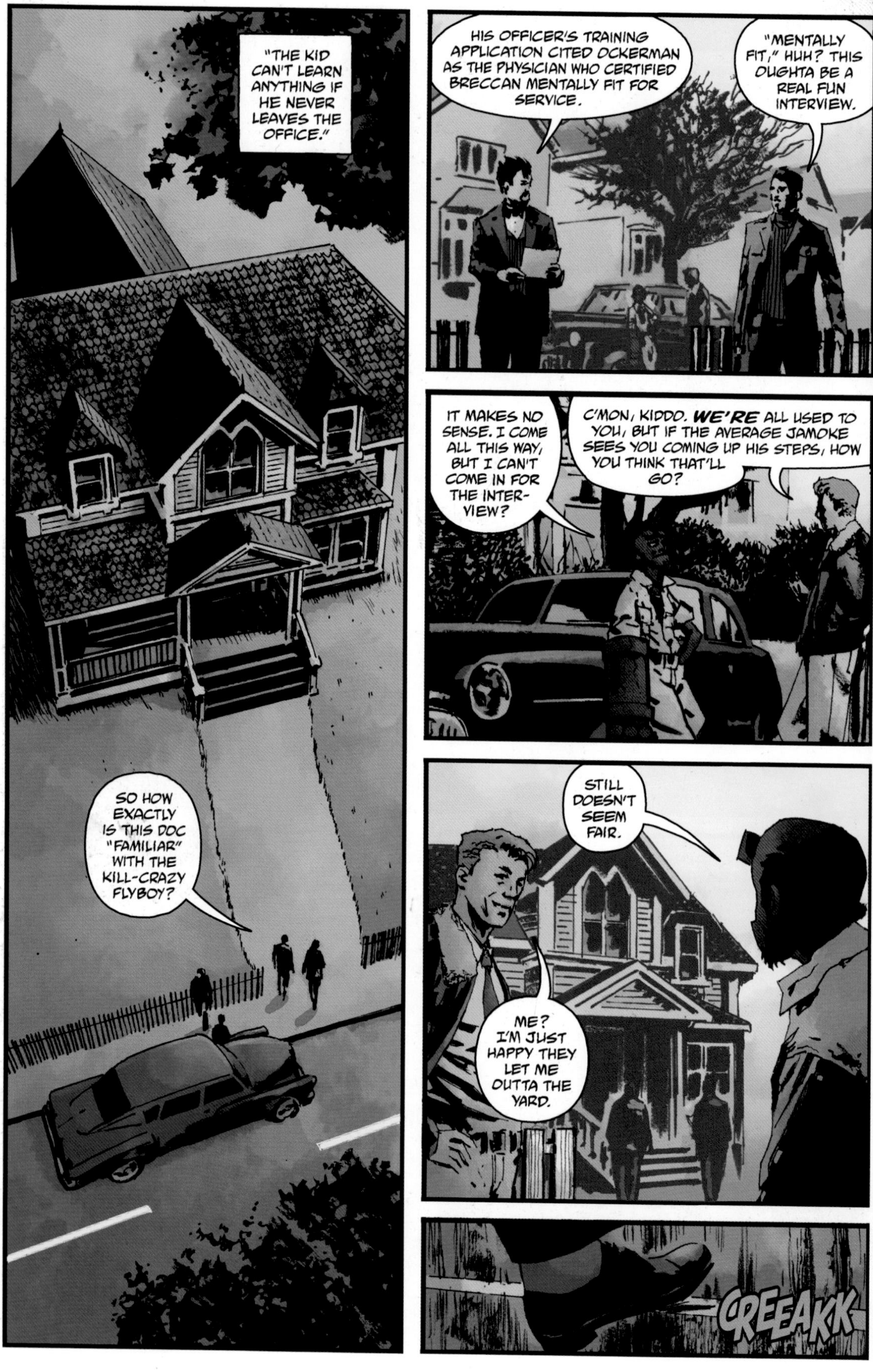
"THE KID CAN'T LEARN ANYTHING IF HE NEVER LEAVES THE OFFICE."
SO HOW EXACTLY IS THIS DOC "FAMILIAR" WITH THE KILL-CRAZY FLYBOY?
HIS OFFICER'S TRAINING APPLICATION CITED OCKERMAN AS THE PHYSICIAN WHO CERTIFIED BRECCAN MENTALLY FIT FOR SERVICE.
"MENTALLY FIT," HUH? THIS OUGHTA BE A REAL FUN INTERVIEW.
IT MAKES NO SENSE. I COME ALL THIS WAY, BUT I CAN'T COME IN FOR THE INTER-VIEW?
C'MON, KIDDO. WE'RE ALL USED TO YOU, BUT IF THE AVERAGE JAMOKE SEES YOU COMING UP HIS STEPS, HOW YOU THINK THAT'LL GO?
STILL DOESN'T SEEM FAIR.
ME? I'M JUST HAPPY THEY LET ME OUTTA THE YARD.
CREEAKK

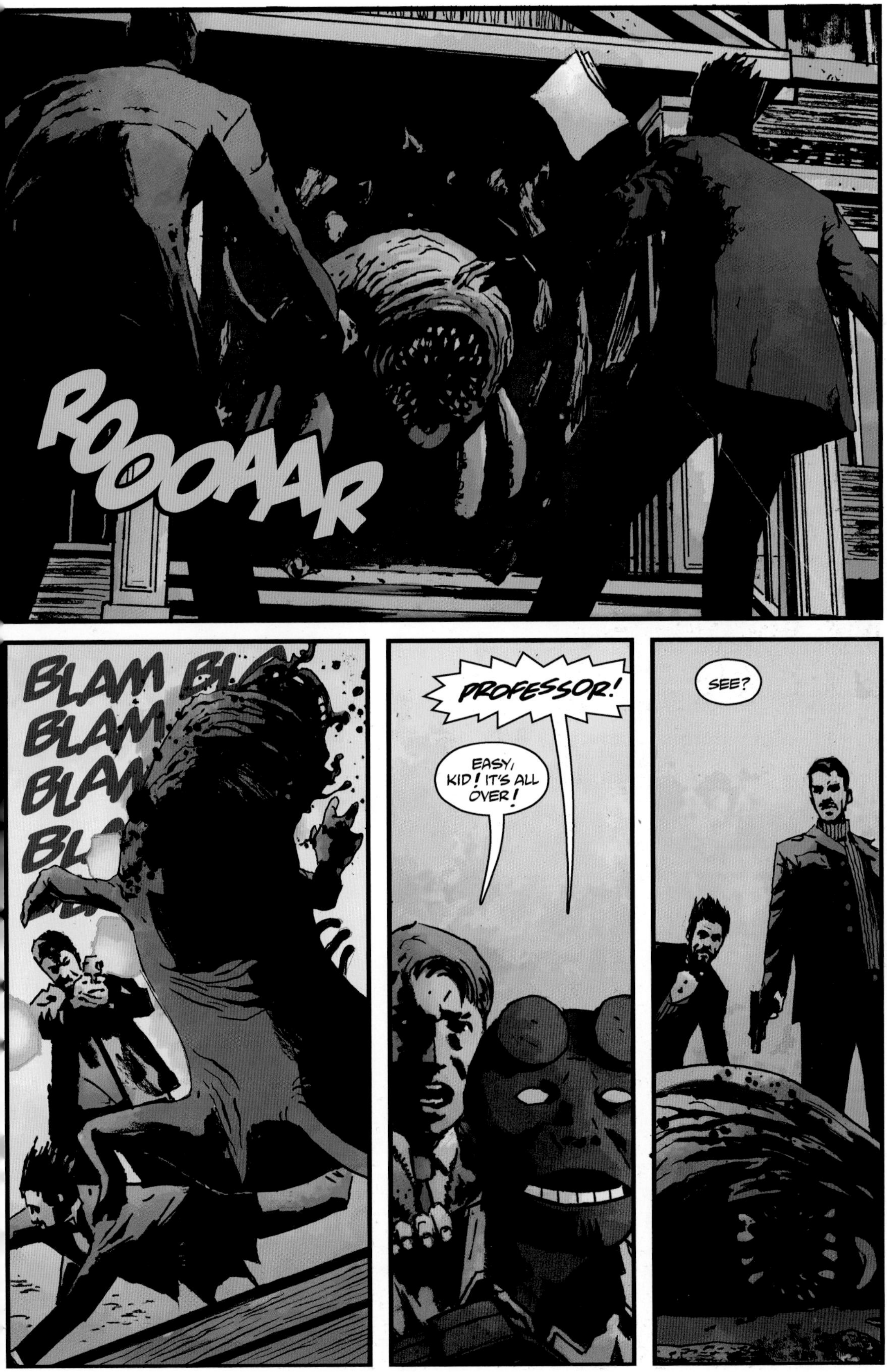
ROOOAAR
BLAM BLA
BLAM
BLAM
BLA
PROFESSOR!
EASY, KID! IT'S ALL OVER!
SEE?

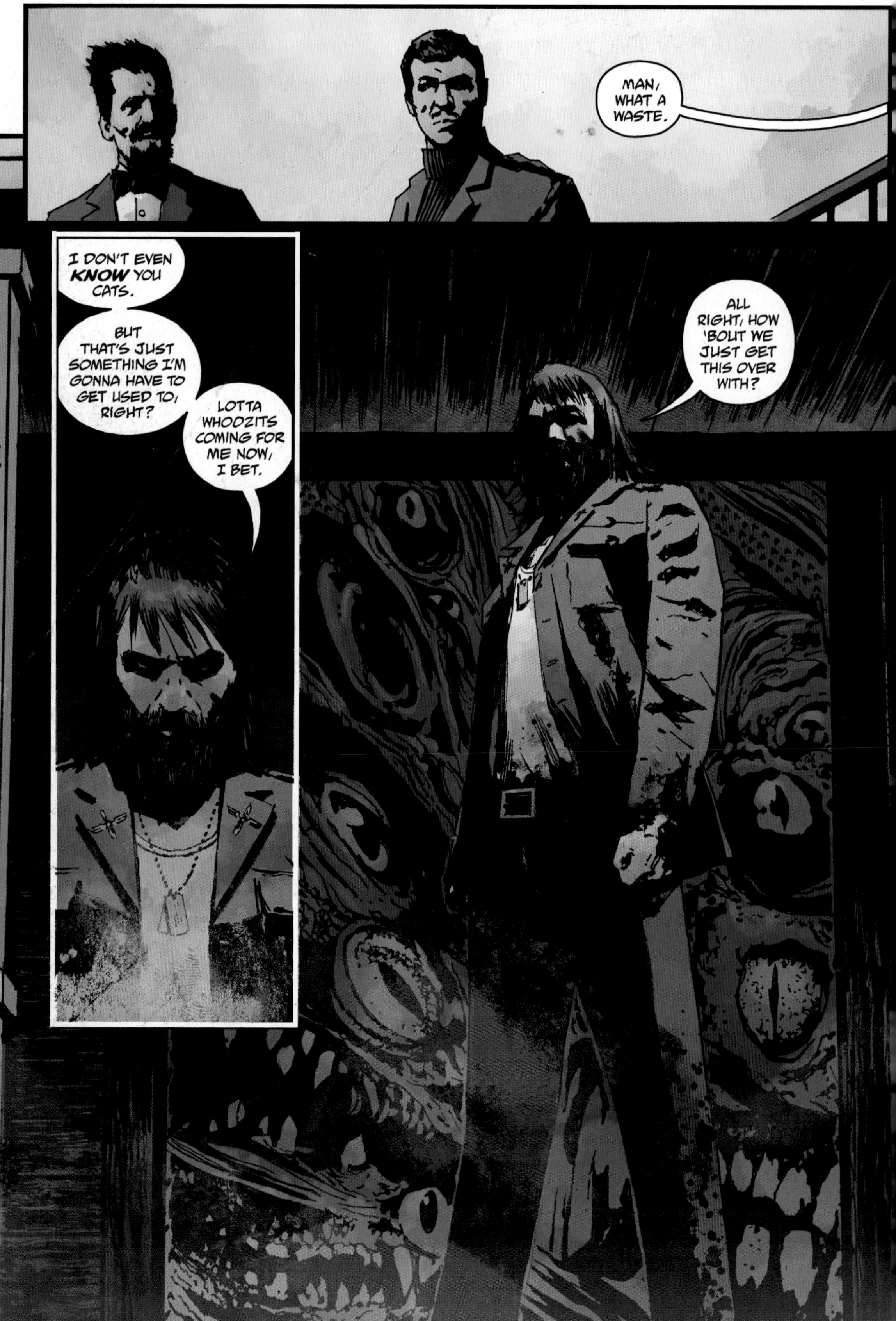
MAN, WHAT A WASTE.
I DON'T EVEN KNOW YOU CATS.
BUT THAT'S JUST SOMETHING I'M GONNA HAVE TO GET USED TO, RIGHT?
LOTTA WHOOZITS COMING FOR ME NOW, I BET.
ALL RIGHT, HOW 'BOUT WE JUST GET THIS OVER WITH?

I KNOW YOU.

PROJECT "SLEDGEHAMMER" IN DRYDOCK. YOU'RE PARKED DOWN IN THE SECOND SUB-BASEMENT.

WHICH MEANS *I'M* IN THE SECOND SUB-BASEMENT. AND JUST HOW DID THAT--?

OKAY, CORRIGAN, GET A GRIP. WEIRDER THINGS HAVE HAPPENED TO YOU BEFORE. JUST FIND THE ELEVATOR, GET OUT OF HERE, AND *THEN* YOU CAN FREAK OUT.

EXCEPT... WE DON'T HAVE ANY POWER.

?

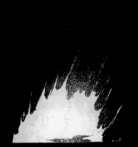

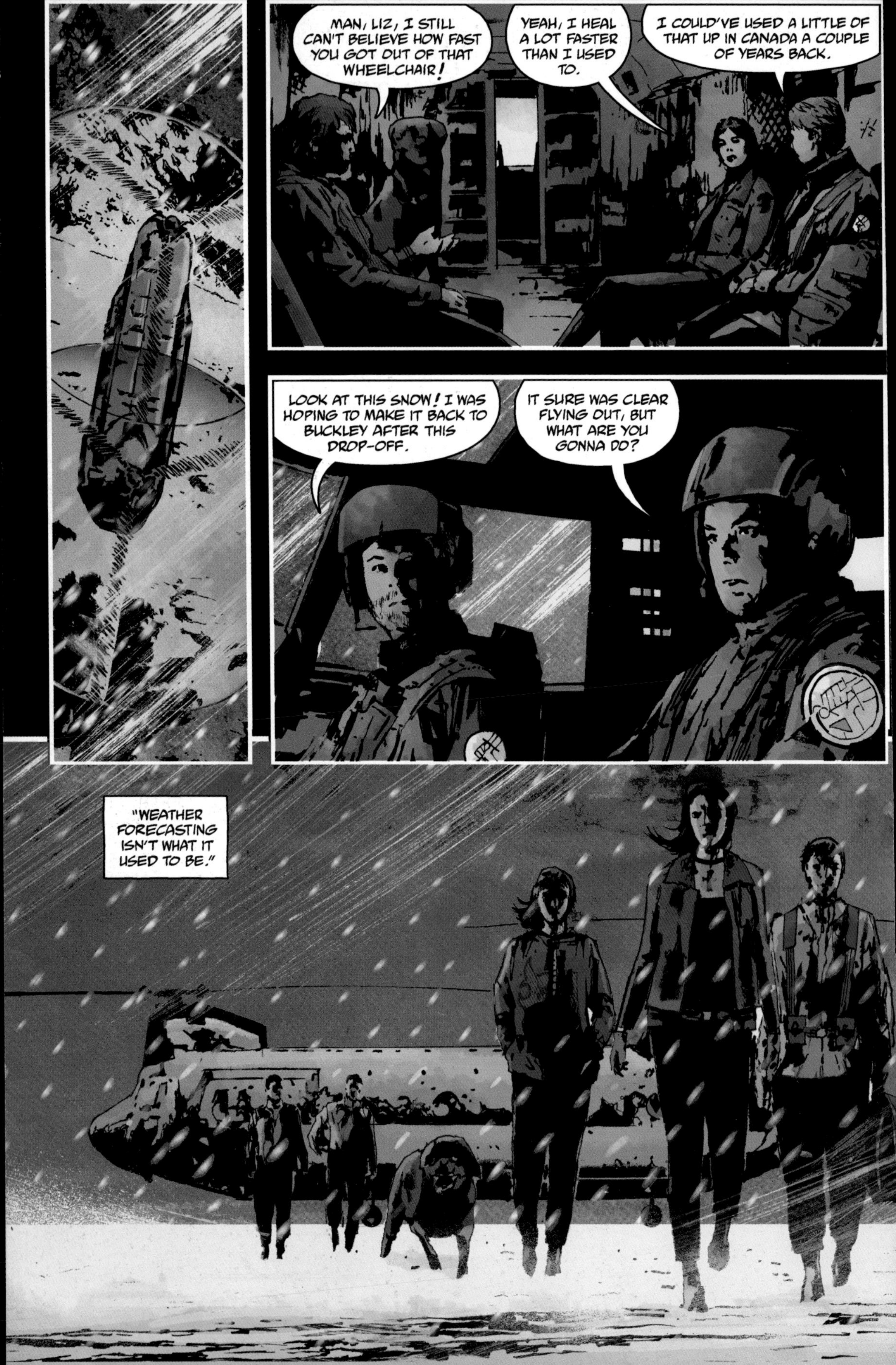
MAN, LIZ, I STILL CAN'T BELIEVE HOW FAST YOU GOT OUT OF THAT WHEELCHAIR!
YEAH, I HEAL A LOT FASTER THAN I USED TO.
I COULD'VE USED A LITTLE OF THAT UP IN CANADA A COUPLE OF YEARS BACK.
LOOK AT THIS SNOW! I WAS HOPING TO MAKE IT BACK TO BUCKLEY AFTER THIS DROP-OFF.
IT SURE WAS CLEAR FLYING OUT, BUT WHAT ARE YOU GONNA DO?
"WEATHER FORECASTING ISN'T WHAT IT USED TO BE."

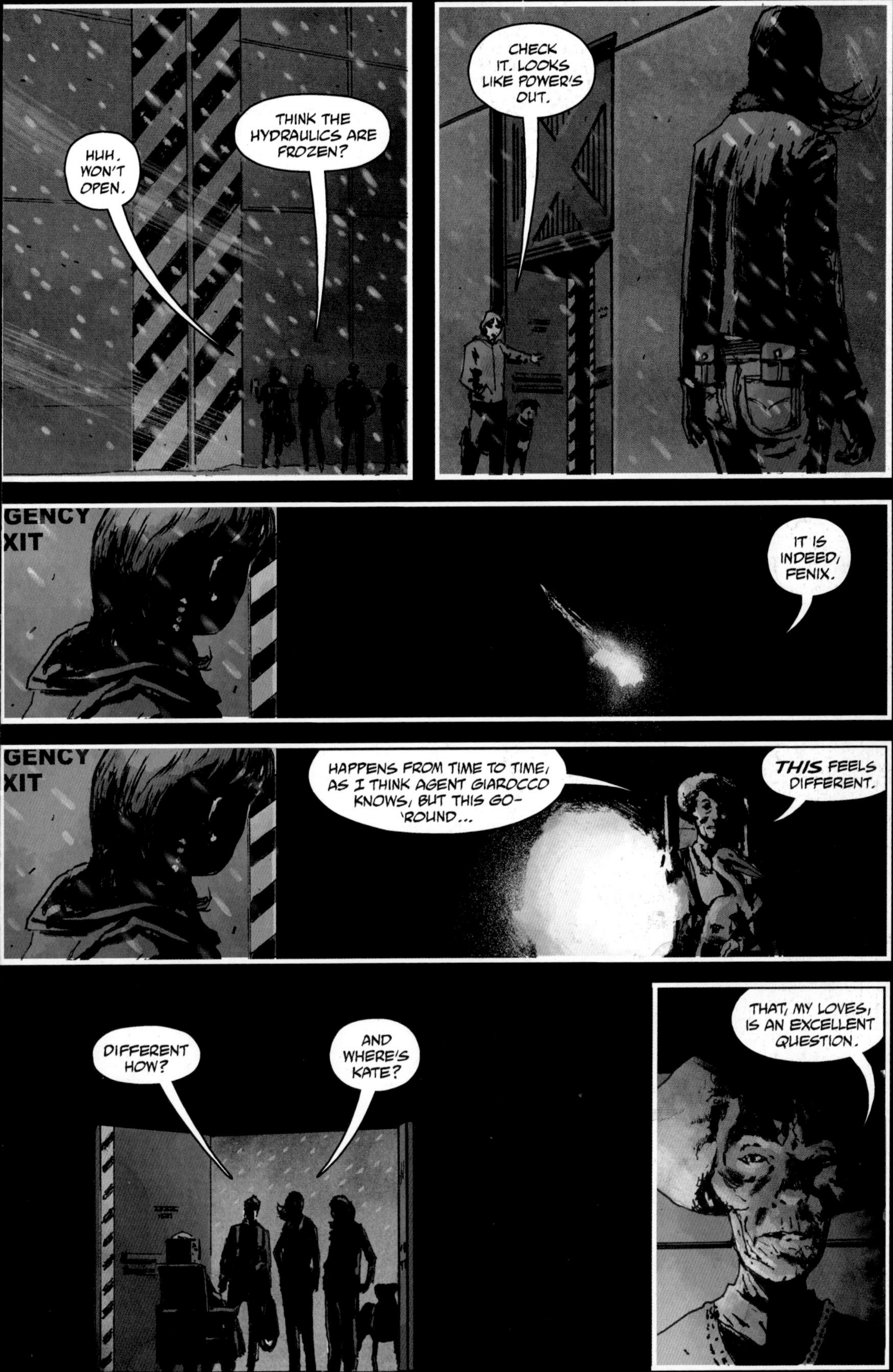
HUH. WON'T OPEN.
THINK THE HYDRAULICS ARE FROZEN?
CHECK IT. LOOKS LIKE POWER'S OUT.
GENCY XIT
IT IS INDEED, FENIX.
GENCY XIT
HAPPENS FROM TIME TO TIME, AS I THINK AGENT GIAROCCO KNOWS, BUT THIS GO-'ROUND...
THIS FEELS DIFFERENT.
DIFFERENT HOW?
AND WHERE'S KATE?
THAT, MY LOVES, IS AN EXCELLENT QUESTION.

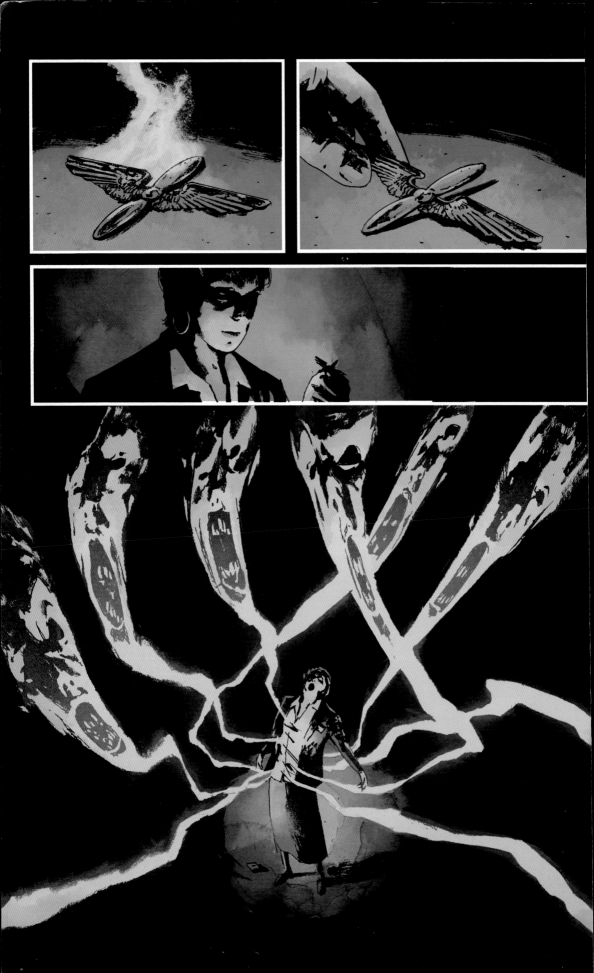

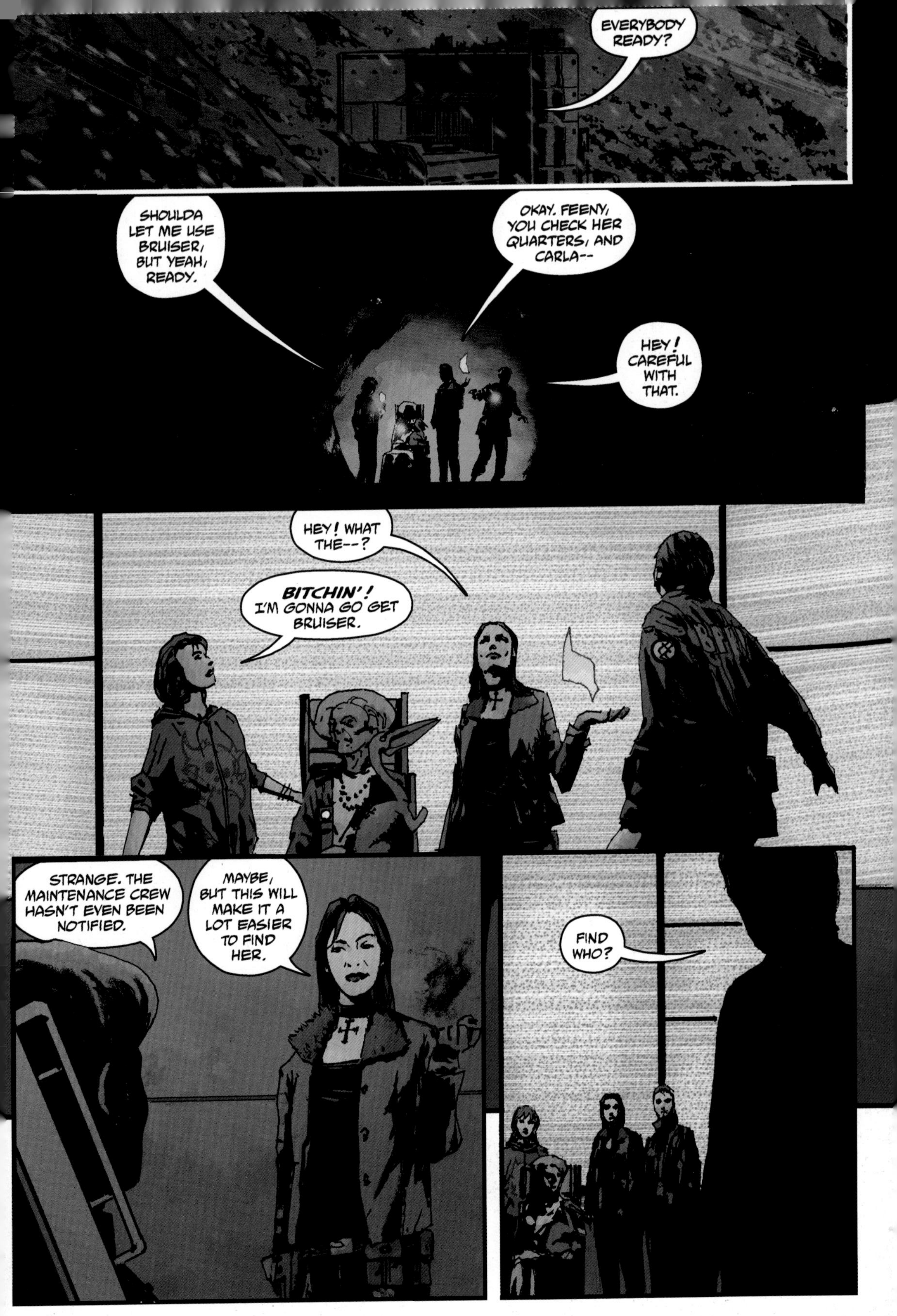
EVERYBODY READY?
SHOULDA LET ME USE BRUISER, BUT YEAH, READY.
OKAY. FEENY, YOU CHECK HER QUARTERS, AND CARLA--
HEY! CAREFUL WITH THAT.
HEY! WHAT THE--?
BITCHIN'! I'M GONNA GO GET BRUISER.
STRANGE. THE MAINTENANCE CREW HASN'T EVEN BEEN NOTIFIED.
MAYBE, BUT THIS WILL MAKE IT A LOT EASIER TO FIND HER.
FIND WHO?

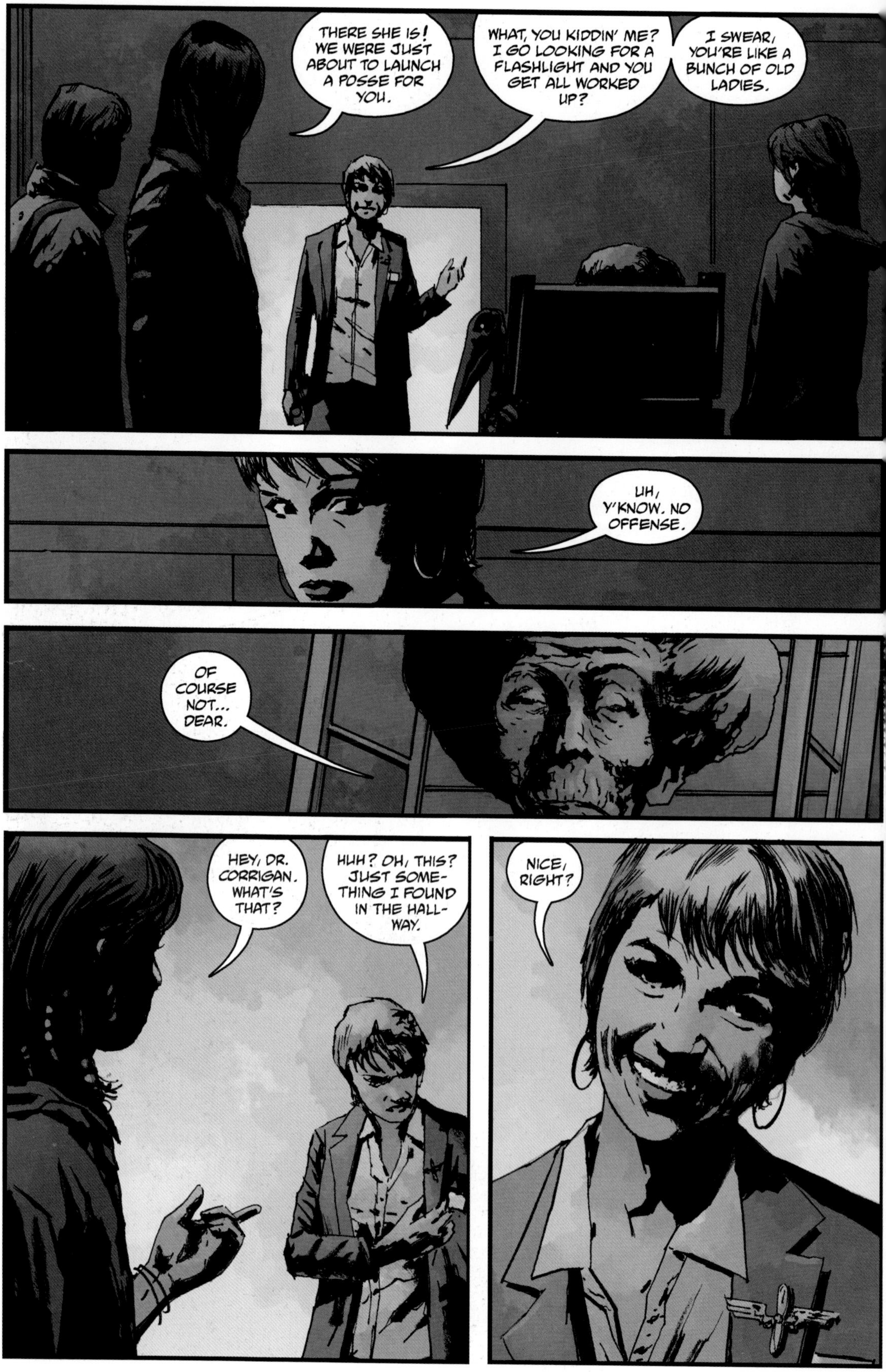
THERE SHE IS! WE WERE JUST ABOUT TO LAUNCH A POSSE FOR YOU.
WHAT, YOU KIDDIN' ME? I GO LOOKING FOR A FLASHLIGHT AND YOU GET ALL WORKED UP?
I SWEAR, YOU'RE LIKE A BUNCH OF OLD LADIES.
UH, Y'KNOW. NO OFFENSE.
OF COURSE NOT... DEAR.
HEY, DR. CORRIGAN. WHAT'S THAT?
HUH? OH, THIS? JUST SOME-THING I FOUND IN THE HALL-WAY.
NICE, RIGHT?

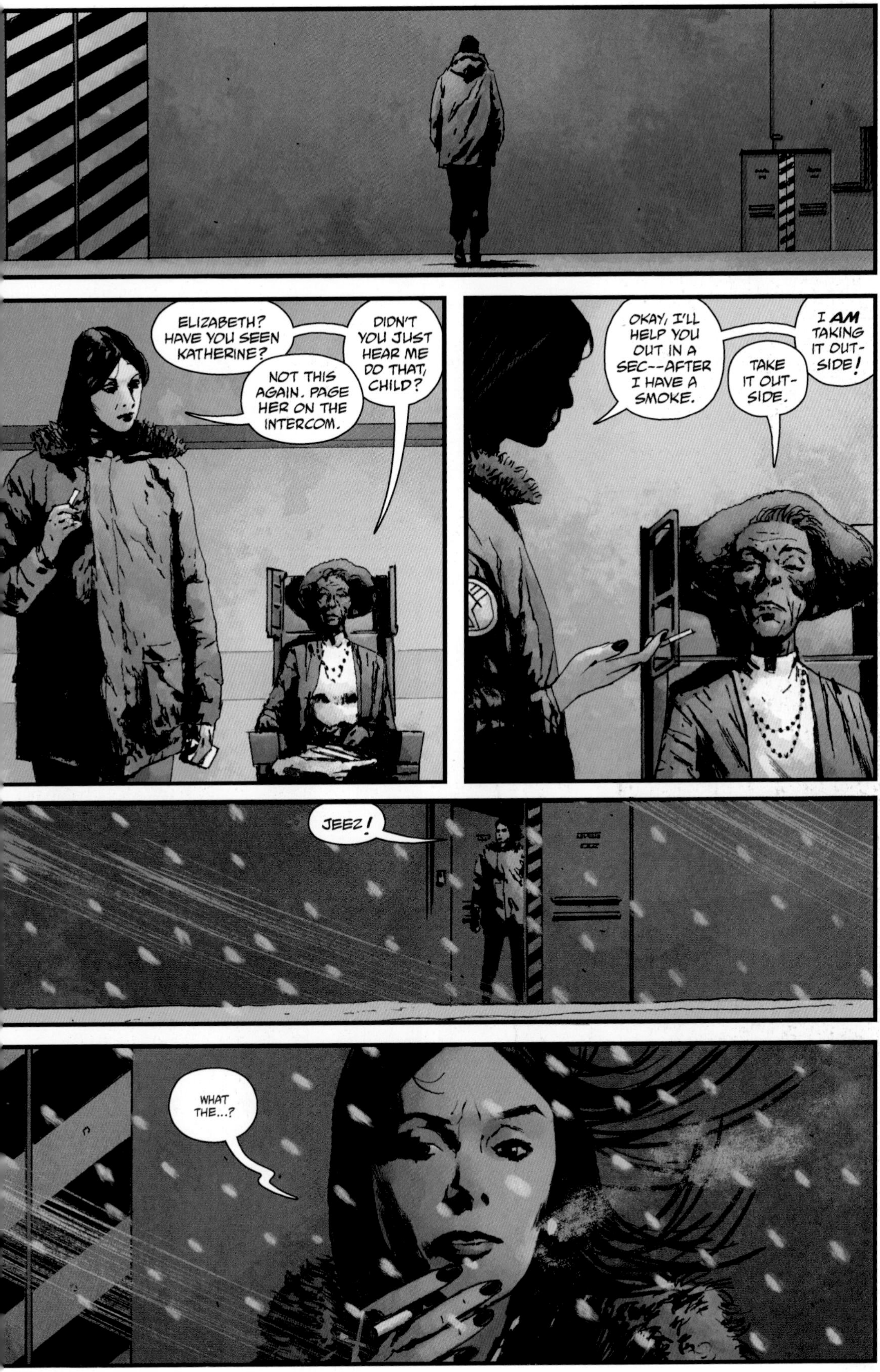
ELIZABETH? HAVE YOU SEEN KATHERINE?
NOT THIS AGAIN. PAGE HER ON THE INTERCOM.
DIDN'T YOU JUST HEAR ME DO THAT, CHILD?
OKAY, I'LL HELP YOU OUT IN A SEC--AFTER I HAVE A SMOKE.
TAKE IT OUT-SIDE.
I AM TAKING IT OUT-SIDE!
JEEZ!
WHAT THE...?

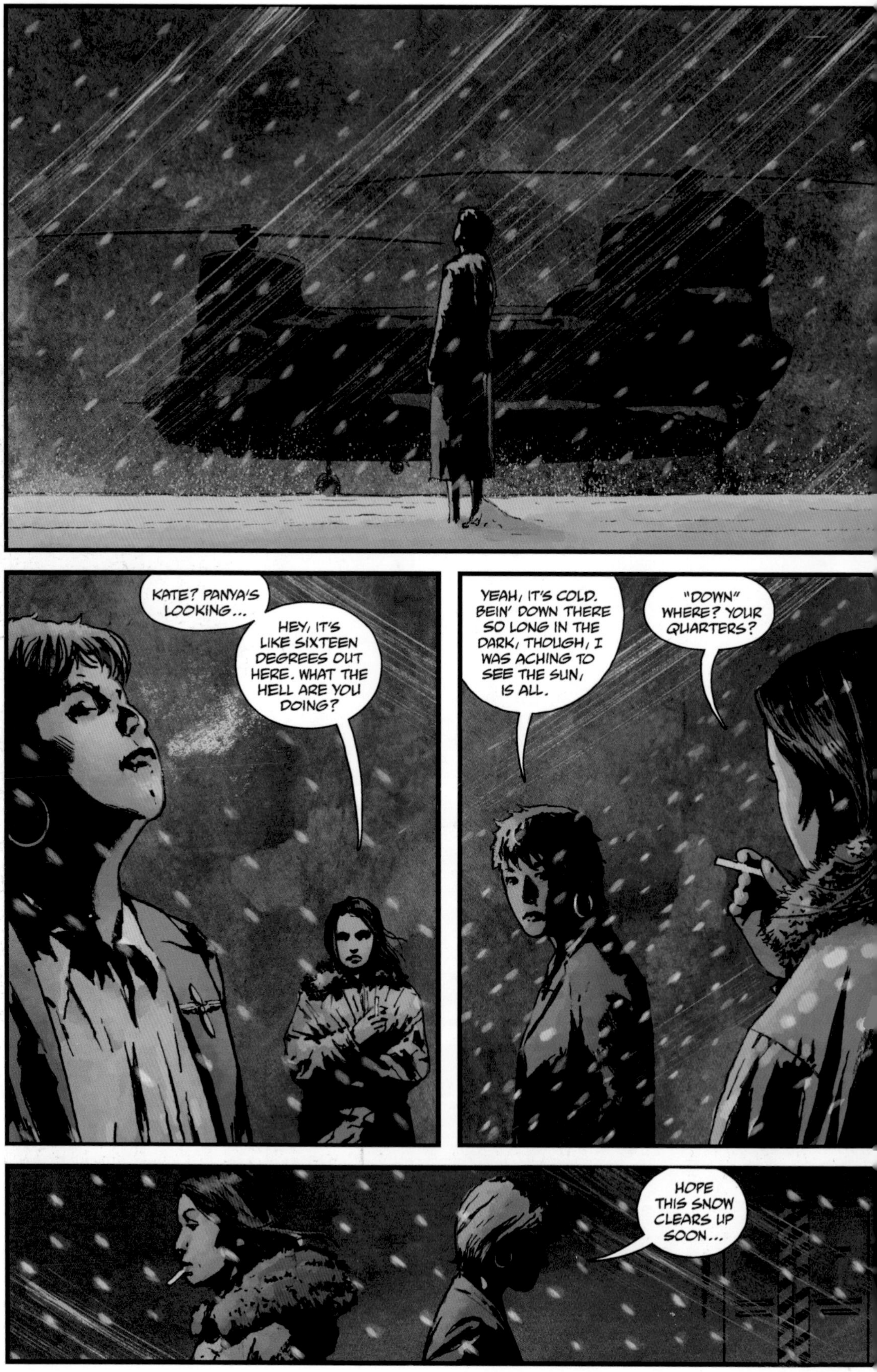
KATE? PANYA'S LOOKING...
HEY, IT'S LIKE SIXTEEN DEGREES OUT HERE. WHAT THE HELL ARE YOU DOING?
YEAH, IT'S COLD. BEIN' DOWN THERE SO LONG IN THE DARK, THOUGH, I WAS ACHING TO SEE THE SUN, IS ALL.
"DOWN" WHERE? YOUR QUARTERS?
HOPE THIS SNOW CLEARS UP SOON...

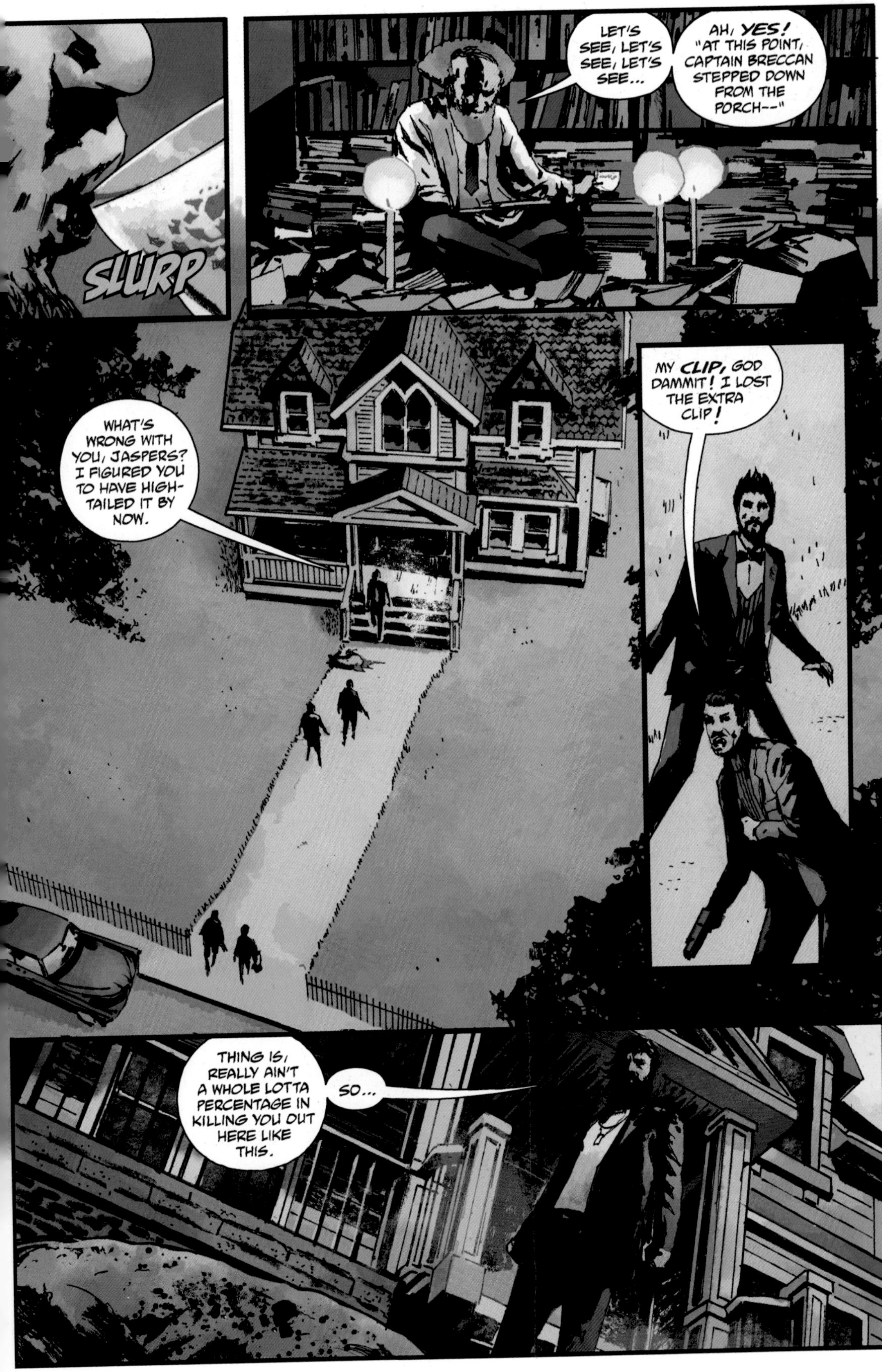
SLURP
LET'S SEE, LET'S SEE, LET'S SEE...
AH, YES! "AT THIS POINT, CAPTAIN BRECCAN STEPPED DOWN FROM THE PORCH--"
WHAT'S WRONG WITH YOU, JASPERS? I FIGURED YOU TO HAVE HIGH-TAILED IT BY NOW.
MY CLIP, GOD DAMMIT! I LOST THE EXTRA CLIP!
THING IS, REALLY AIN'T A WHOLE LOTTA PERCENTAGE IN KILLING YOU OUT HERE LIKE THIS.
SO...

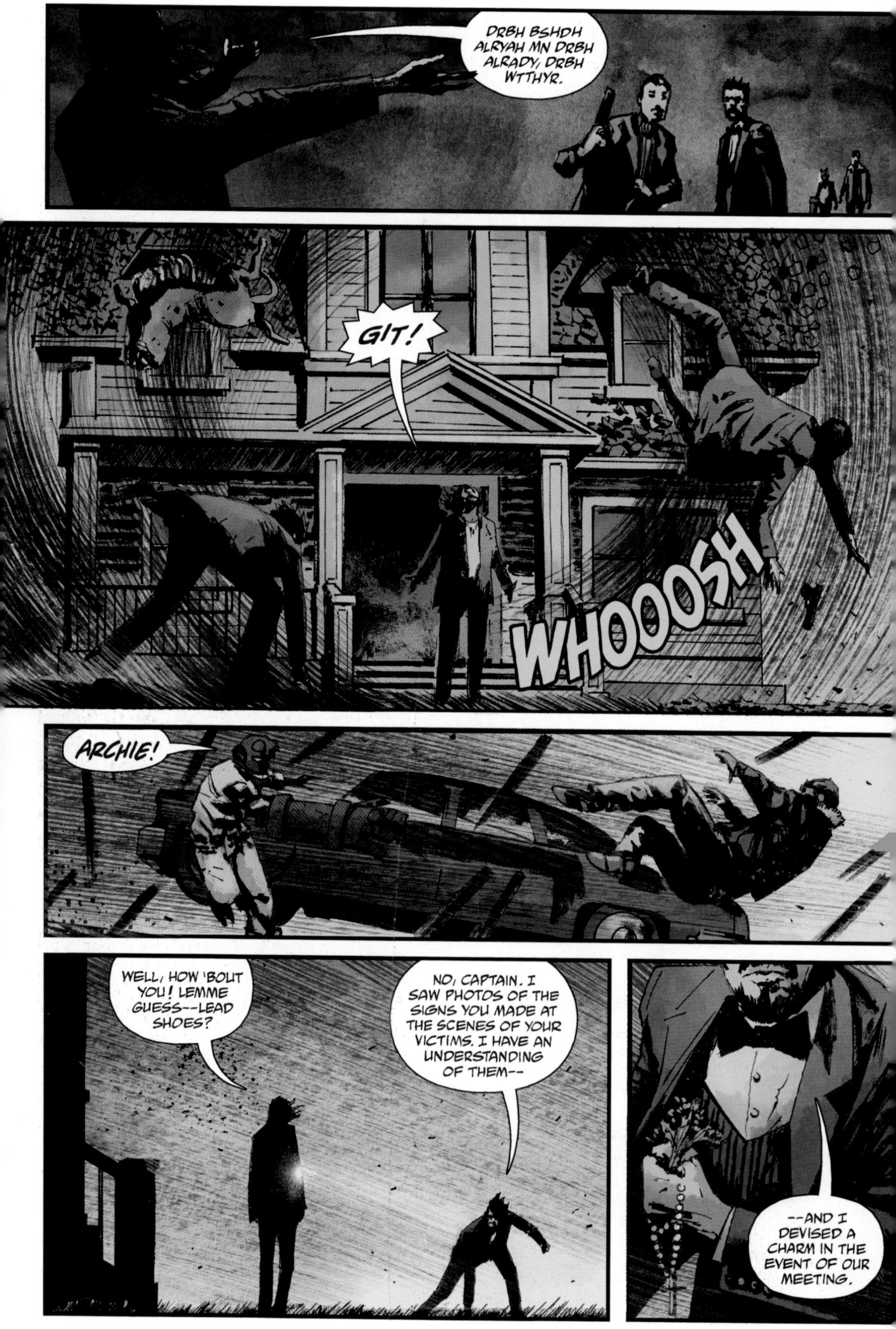
DRBH BSHDH ALRYAH MN DRBH ALRADY, DRBH WTTHYR.
GIT!
WHOOOSH
ARCHIE!
WELL, HOW 'BOUT YOU! LEMME GUESS--LEAD SHOES?
NO, CAPTAIN. I SAW PHOTOS OF THE SIGNS YOU MADE AT THE SCENES OF YOUR VICTIMS. I HAVE AN UNDERSTANDING OF THEM--
--AND I DEVISED A CHARM IN THE EVENT OF OUR MEETING.

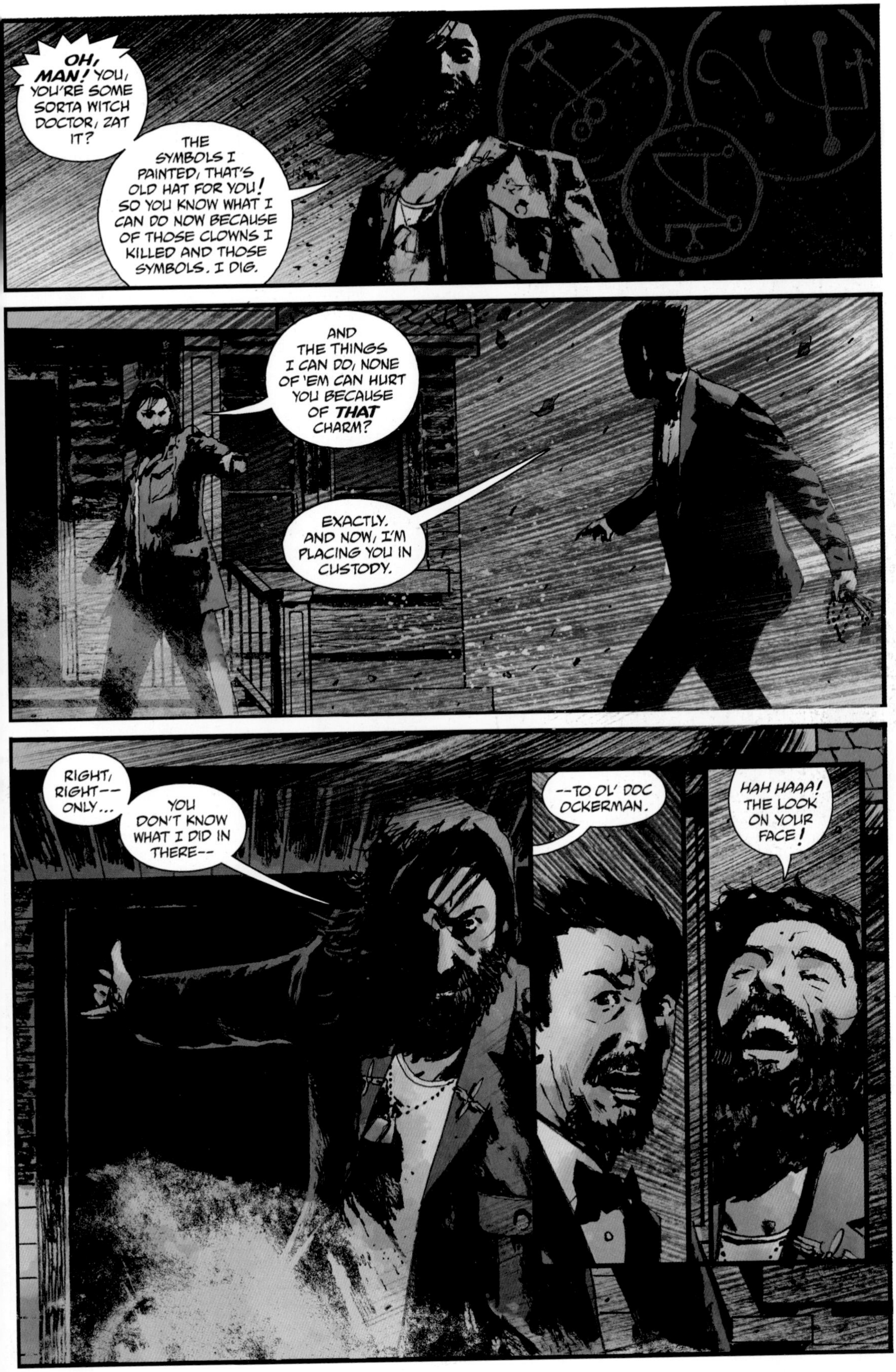
OH, MAN! YOU, YOU'RE SOME SORTA WITCH DOCTOR, ZAT IT?
THE SYMBOLS I PAINTED, THAT'S OLD HAT FOR YOU! SO YOU KNOW WHAT I CAN DO NOW BECAUSE OF THOSE CLOWNS I KILLED AND THOSE SYMBOLS. I DIG.
AND THE THINGS I CAN DO, NONE OF 'EM CAN HURT YOU BECAUSE OF THAT CHARM?
EXACTLY. AND NOW, I'M PLACING YOU IN CUSTODY.
RIGHT, RIGHT-- ONLY...
YOU DON'T KNOW WHAT I DID IN THERE--
--TO OL' DOC OCKERMAN.
HAH HAAA! THE LOOK ON YOUR FACE!

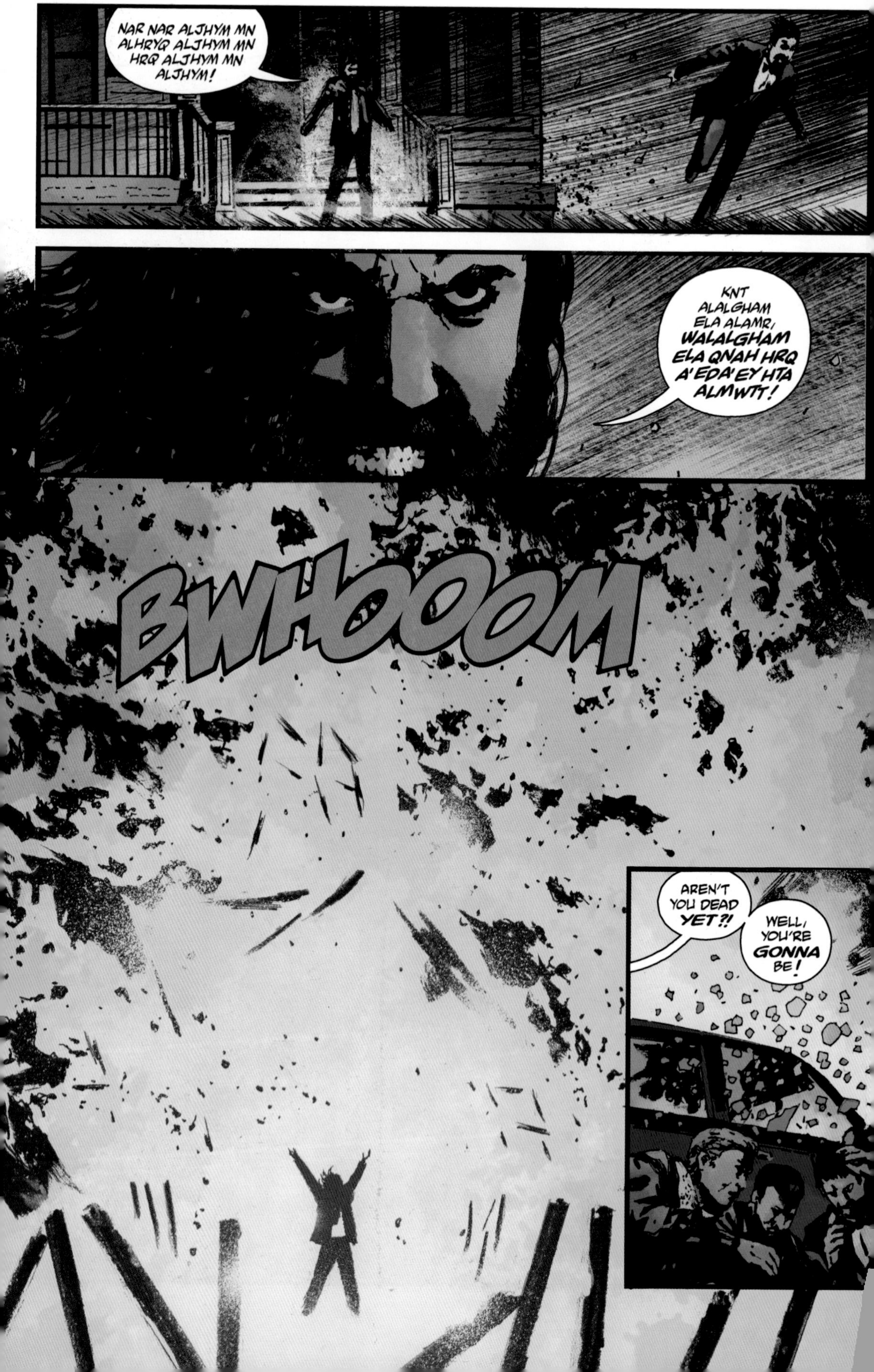

NAR NAR ALJHYM MN ALHRYQ ALJHYM MN HRQ ALJHYM MN ALJHYM!
KNT ALALGHAM ELA ALAMR, WALALGHAM ELA QNAH HRQ A'EDA'EY HTA ALMWTT!
BWHOOOM
AREN'T YOU DEAD YET?!
WELL, YOU'RE GONNA BE!

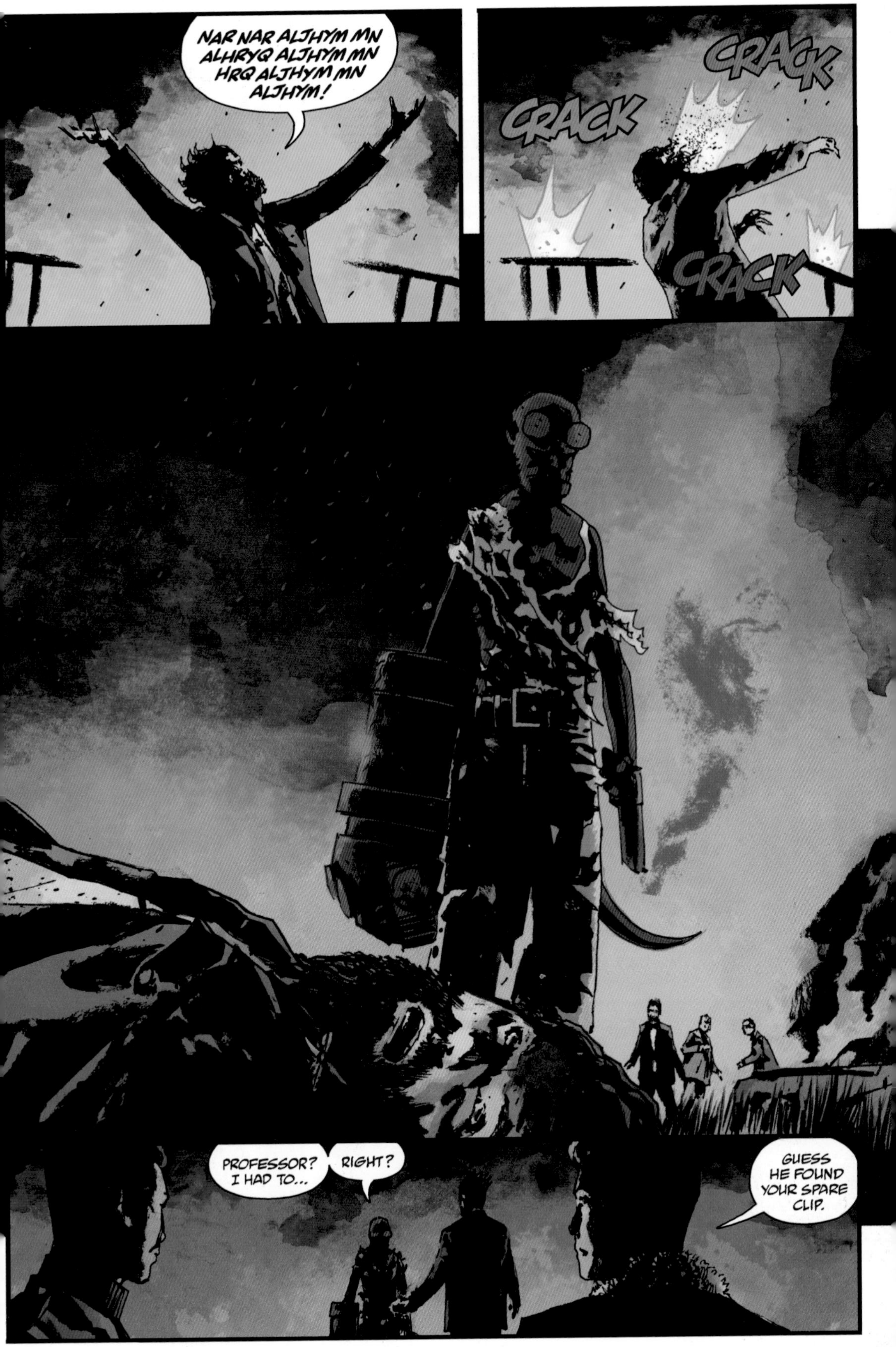
NAR NAR ALJHYM MN ALHRYQ ALJHYM MN HRQ ALJHYM MN ALJHYM!
CRACK
CRACK
CRACK
PROFESSOR? I HAD TO...
RIGHT?
GUESS HE FOUND YOUR SPARE CLIP.

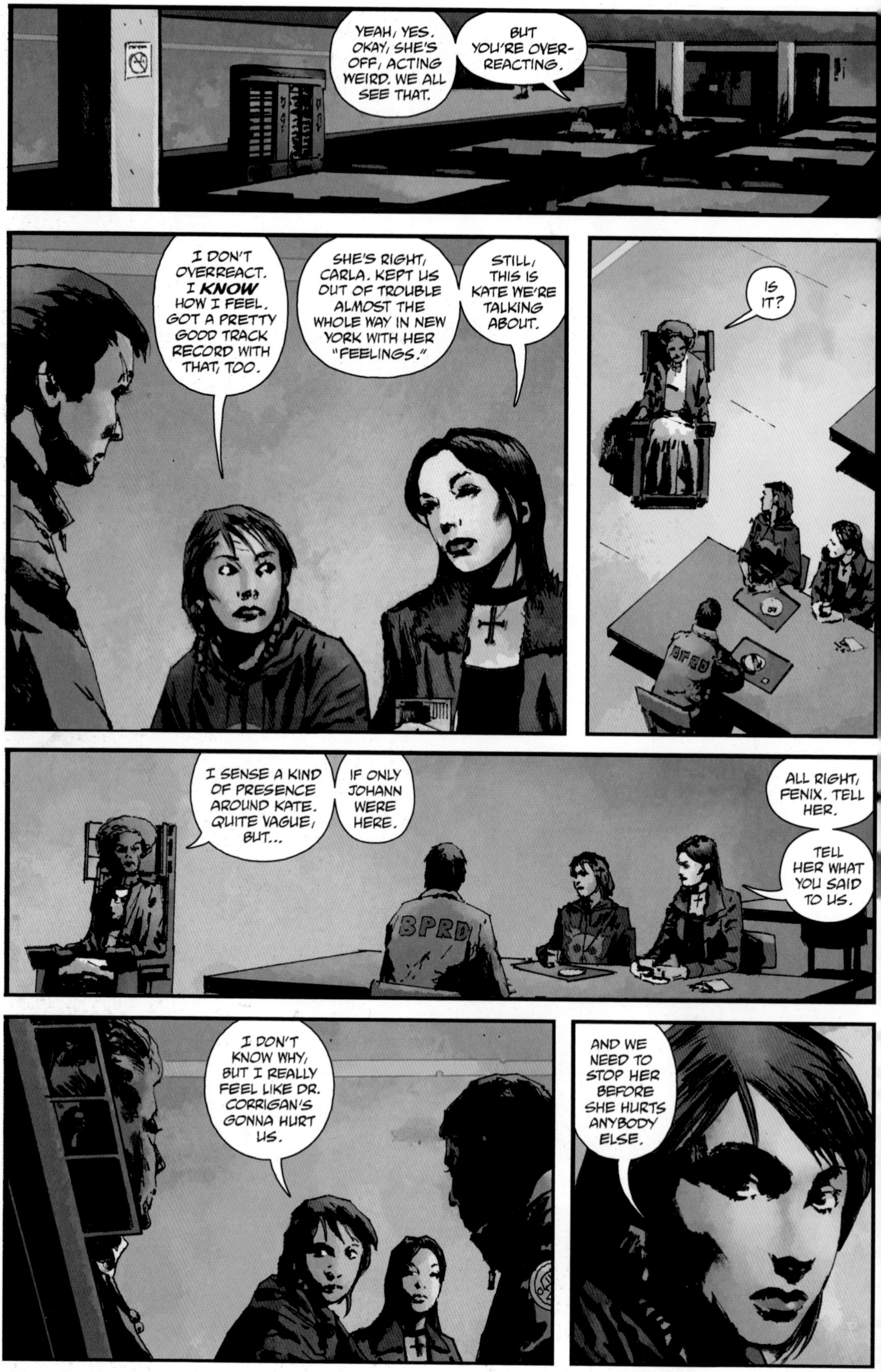
YEAH, YES. OKAY, SHE'S OFF, ACTING WEIRD. WE ALL SEE THAT.
BUT YOU'RE OVER-REACTING.
I DON'T OVERREACT. I ***KNOW*** HOW I FEEL. GOT A PRETTY GOOD TRACK RECORD WITH THAT, TOO.
SHE'S RIGHT, CARLA. KEPT US OUT OF TROUBLE ALMOST THE WHOLE WAY IN NEW YORK WITH HER "FEELINGS."
STILL, THIS IS KATE WE'RE TALKING ABOUT.
IS IT?
I SENSE A KIND OF PRESENCE AROUND KATE. QUITE VAGUE, BUT...
IF ONLY JOHANN WERE HERE.
ALL RIGHT, FENIX. TELL HER.
TELL HER WHAT YOU SAID TO US.
BPRD
I DON'T KNOW WHY, BUT I REALLY FEEL LIKE DR. CORRIGAN'S GONNA HURT US.
AND WE NEED TO STOP HER BEFORE SHE HURTS ANYBODY ELSE.

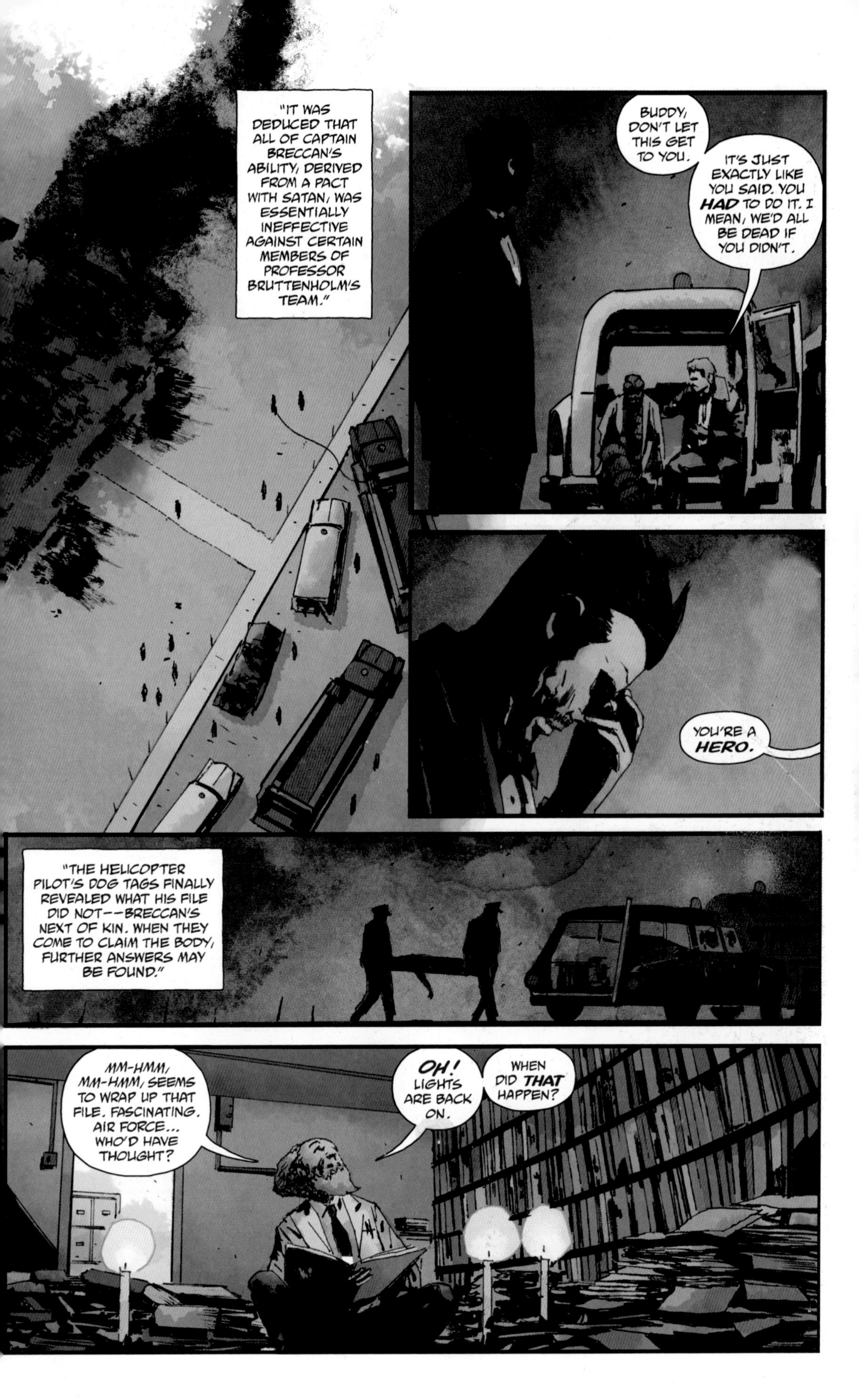

"IT WAS DEDUCED THAT ALL OF CAPTAIN BRECCAN'S ABILITY, DERIVED FROM A PACT WITH SATAN, WAS ESSENTIALLY INEFFECTIVE AGAINST CERTAIN MEMBERS OF PROFESSOR BRUTTENHOLM'S TEAM."
BUDDY, DON'T LET THIS GET TO YOU.
IT'S JUST EXACTLY LIKE YOU SAID. YOU HAD TO DO IT. I MEAN, WE'D ALL BE DEAD IF YOU DIDN'T.
YOU'RE A HERO.
"THE HELICOPTER PILOT'S DOG TAGS FINALLY REVEALED WHAT HIS FILE DID NOT--BRECCAN'S NEXT OF KIN. WHEN THEY COME TO CLAIM THE BODY, FURTHER ANSWERS MAY BE FOUND."
MM-HMM, MM-HMM, SEEMS TO WRAP UP THAT FILE. FASCINATING. AIR FORCE... WHO'D HAVE THOUGHT?
OH! LIGHTS ARE BACK ON.
WHEN DID THAT HAPPEN?

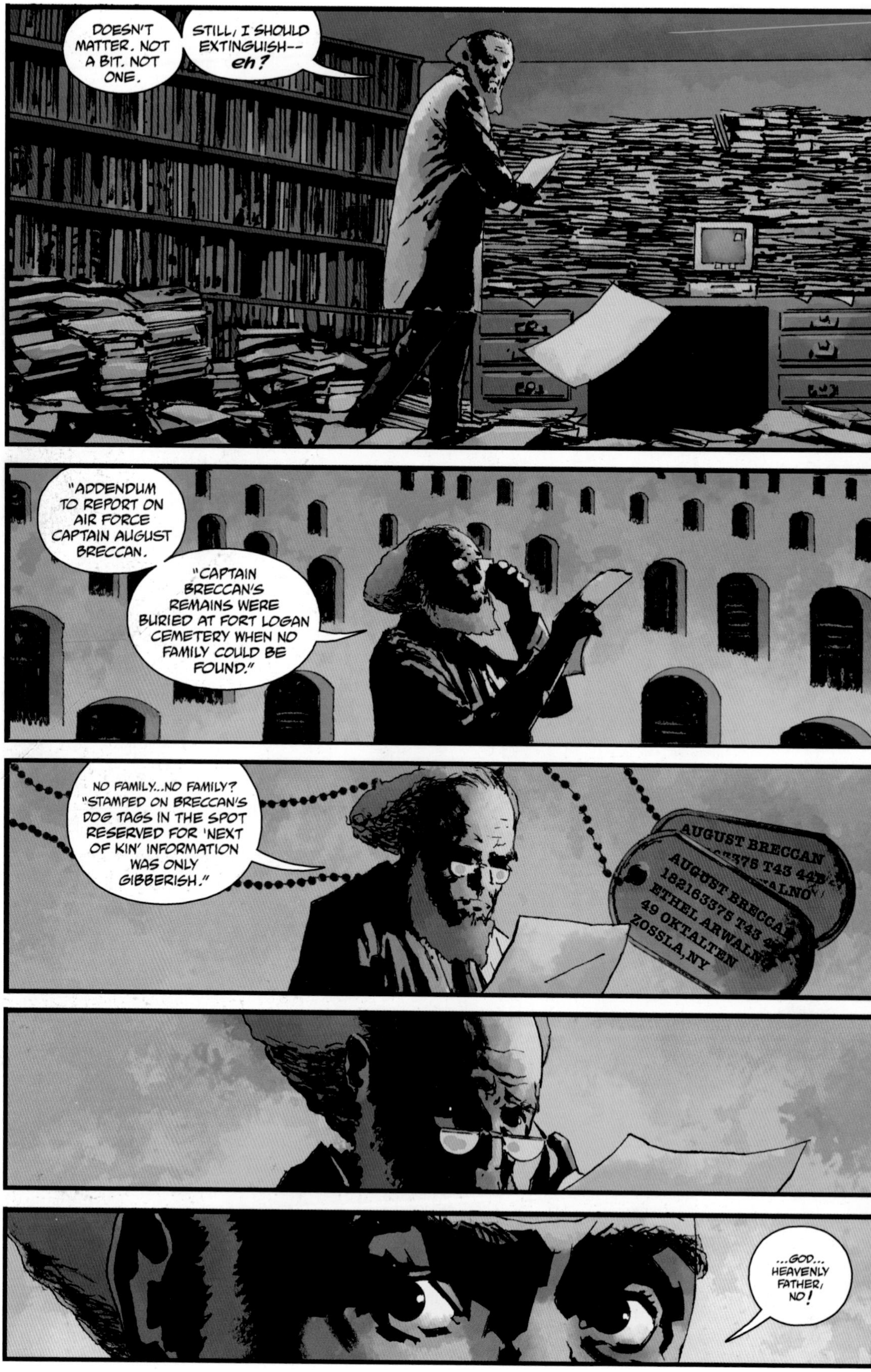
DOESN'T MATTER. NOT A BIT. NOT ONE.
STILL, I SHOULD EXTINGUISH-- eh?
"ADDENDUM TO REPORT ON AIR FORCE CAPTAIN AUGUST BRECCAN.
"CAPTAIN BRECCAN'S REMAINS WERE BURIED AT FORT LOGAN CEMETERY WHEN NO FAMILY COULD BE FOUND."
NO FAMILY...NO FAMILY? "STAMPED ON BRECCAN'S DOG TAGS IN THE SPOT RESERVED FOR 'NEXT OF KIN' INFORMATION WAS ONLY GIBBERISH."
AUGUST BRECCAN
AUGUST BRECCAN
18163375 T43 4
ETHEL ARWALN
49 OKTALTEN
ZOSSLA, NY
...GOD... HEAVENLY FATHER, NO!

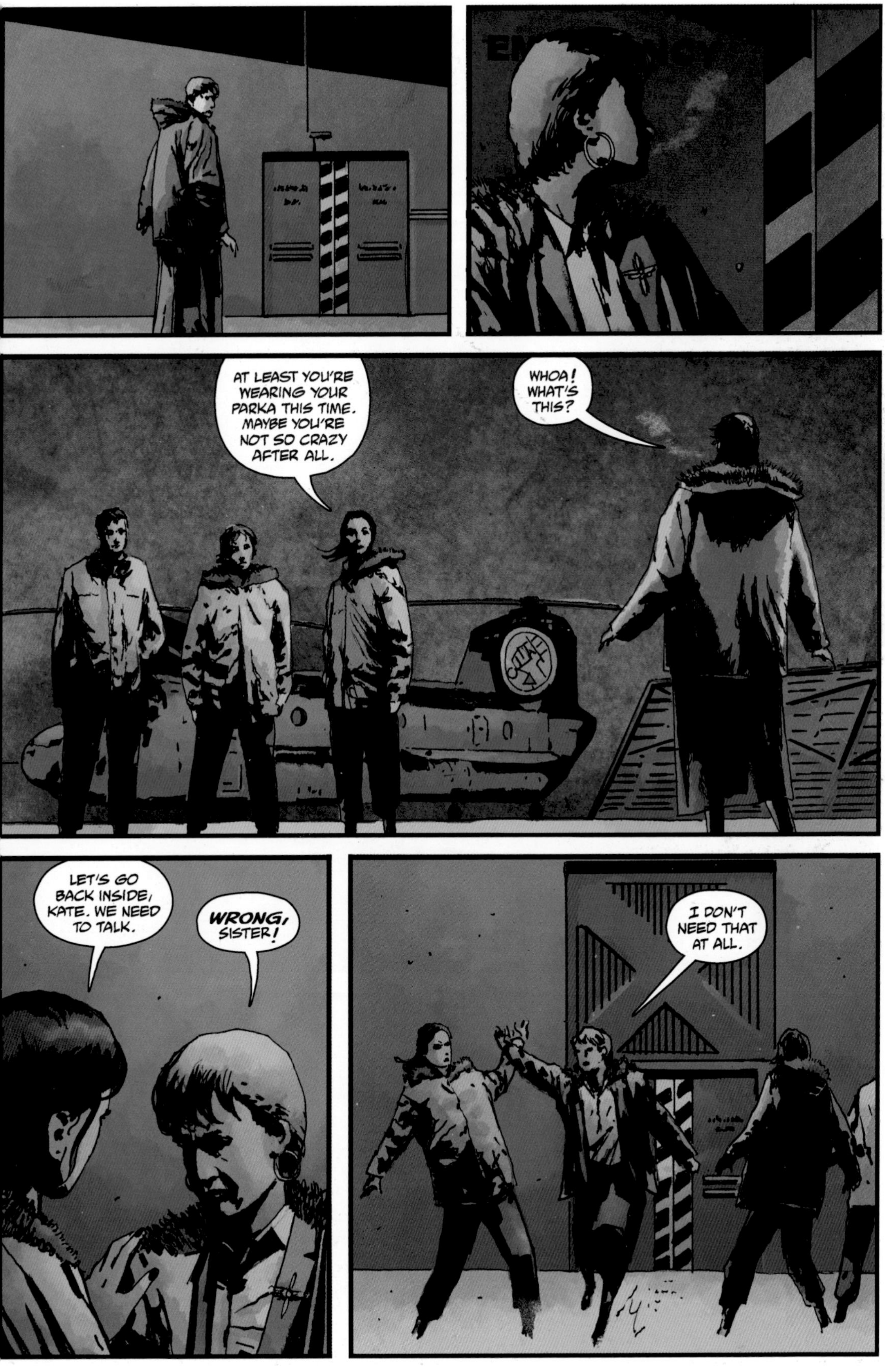
AT LEAST YOU'RE WEARING YOUR PARKA THIS TIME. MAYBE YOU'RE NOT SO CRAZY AFTER ALL.
WHOA! WHAT'S THIS?
LET'S GO BACK INSIDE, KATE. WE NEED TO TALK.
WRONG, SISTER!
I DON'T NEED THAT AT ALL.

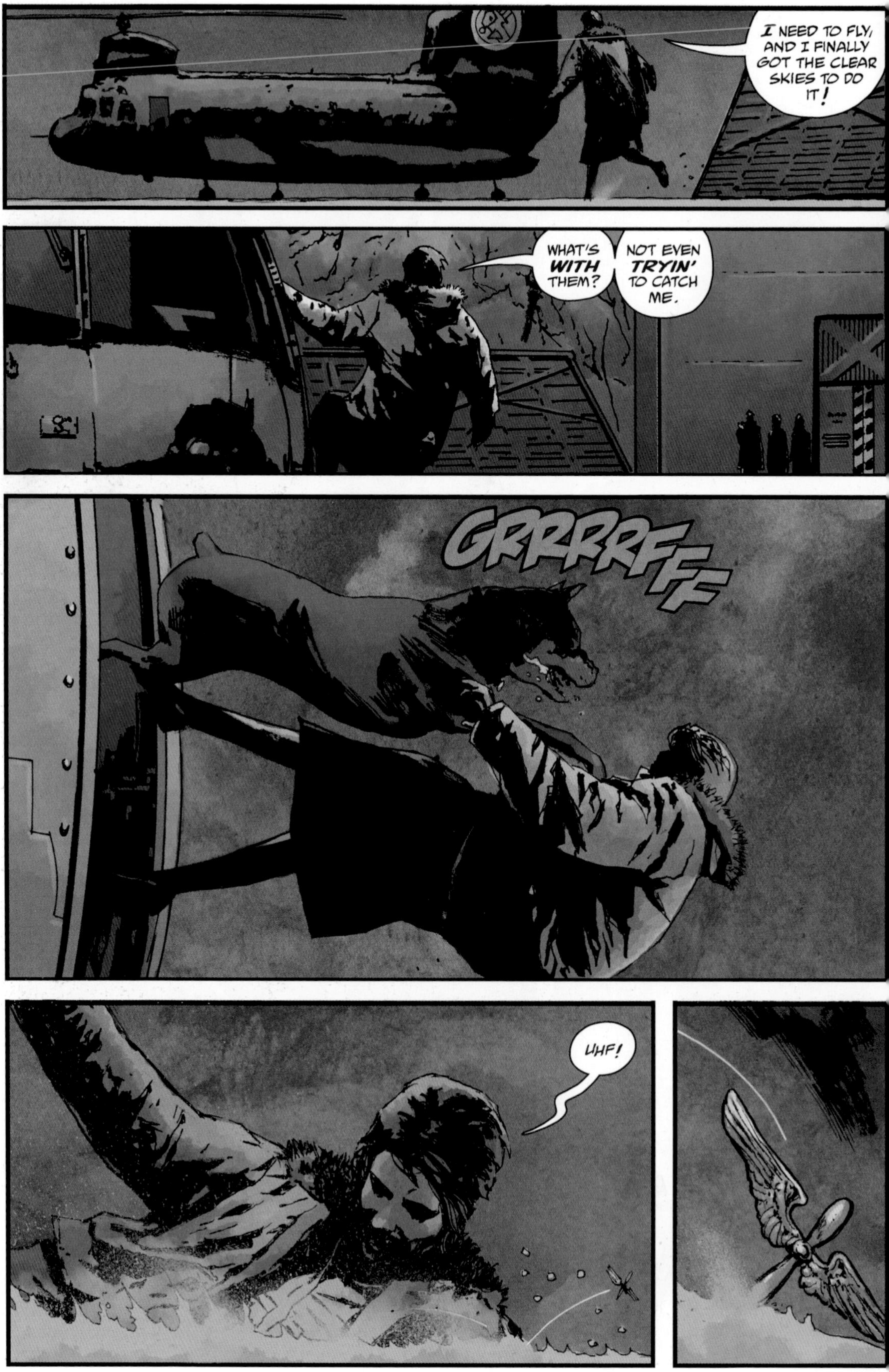

I NEED TO FLY, AND I FINALLY GOT THE CLEAR SKIES TO DO IT!
WHAT'S WITH THEM?
NOT EVEN TRYIN' TO CATCH ME.
GRRRRFFF
UHF!

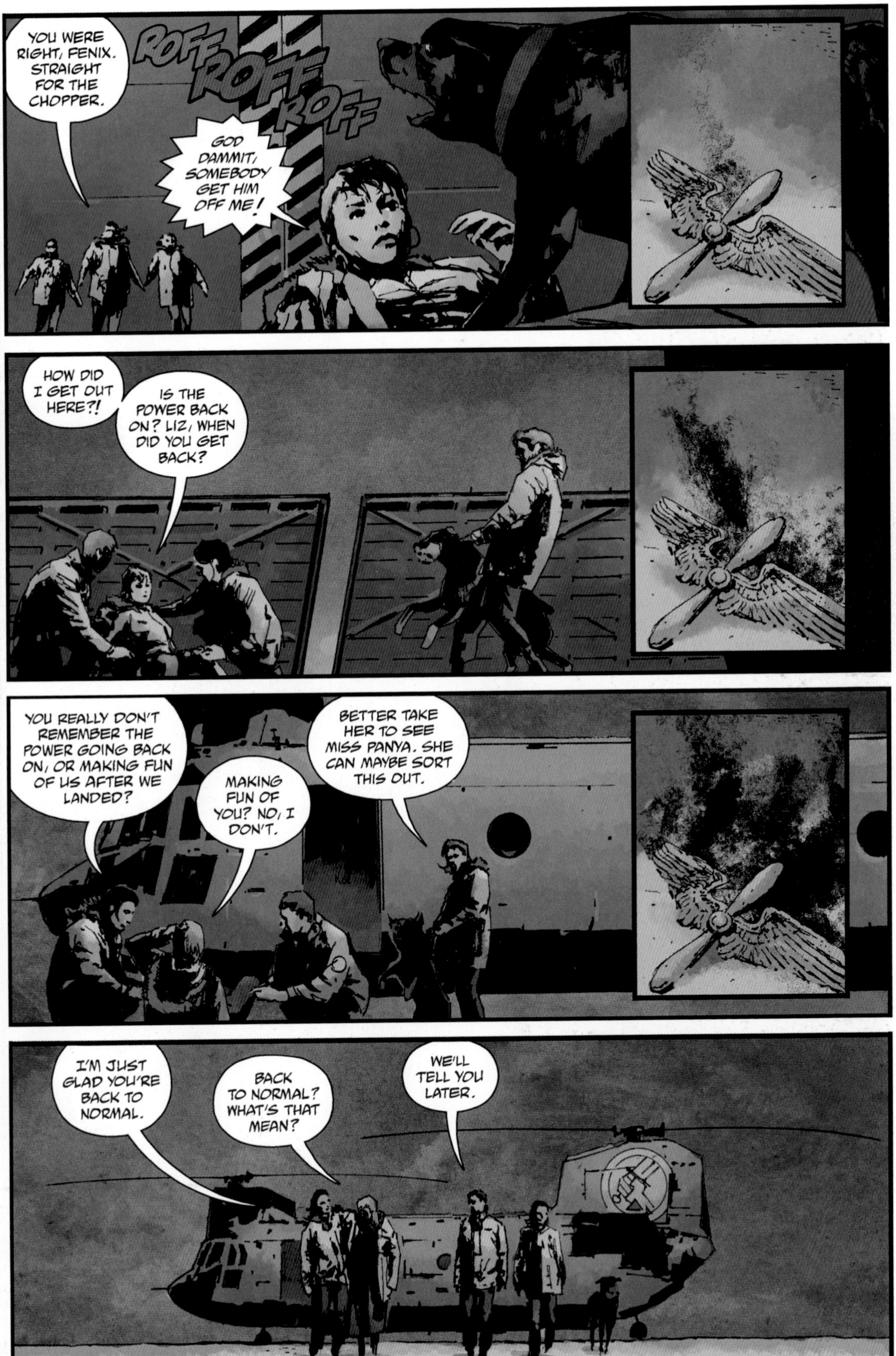
YOU WERE RIGHT, FENIX. STRAIGHT FOR THE CHOPPER.
ROFF ROFF ROFF
GOD DAMMIT, SOMEBODY GET HIM OFF ME!
HOW DID I GET OUT HERE?!
IS THE POWER BACK ON? LIZ, WHEN DID YOU GET BACK?
YOU REALLY DON'T REMEMBER THE POWER GOING BACK ON, OR MAKING FUN OF US AFTER WE LANDED?
MAKING FUN OF YOU? NO, I DON'T.
BETTER TAKE HER TO SEE MISS PANYA. SHE CAN MAYBE SORT THIS OUT.
I'M JUST GLAD YOU'RE BACK TO NORMAL.
BACK TO NORMAL? WHAT'S THAT MEAN?
WE'LL TELL YOU LATER.

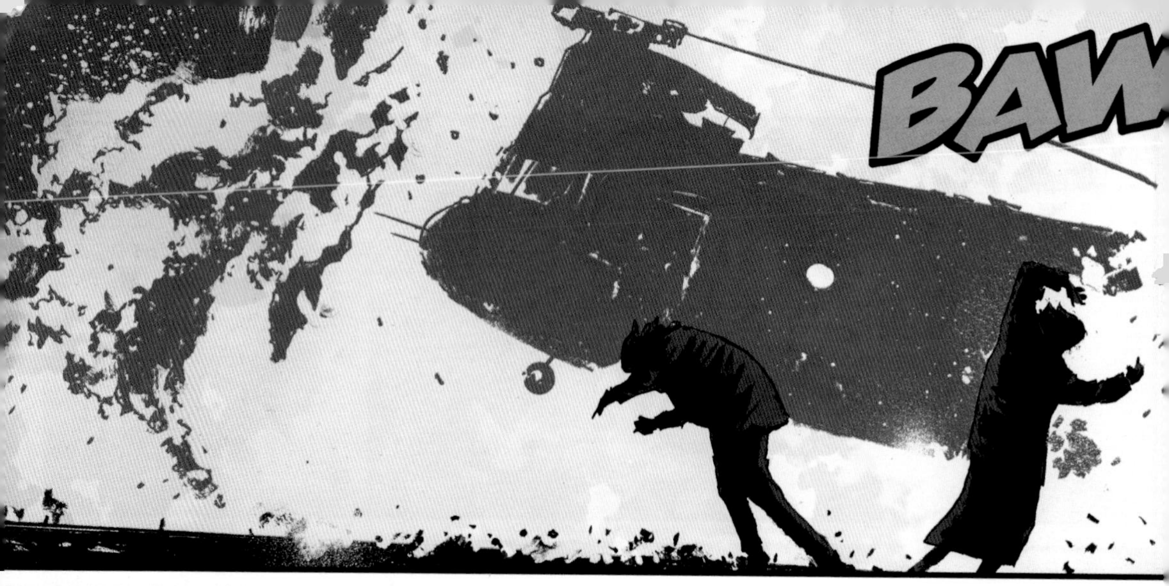
BAW

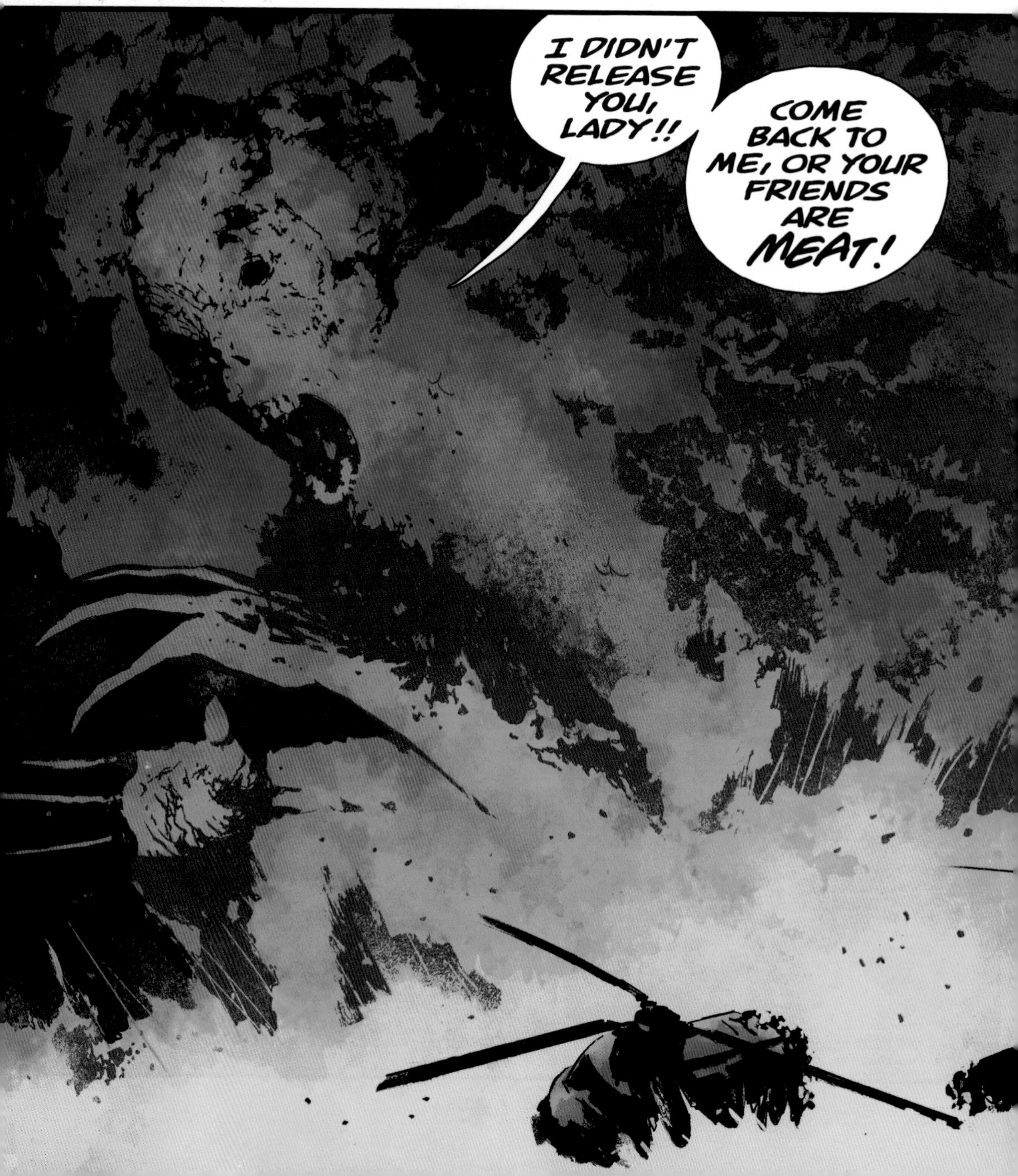
I DIDN'T RELEASE YOU, LADY!!
COME BACK TO ME, OR YOUR FRIENDS ARE MEAT!

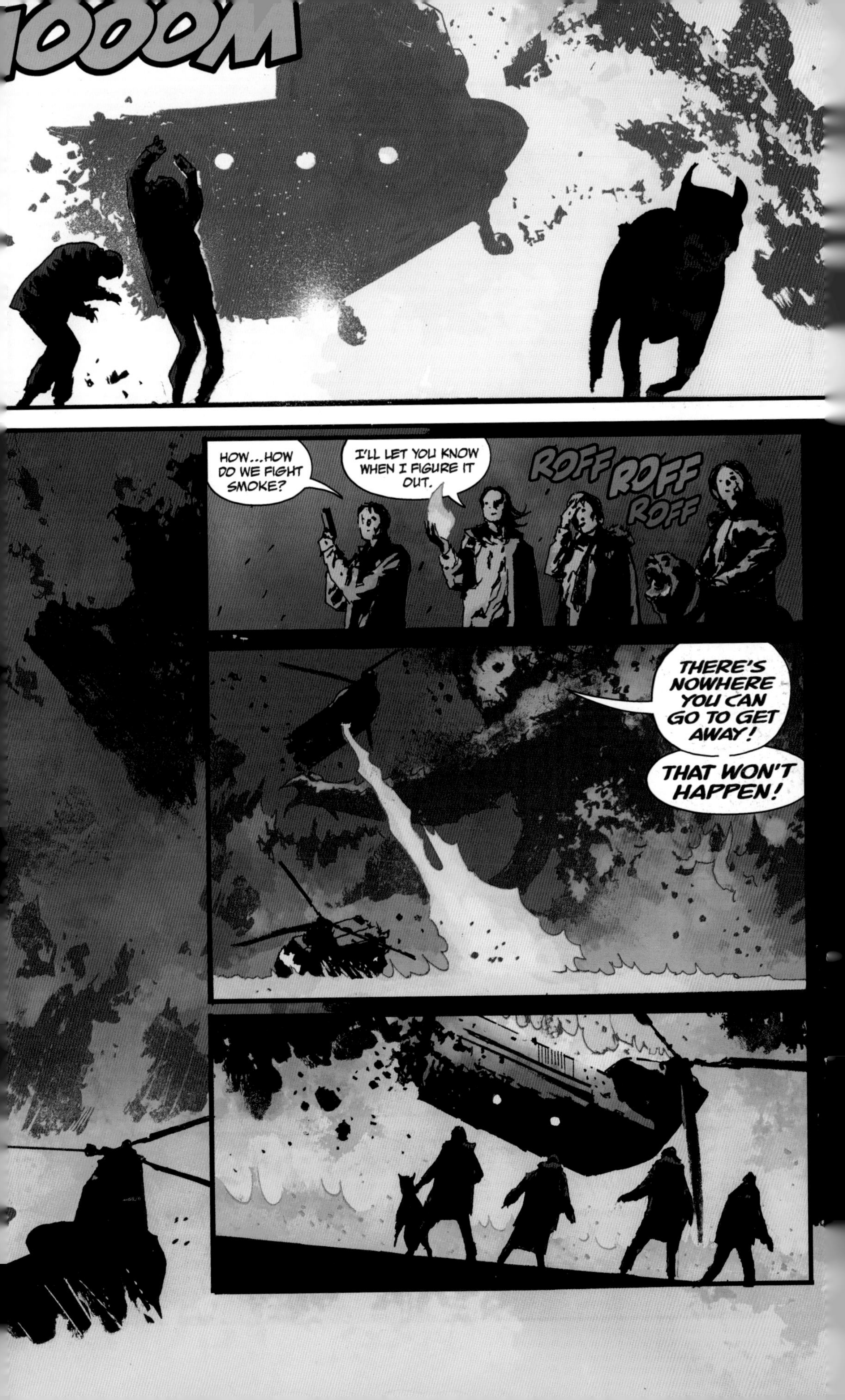
OOOOM
HOW...HOW DO WE FIGHT SMOKE?
I'LL LET YOU KNOW WHEN I FIGURE IT OUT.
ROFF ROFF ROFF
THERE'S NOWHERE YOU CAN GO TO GET AWAY!
THAT WON'T HAPPEN!

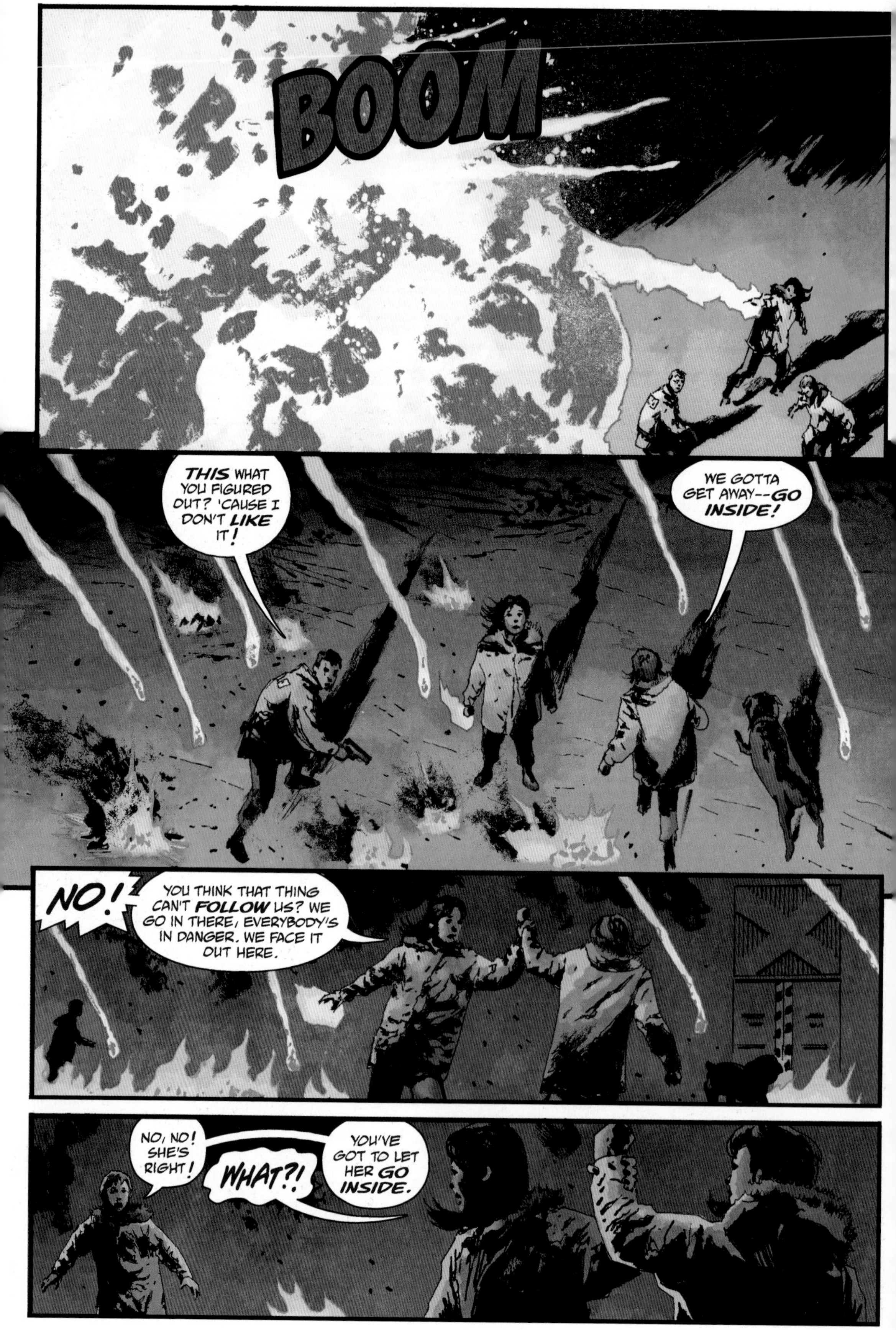
BOOM
THIS WHAT YOU FIGURED OUT? 'CAUSE I DON'T LIKE IT!
WE GOTTA GET AWAY--GO INSIDE!
NO!
YOU THINK THAT THING CAN'T FOLLOW US? WE GO IN THERE, EVERYBODY'S IN DANGER. WE FACE IT OUT HERE.
NO, NO! SHE'S RIGHT!
WHAT?!
YOU'VE GOT TO LET HER GO INSIDE.

"SHE SAID IT BEFORE! PANYA MIGHT KNOW WHAT TO DO!"

HEY! YOU DON'T WANNA GO OUT THERE!

NO, NO, NO, NO, NO. YOU'RE WRONG, GIRL. YOU'RE WRONG ABOUT THAT. I ABSOLUTELY DO!

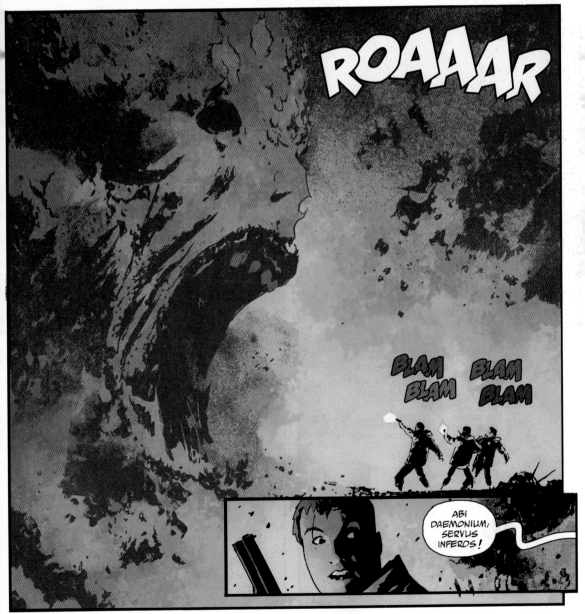

ROAAAR

BLAM BLAM   BLAM BLAM

ABI DAEMONIUM, SERVUS INFEROS!

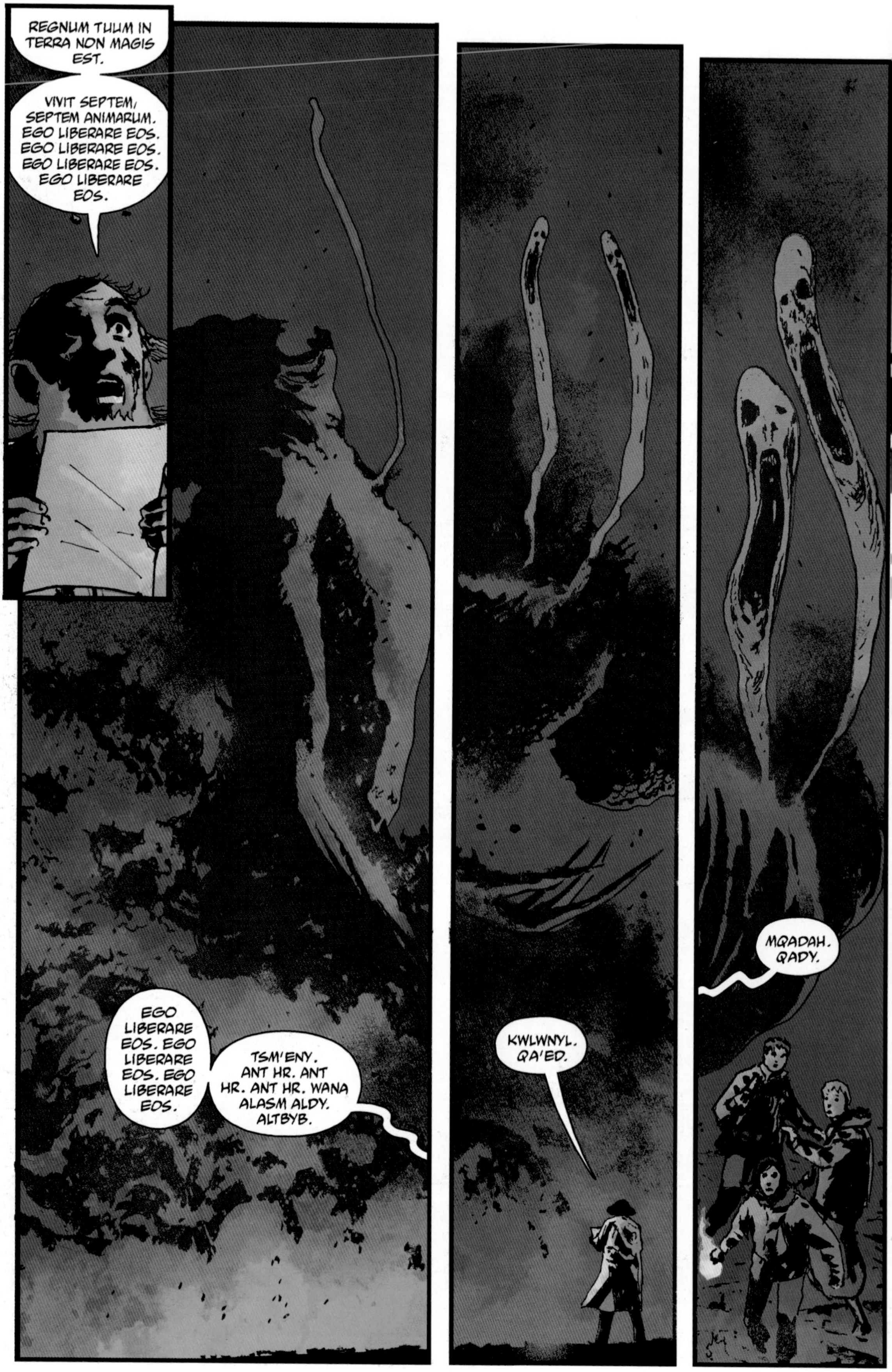

REGNUM TUUM IN TERRA NON MAGIS EST.
VIVIT SEPTEM, SEPTEM ANIMARUM. EGO LIBERARE EOS. EGO LIBERARE EOS. EGO LIBERARE EOS. EGO LIBERARE EOS.
EGO LIBERARE EOS. EGO LIBERARE EOS. EGO LIBERARE EOS.
TSM'ENY. ANT HR. ANT HR. ANT HR. WANA ALASM ALDY. ALTBYB.
KWLWNYL. QA'ED.
MQADAH. QADY.

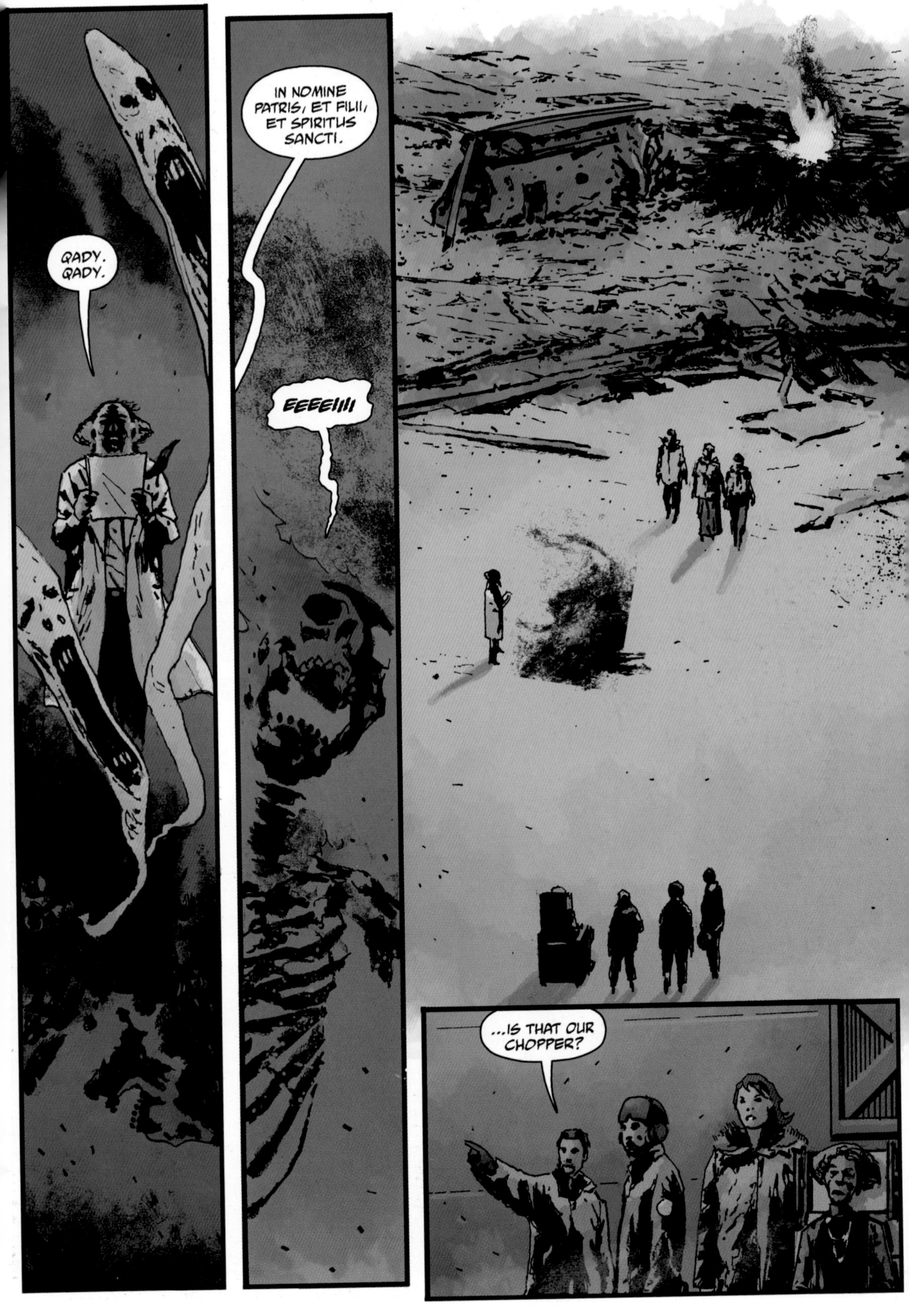
QADY. QADY.
IN NOMINE PATRIS, ET FILII, ET SPIRITUS SANCTI.
EEEEIIII
...IS THAT OUR CHOPPER?

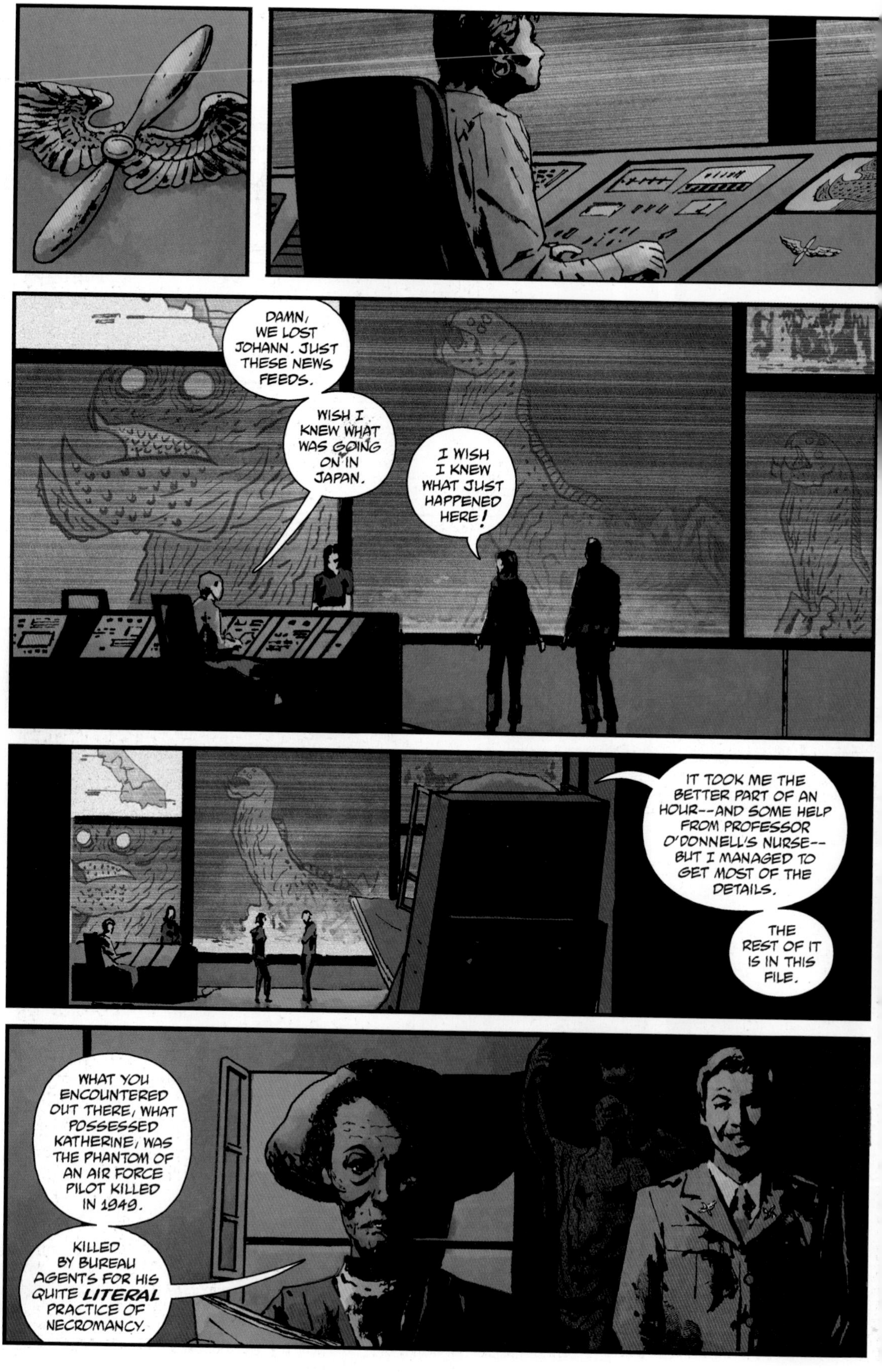
DAMN, WE LOST JOHANN. JUST THESE NEWS FEEDS.
WISH I KNEW WHAT WAS GOING ON IN JAPAN.
I WISH I KNEW WHAT JUST HAPPENED HERE!
IT TOOK ME THE BETTER PART OF AN HOUR--AND SOME HELP FROM PROFESSOR O'DONNELL'S NURSE--BUT I MANAGED TO GET MOST OF THE DETAILS.
THE REST OF IT IS IN THIS FILE.
WHAT YOU ENCOUNTERED OUT THERE, WHAT POSSESSED KATHERINE, WAS THE PHANTOM OF AN AIR FORCE PILOT KILLED IN 1949.
KILLED BY BUREAU AGENTS FOR HIS QUITE ***LITERAL*** PRACTICE OF NECROMANCY.

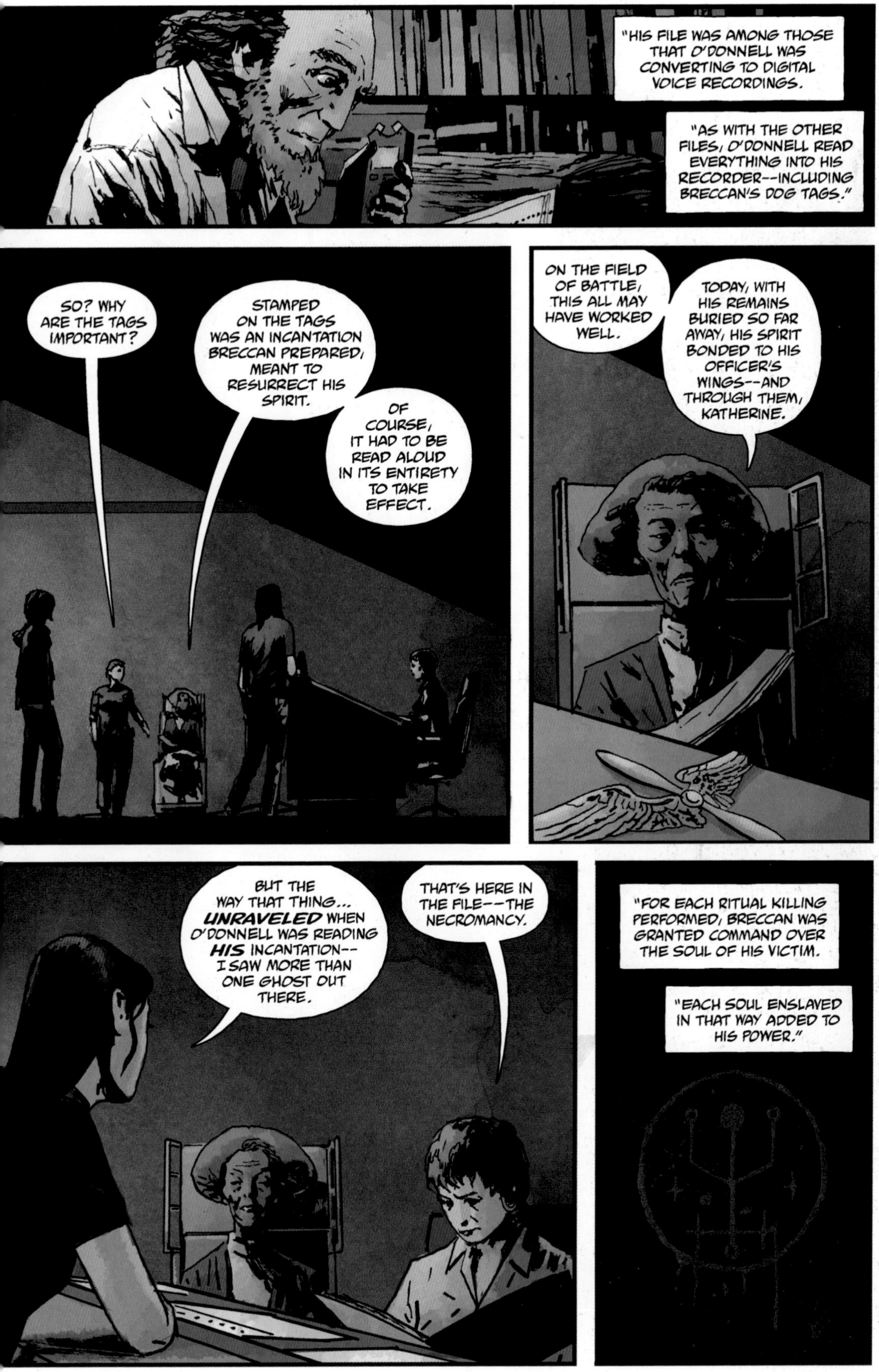
"HIS FILE WAS AMONG THOSE THAT O'DONNELL WAS CONVERTING TO DIGITAL VOICE RECORDINGS.
"AS WITH THE OTHER FILES, O'DONNELL READ EVERYTHING INTO HIS RECORDER--INCLUDING BRECCAN'S DOG TAGS."
SO? WHY ARE THE TAGS IMPORTANT?
STAMPED ON THE TAGS WAS AN INCANTATION BRECCAN PREPARED, MEANT TO RESURRECT HIS SPIRIT.
OF COURSE, IT HAD TO BE READ ALOUD IN ITS ENTIRETY TO TAKE EFFECT.
ON THE FIELD OF BATTLE, THIS ALL MAY HAVE WORKED WELL.
TODAY, WITH HIS REMAINS BURIED SO FAR AWAY, HIS SPIRIT BONDED TO HIS OFFICER'S WINGS--AND THROUGH THEM, KATHERINE.
BUT THE WAY THAT THING... UNRAVELED WHEN O'DONNELL WAS READING HIS INCANTATION-- I SAW MORE THAN ONE GHOST OUT THERE.
THAT'S HERE IN THE FILE--THE NECROMANCY.
"FOR EACH RITUAL KILLING PERFORMED, BRECCAN WAS GRANTED COMMAND OVER THE SOUL OF HIS VICTIM.
"EACH SOUL ENSLAVED IN THAT WAY ADDED TO HIS POWER."

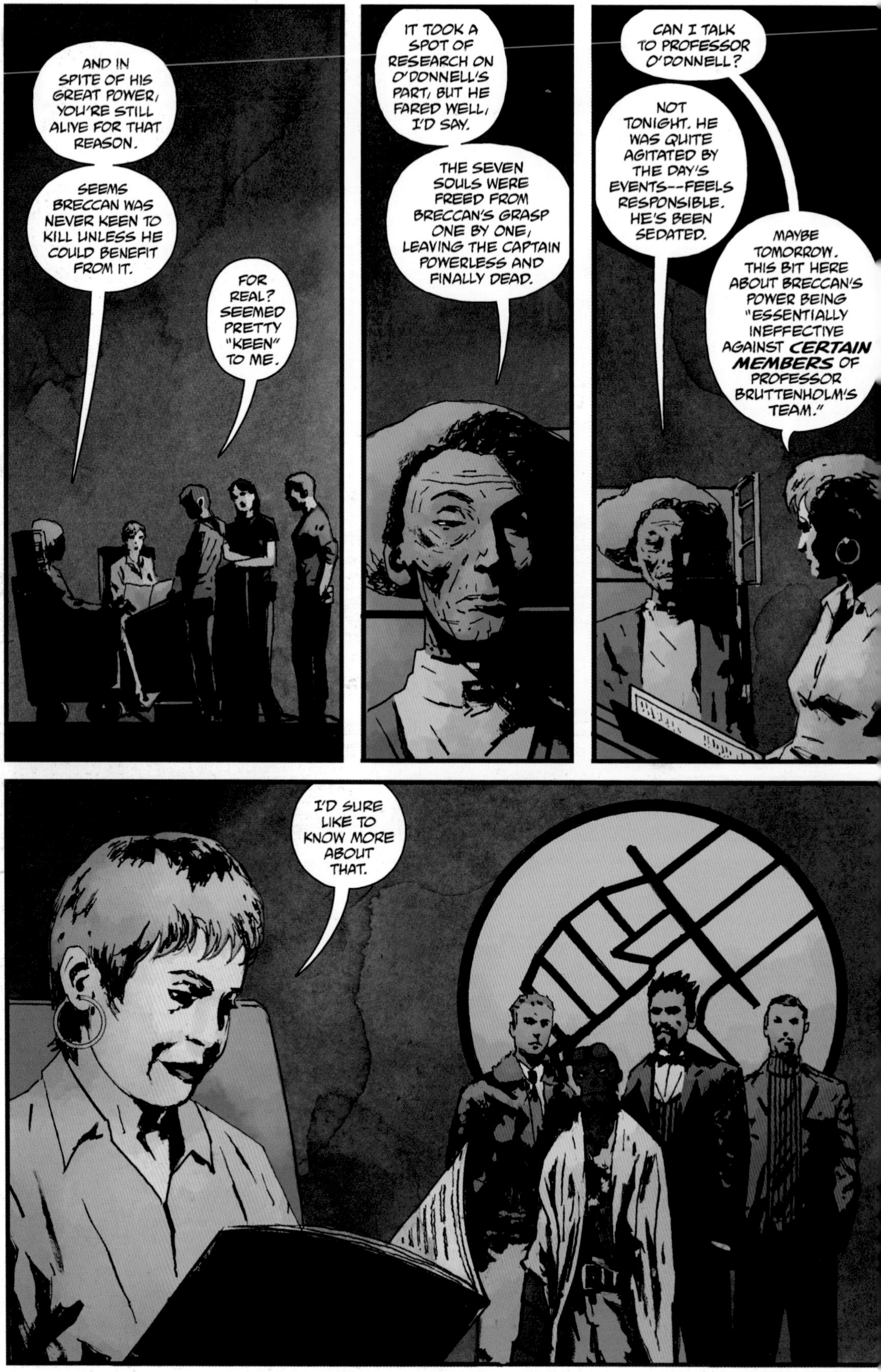

AND IN SPITE OF HIS GREAT POWER, YOU'RE STILL ALIVE FOR THAT REASON.
SEEMS BRECCAN WAS NEVER KEEN TO KILL UNLESS HE COULD BENEFIT FROM IT.
FOR REAL? SEEMED PRETTY "KEEN" TO ME.
IT TOOK A SPOT OF RESEARCH ON O'DONNELL'S PART, BUT HE FARED WELL, I'D SAY.
THE SEVEN SOULS WERE FREED FROM BRECCAN'S GRASP ONE BY ONE, LEAVING THE CAPTAIN POWERLESS AND FINALLY DEAD.
CAN I TALK TO PROFESSOR O'DONNELL?
NOT TONIGHT. HE WAS QUITE AGITATED BY THE DAY'S EVENTS--FEELS RESPONSIBLE. HE'S BEEN SEDATED.
MAYBE TOMORROW. THIS BIT HERE ABOUT BRECCAN'S POWER BEING "ESSENTIALLY INEFFECTIVE AGAINST ***CERTAIN MEMBERS*** OF PROFESSOR BRUTTENHOLM'S TEAM."
I'D SURE LIKE TO KNOW MORE ABOUT THAT.

THE EN

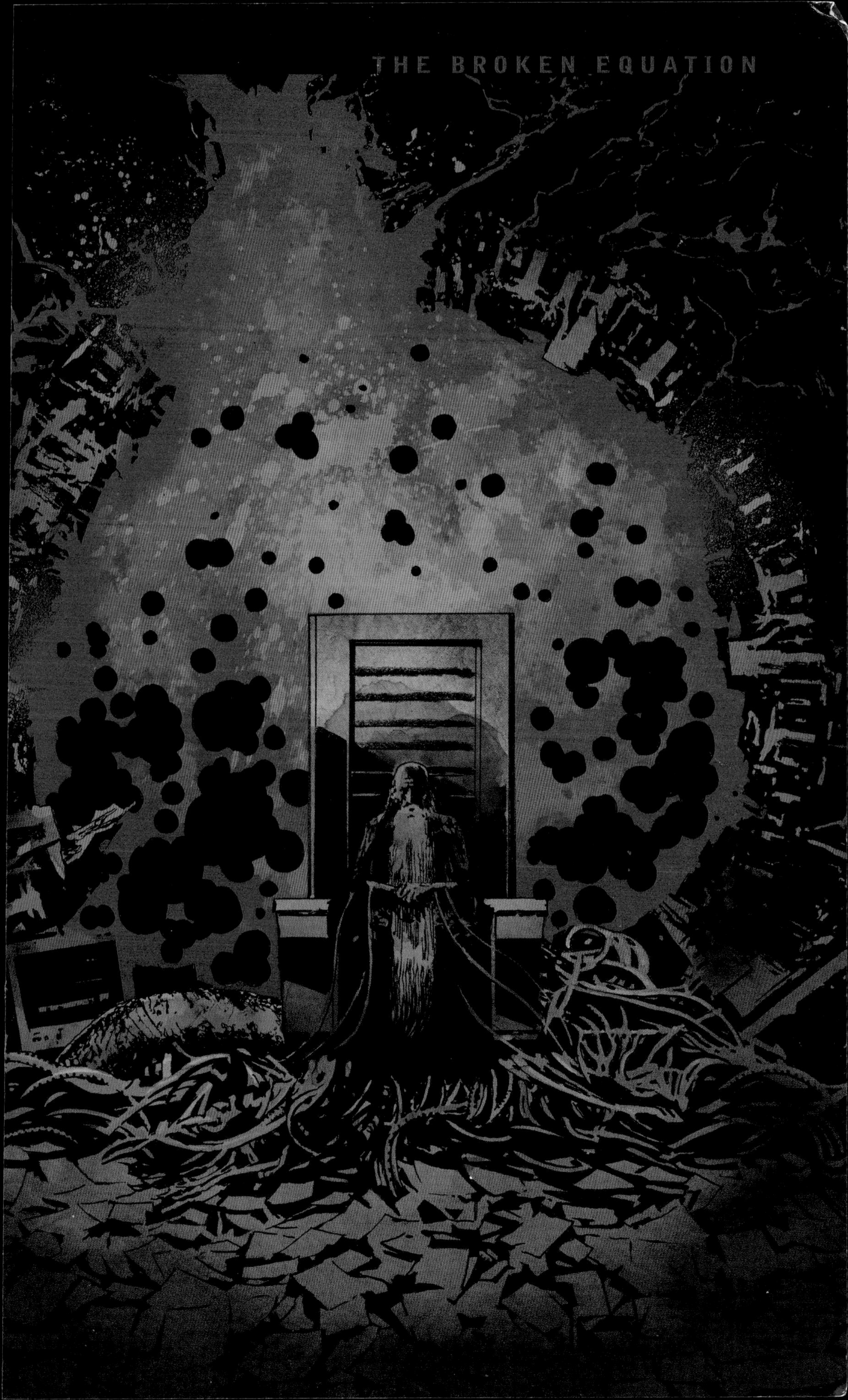
THE BROKEN EQUATION

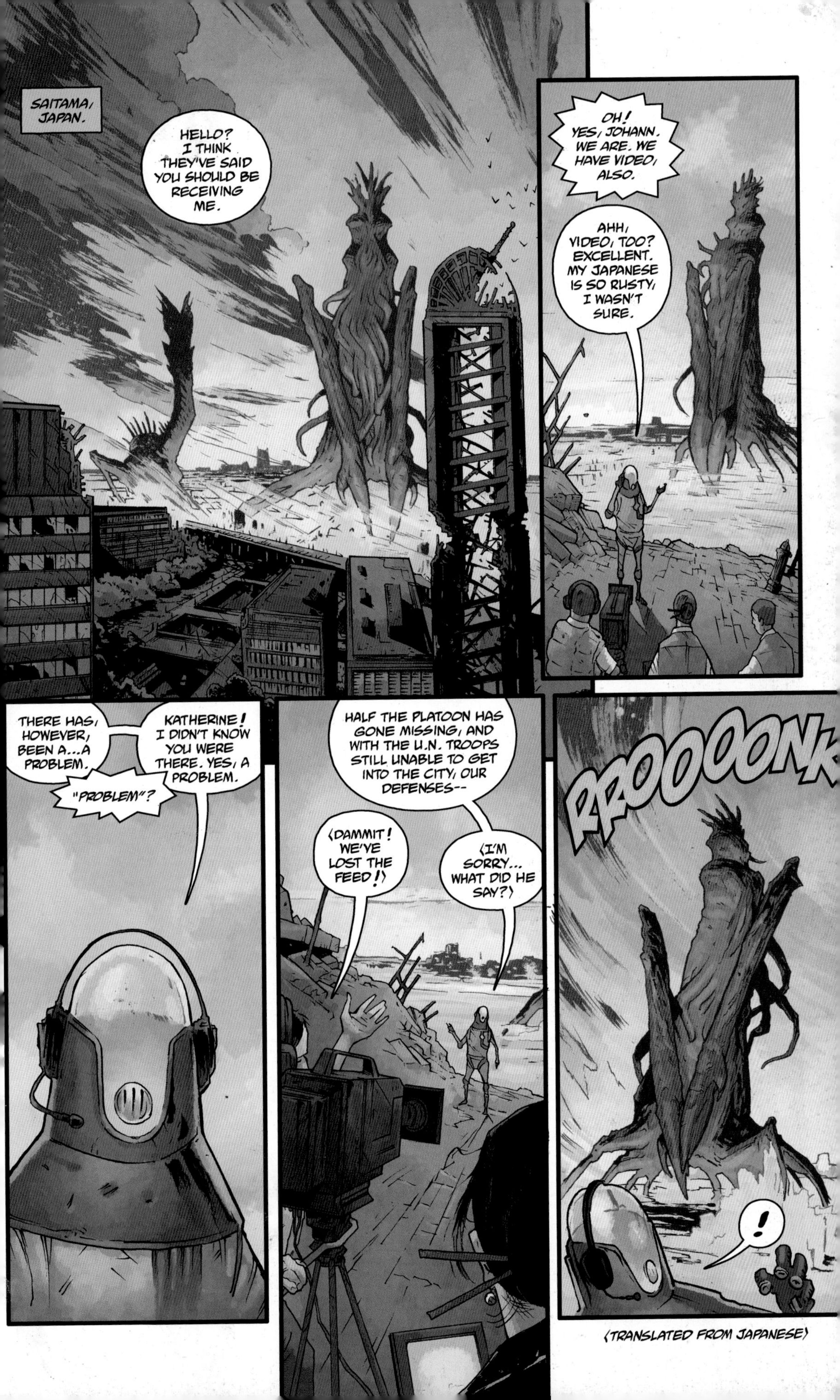
SAITAMA, JAPAN.
HELLO? I THINK THEY'VE SAID YOU SHOULD BE RECEIVING ME.
OH! YES, JOHANN. WE ARE. WE HAVE VIDEO, ALSO.
AHH, VIDEO, TOO? EXCELLENT. MY JAPANESE IS SO RUSTY, I WASN'T SURE.
THERE HAS, HOWEVER, BEEN A...A PROBLEM.
KATHERINE! I DIDN'T KNOW YOU WERE THERE. YES, A PROBLEM.
"PROBLEM"?
HALF THE PLATOON HAS GONE MISSING, AND WITH THE U.N. TROOPS STILL UNABLE TO GET INTO THE CITY, OUR DEFENSES--
‹DAMMIT! WE'VE LOST THE FEED!›
‹I'M SORRY... WHAT DID HE SAY?›
RROOOONK
!
‹TRANSLATED FROM JAPANESE›

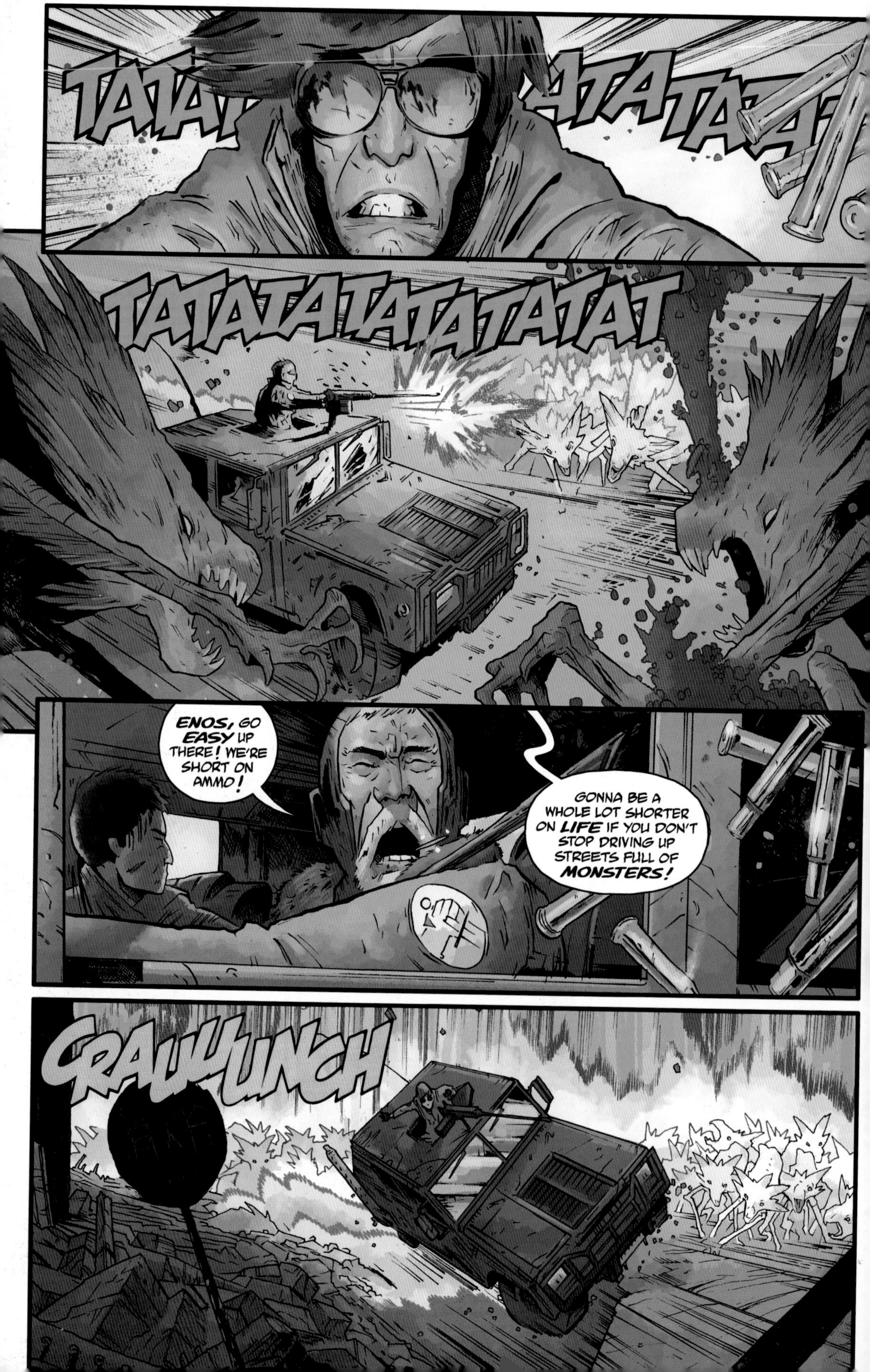
TATAT TATATATA
TATATATATATATAT
ENOS, GO EASY UP THERE! WE'RE SHORT ON AMMO!
GONNA BE A WHOLE LOT SHORTER ON LIFE IF YOU DON'T STOP DRIVING UP STREETS FULL OF MONSTERS!
CRAWWUNCH

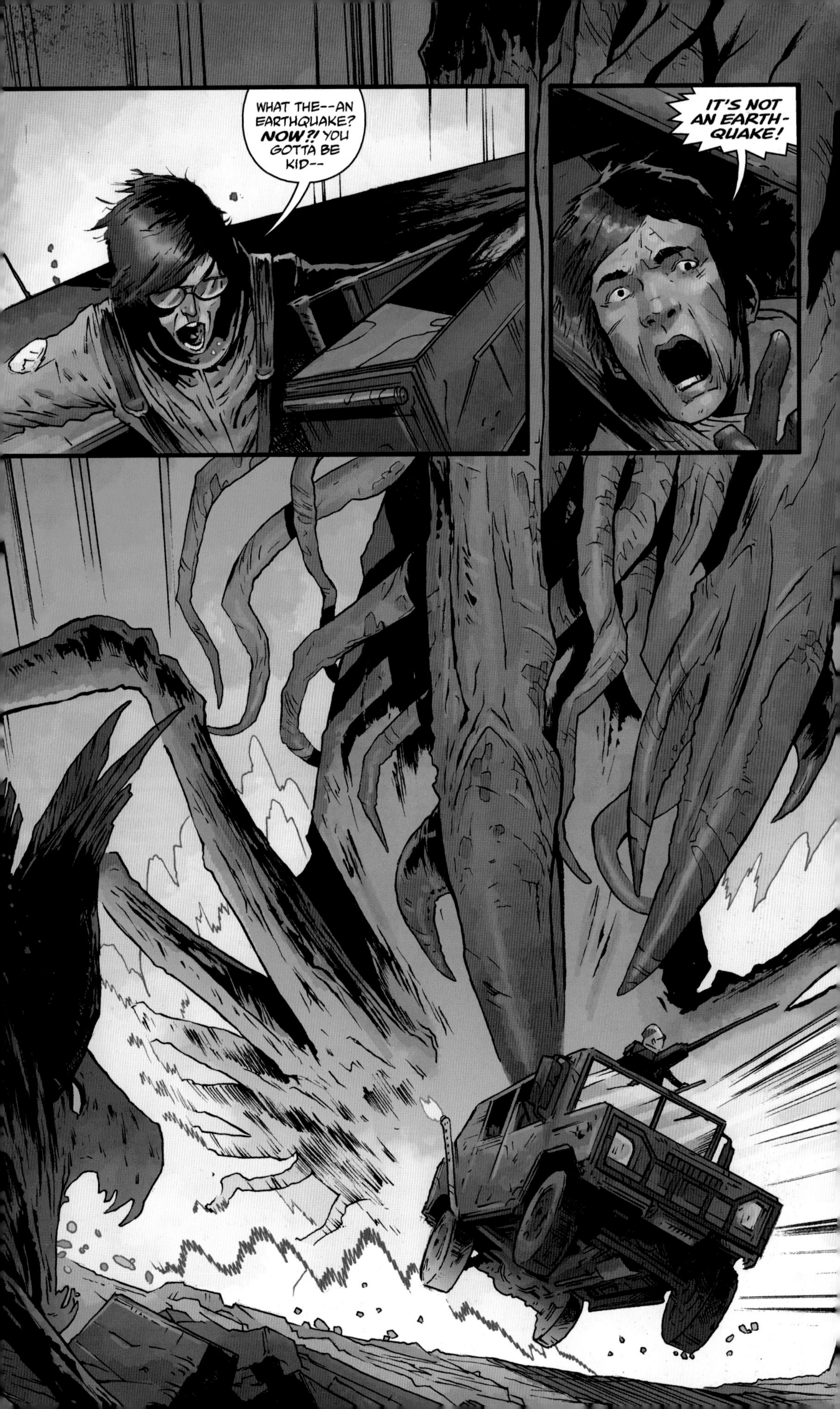
WHAT THE--AN EARTHQUAKE? **NOW?!** YOU GOTTA BE KID--
IT'S NOT AN EARTH-QUAKE!

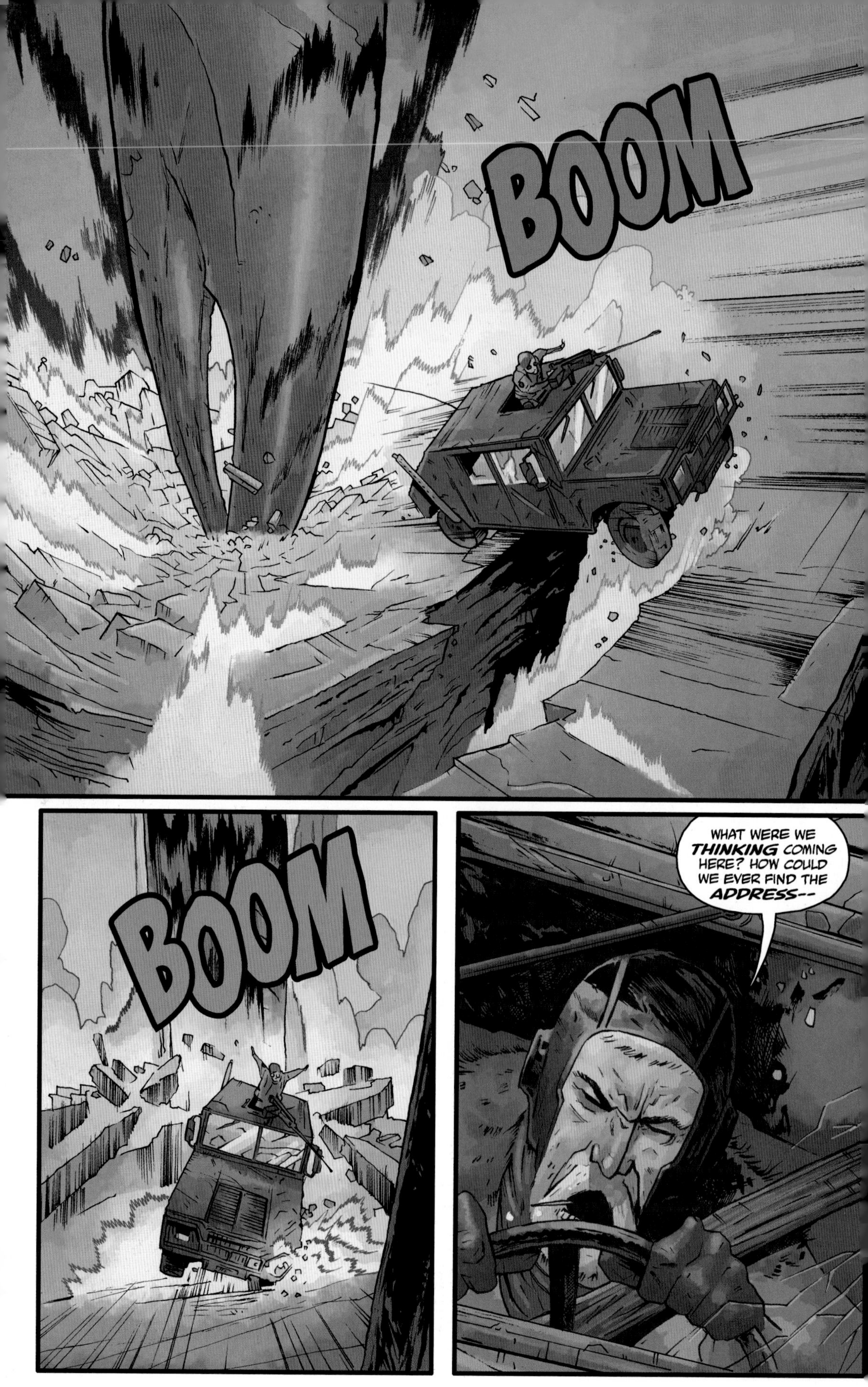
BOOM
BOOM
WHAT WERE WE THINKING COMING HERE? HOW COULD WE EVER FIND THE ADDRESS--

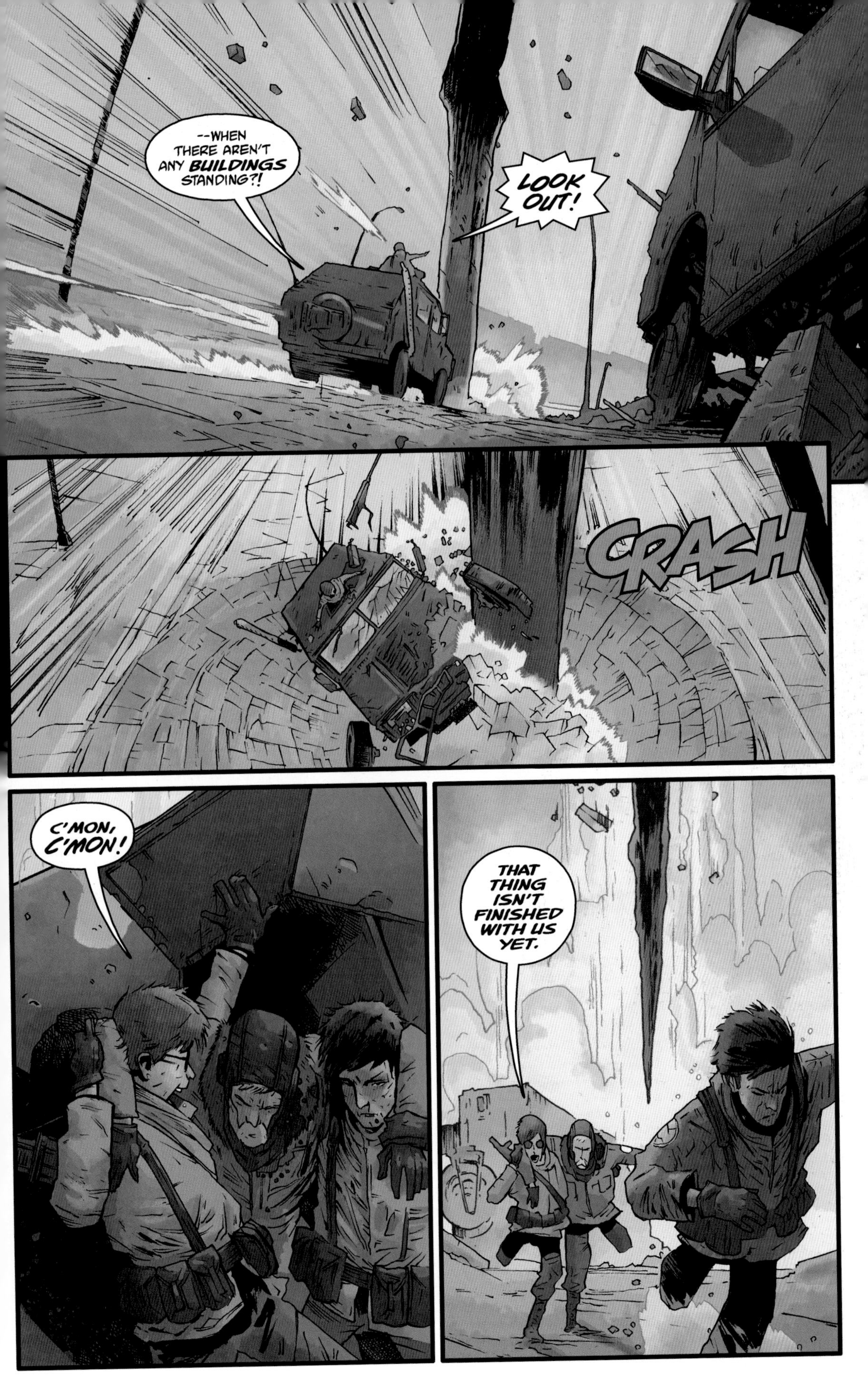
--WHEN THERE AREN'T ANY BUILDINGS STANDING?!
LOOK OUT!
CRASH
C'MON, C'MON!
THAT THING ISN'T FINISHED WITH US YET.

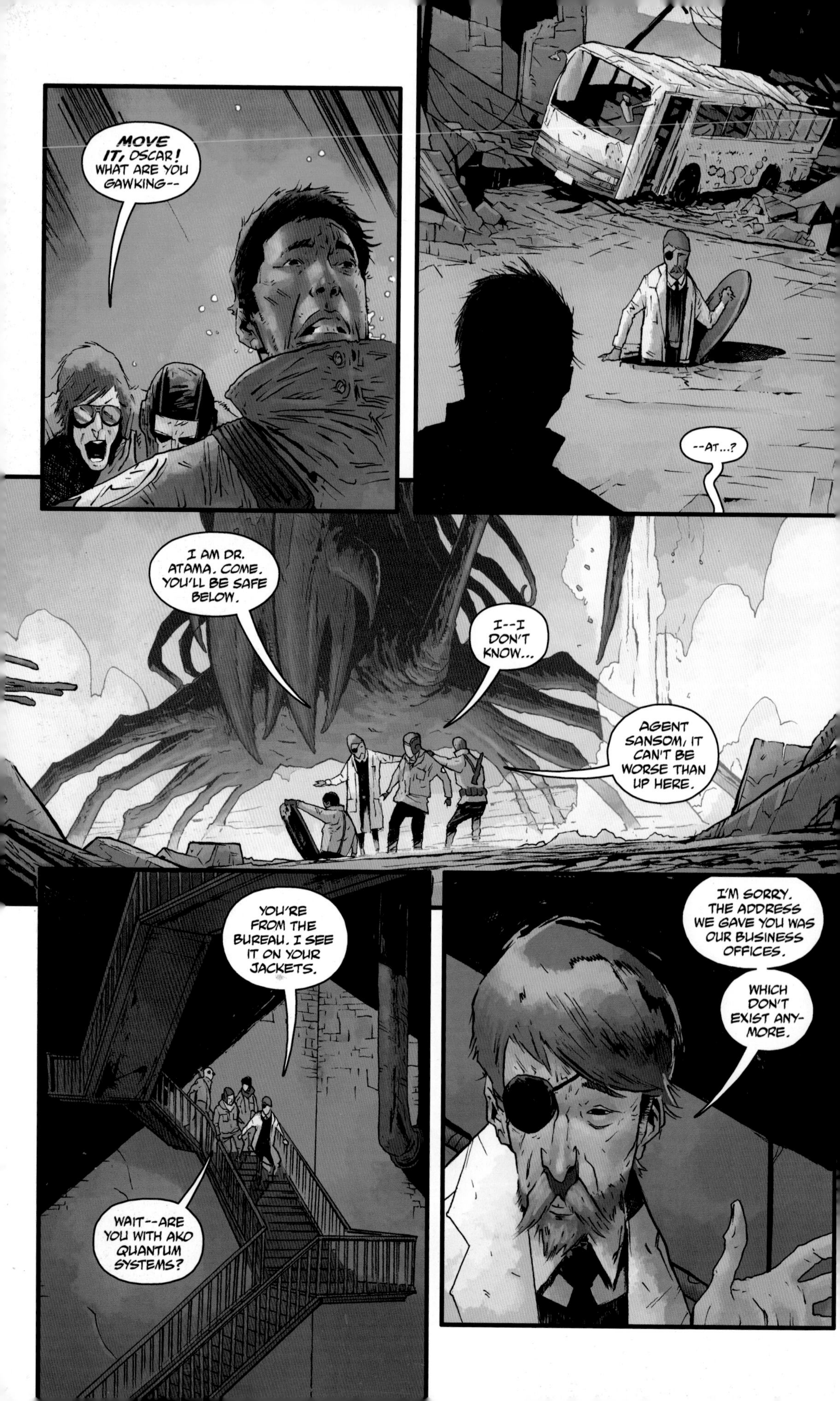
MOVE IT, OSCAR! WHAT ARE YOU GAWKING--
--AT...?
I AM DR. ATAMA. COME. YOU'LL BE SAFE BELOW.
I--I DON'T KNOW...
AGENT SANSOM, IT CAN'T BE WORSE THAN UP HERE.
YOU'RE FROM THE BUREAU. I SEE IT ON YOUR JACKETS.
WAIT--ARE YOU WITH AKO QUANTUM SYSTEMS?
I'M SORRY. THE ADDRESS WE GAVE YOU WAS OUR BUSINESS OFFICES.
WHICH DON'T EXIST ANY-MORE.

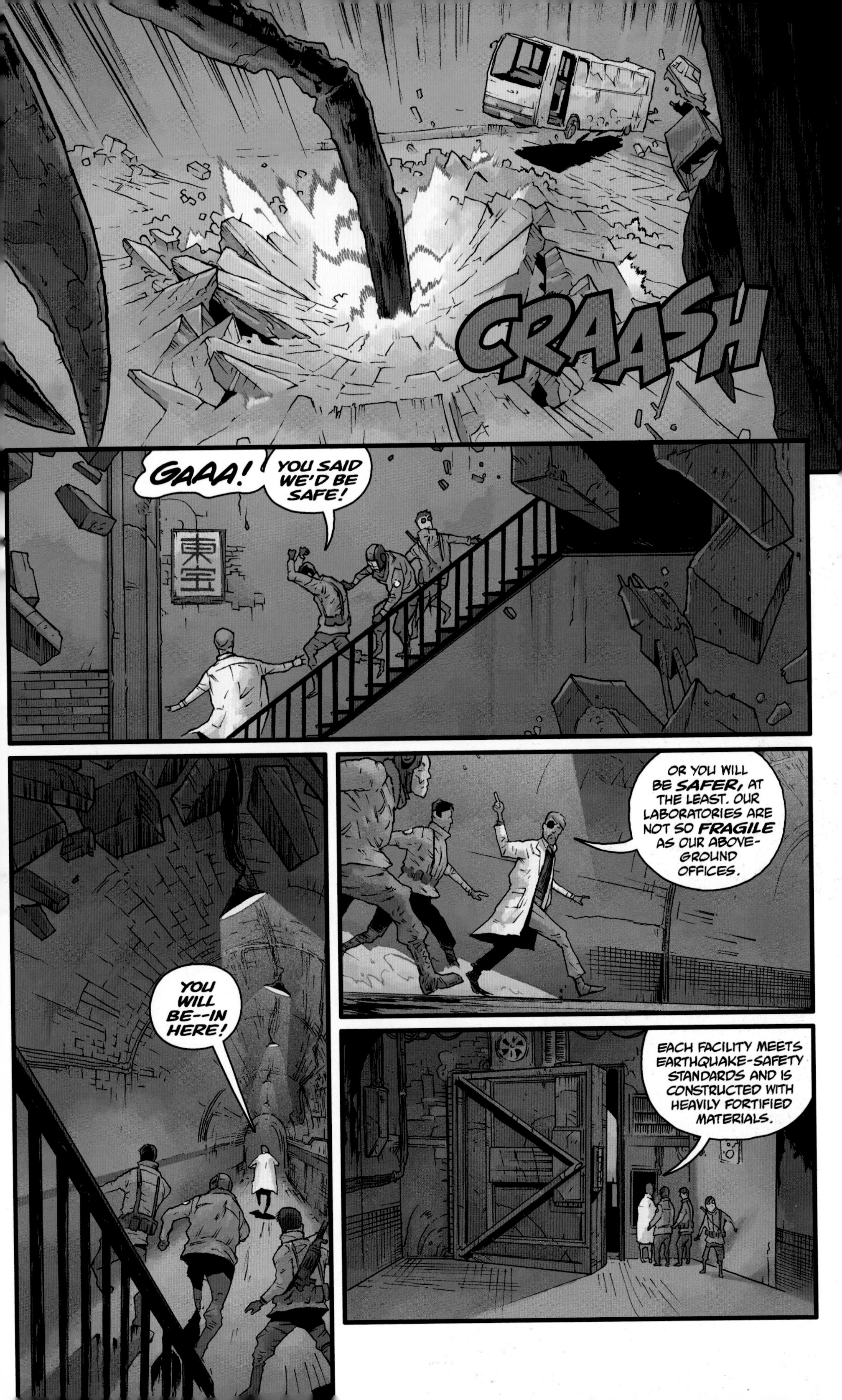
CRAASH
GAAA!
YOU SAID WE'D BE SAFE!
東宝
YOU WILL BE--IN HERE!
OR YOU WILL BE SAFER, AT THE LEAST. OUR LABORATORIES ARE NOT SO FRAGILE AS OUR ABOVE-GROUND OFFICES.
EACH FACILITY MEETS EARTHQUAKE-SAFETY STANDARDS AND IS CONSTRUCTED WITH HEAVILY FORTIFIED MATERIALS.

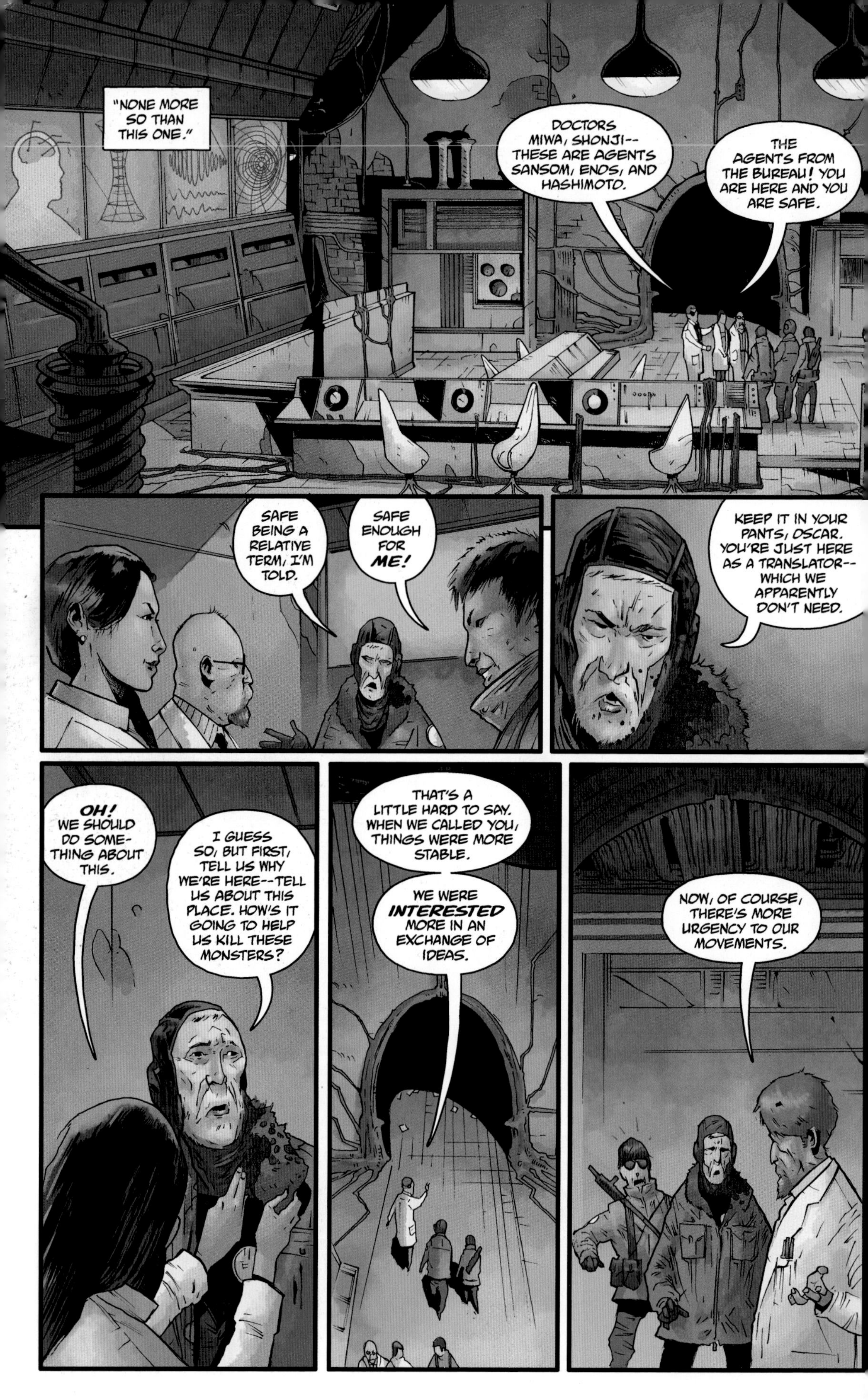
"NONE MORE SO THAN THIS ONE."
DOCTORS MIWA, SHONJI-- THESE ARE AGENTS SANSOM, ENOS, AND HASHIMOTO.
THE AGENTS FROM THE BUREAU! YOU ARE HERE AND YOU ARE SAFE.
SAFE BEING A RELATIVE TERM, I'M TOLD.
SAFE ENOUGH FOR ME!
KEEP IT IN YOUR PANTS, OSCAR. YOU'RE JUST HERE AS A TRANSLATOR-- WHICH WE APPARENTLY DON'T NEED.
OH! WE SHOULD DO SOME-THING ABOUT THIS.
I GUESS SO, BUT FIRST, TELL US WHY WE'RE HERE--TELL US ABOUT THIS PLACE. HOW'S IT GOING TO HELP US KILL THESE MONSTERS?
THAT'S A LITTLE HARD TO SAY. WHEN WE CALLED YOU, THINGS WERE MORE STABLE.
WE WERE INTERESTED MORE IN AN EXCHANGE OF IDEAS.
NOW, OF COURSE, THERE'S MORE URGENCY TO OUR MOVEMENTS.

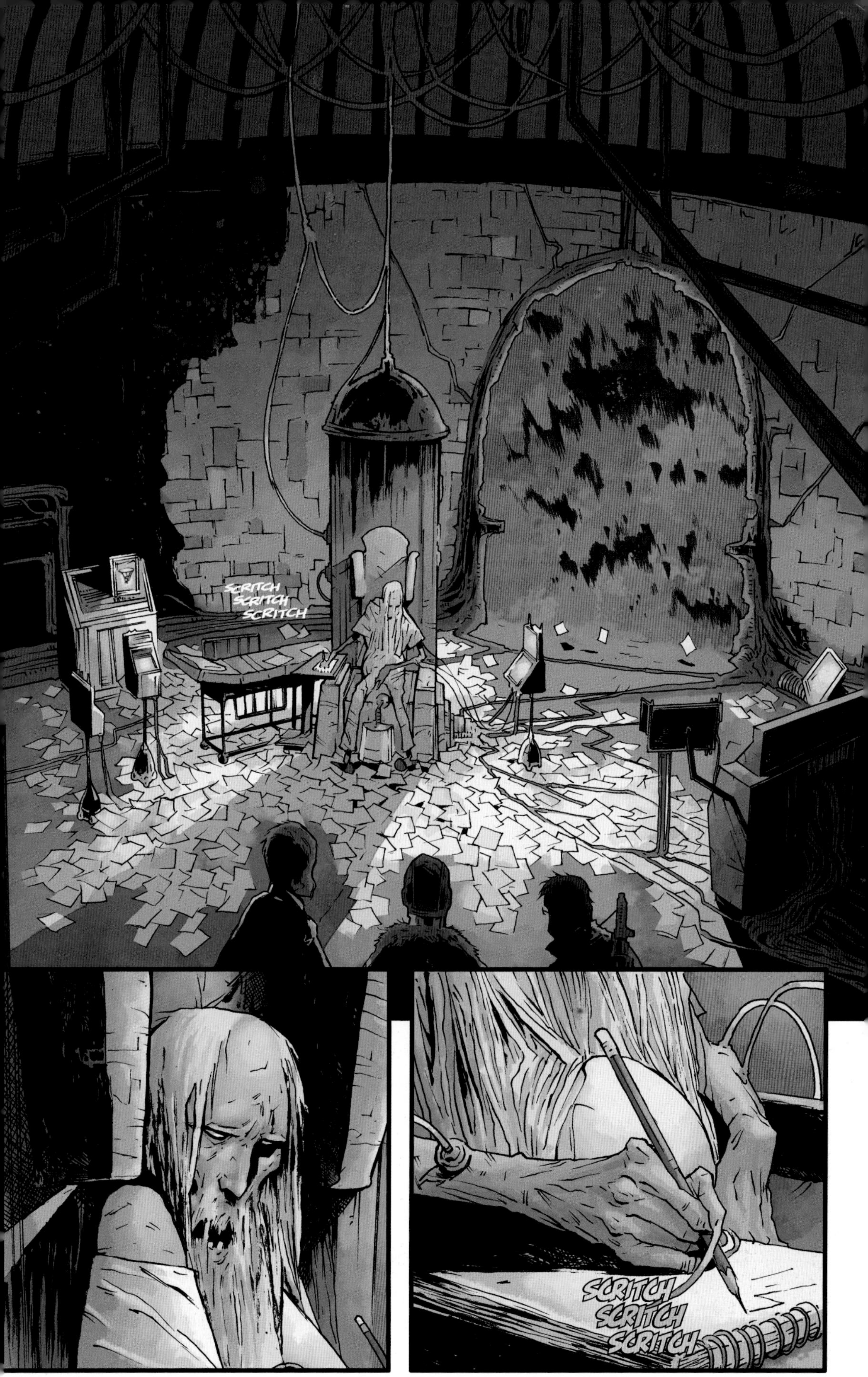
SCRITCH
SCRITCH
SCRITCH
SCRITCH
SCRITCH
SCRITCH

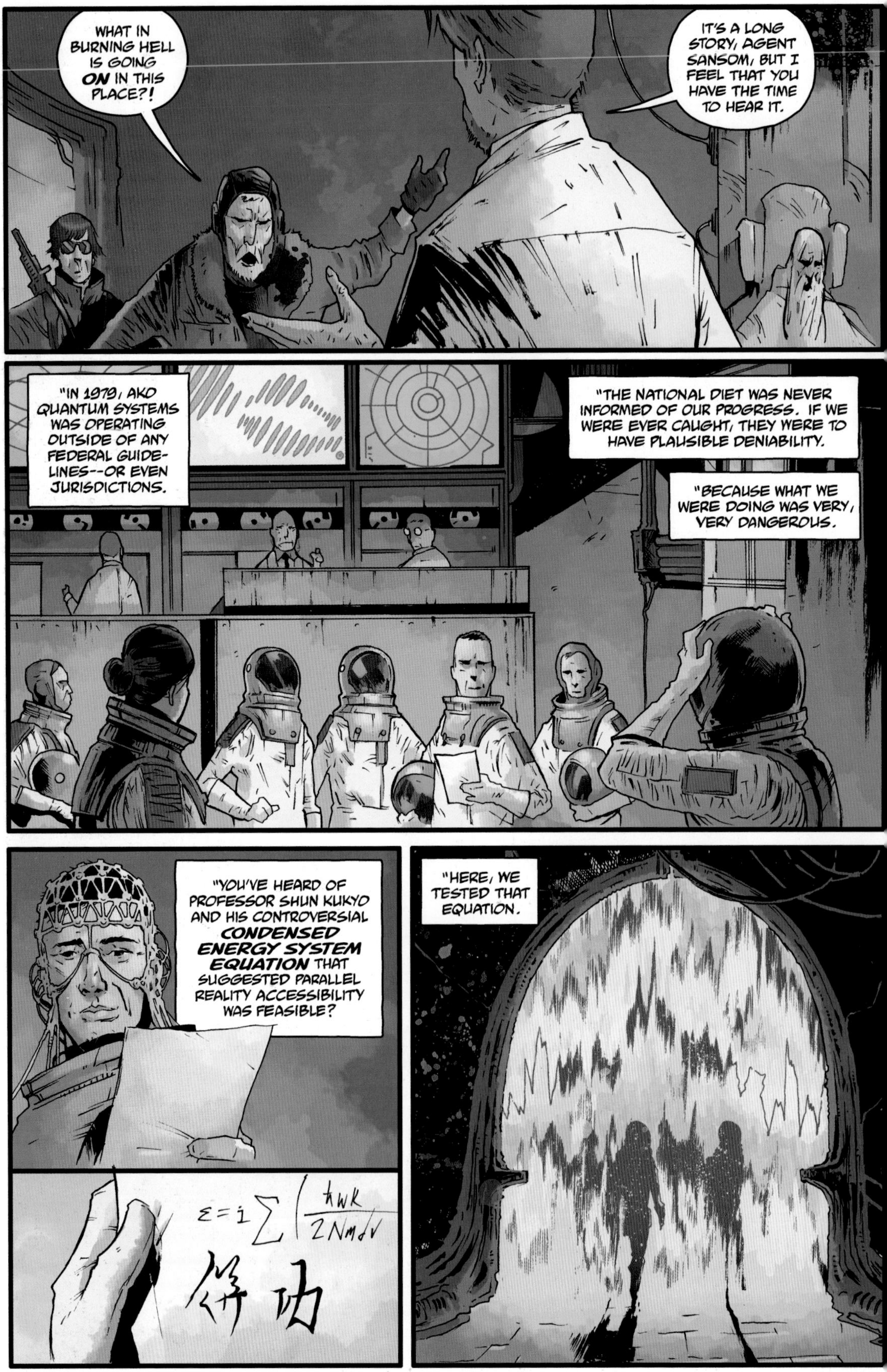

WHAT IN BURNING HELL IS GOING ON IN THIS PLACE?!
IT'S A LONG STORY, AGENT SANSOM, BUT I FEEL THAT YOU HAVE THE TIME TO HEAR IT.
"IN 1979, AKO QUANTUM SYSTEMS WAS OPERATING OUTSIDE OF ANY FEDERAL GUIDE-LINES--OR EVEN JURISDICTIONS.
"THE NATIONAL DIET WAS NEVER INFORMED OF OUR PROGRESS. IF WE WERE EVER CAUGHT, THEY WERE TO HAVE PLAUSIBLE DENIABILITY.
"BECAUSE WHAT WE WERE DOING WAS VERY, VERY DANGEROUS.
"YOU'VE HEARD OF PROFESSOR SHUN KUKYO AND HIS CONTROVERSIAL CONDENSED ENERGY SYSTEM EQUATION THAT SUGGESTED PARALLEL REALITY ACCESSIBILITY WAS FEASIBLE?
"HERE, WE TESTED THAT EQUATION.

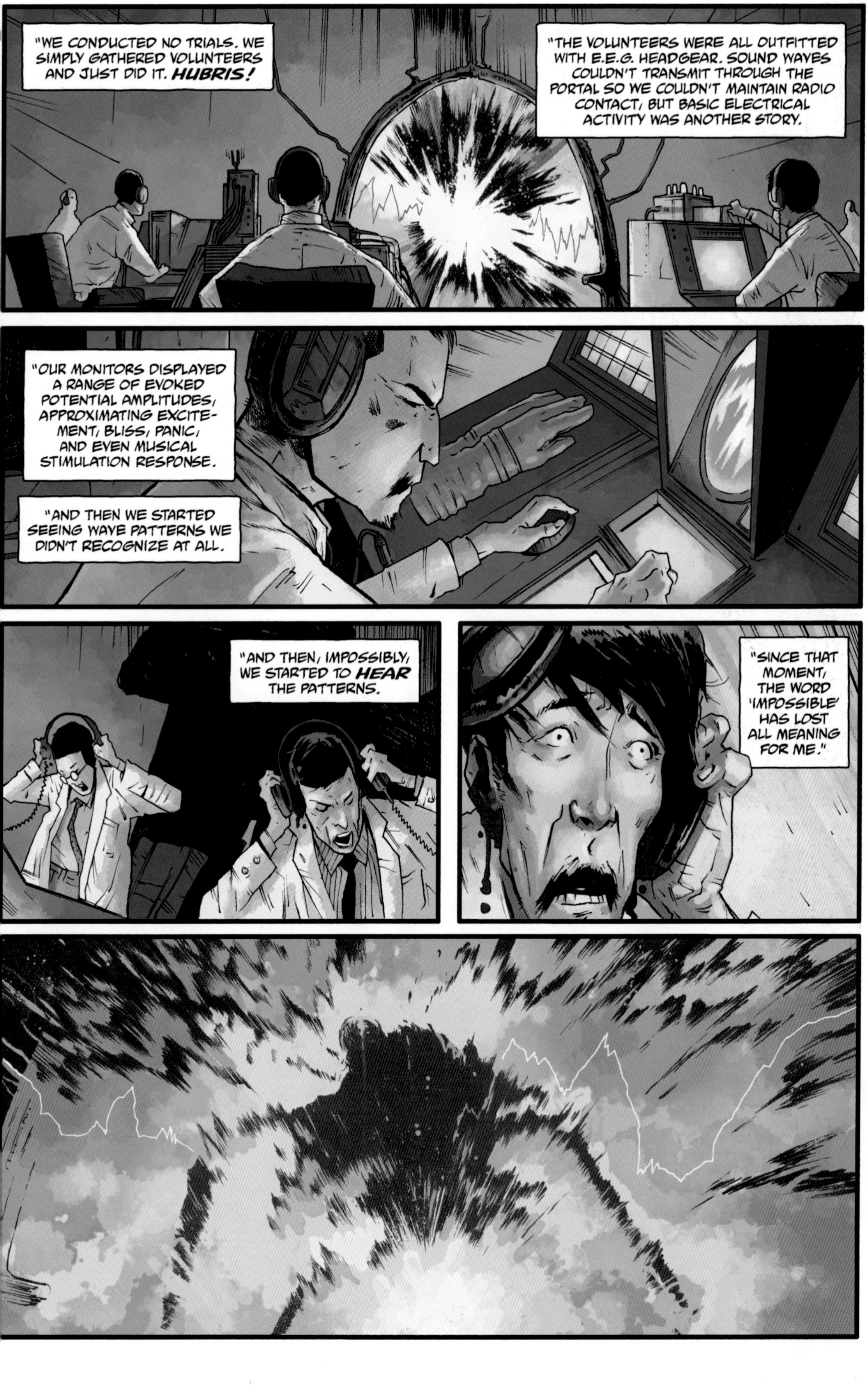
"WE CONDUCTED NO TRIALS. WE SIMPLY GATHERED VOLUNTEERS AND JUST DID IT. HUBRIS!
"THE VOLUNTEERS WERE ALL OUTFITTED WITH E.E.G. HEADGEAR. SOUND WAVES COULDN'T TRANSMIT THROUGH THE PORTAL SO WE COULDN'T MAINTAIN RADIO CONTACT, BUT BASIC ELECTRICAL ACTIVITY WAS ANOTHER STORY.
"OUR MONITORS DISPLAYED A RANGE OF EVOKED POTENTIAL AMPLITUDES, APPROXIMATING EXCITEMENT, BLISS, PANIC, AND EVEN MUSICAL STIMULATION RESPONSE.
"AND THEN WE STARTED SEEING WAVE PATTERNS WE DIDN'T RECOGNIZE AT ALL.
"AND THEN, IMPOSSIBLY, WE STARTED TO HEAR THE PATTERNS.
"SINCE THAT MOMENT, THE WORD 'IMPOSSIBLE' HAS LOST ALL MEANING FOR ME."

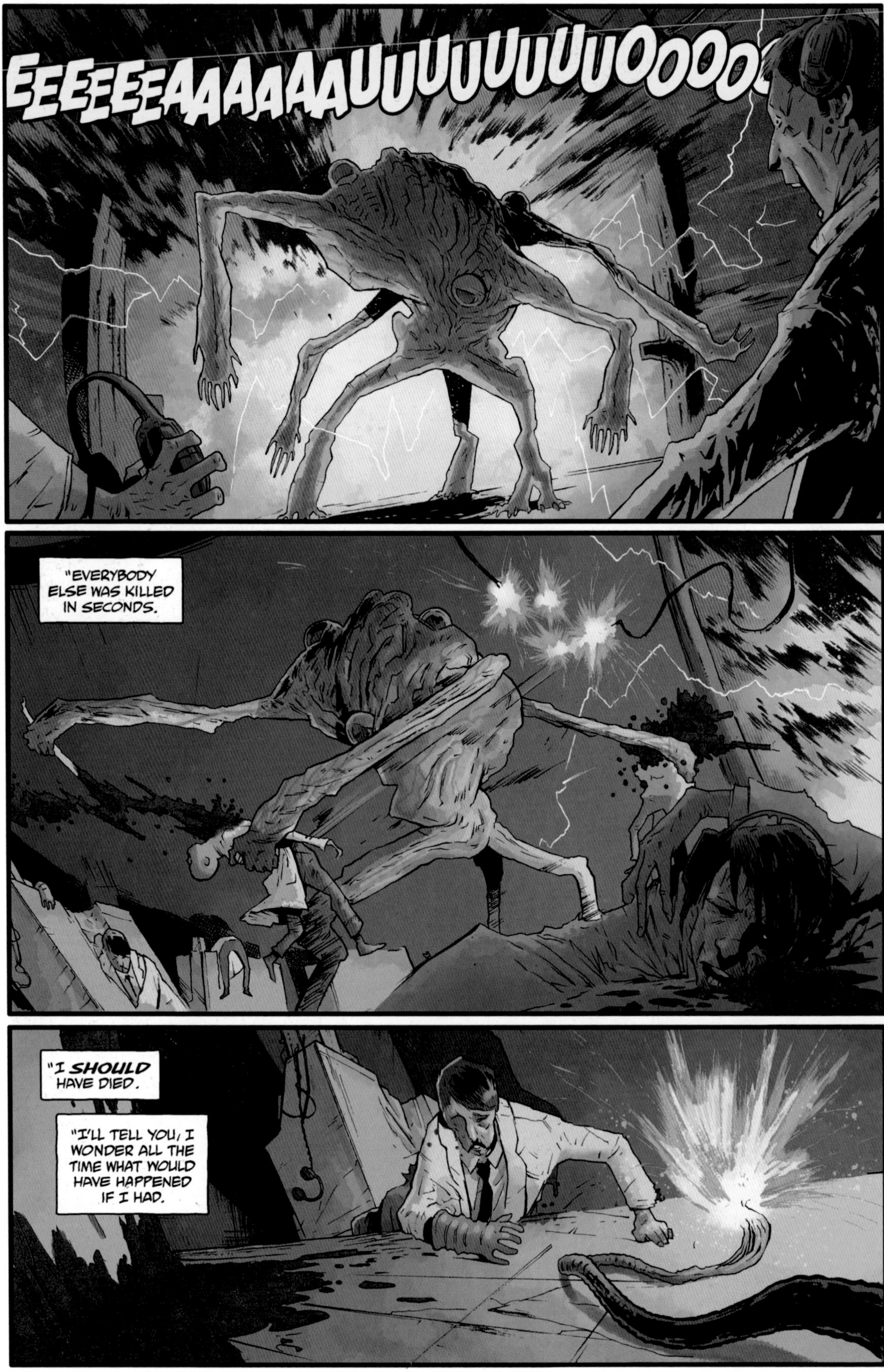
EEEEEEAAAAAAUUUUUUUUUOOOOO
"EVERYBODY ELSE WAS KILLED IN SECONDS.
"I SHOULD HAVE DIED.
"I'LL TELL YOU, I WONDER ALL THE TIME WHAT WOULD HAVE HAPPENED IF I HAD.

"WHAT WOULD THAT CREATURE HAVE DONE HAD I NOT STOPPED IT?

"WHAT ELSE WOULD HAVE COME THROUGH OUR PORTAL IF IT HAD BEEN LEFT RUNNING?

"THIS FACILITY WAS DISMANTLED. WE PULLED OUT ALL THE EQUIPMENT THAT WE COULD; WE SHUT DOWN ALL THE POWER TO THE CHAMBER.

"ITS ENTIRE EXISTENCE WAS ERASED.

"SIX MONTHS LATER, I WAS INFORMED OF AN ANOMALY.

"THE NUCLEAR SAFETY COMMISSION WAS REGISTERING READINGS OF UNUSUAL RADIOACTIVITY UNDER SAITAMA'S SEWERS--

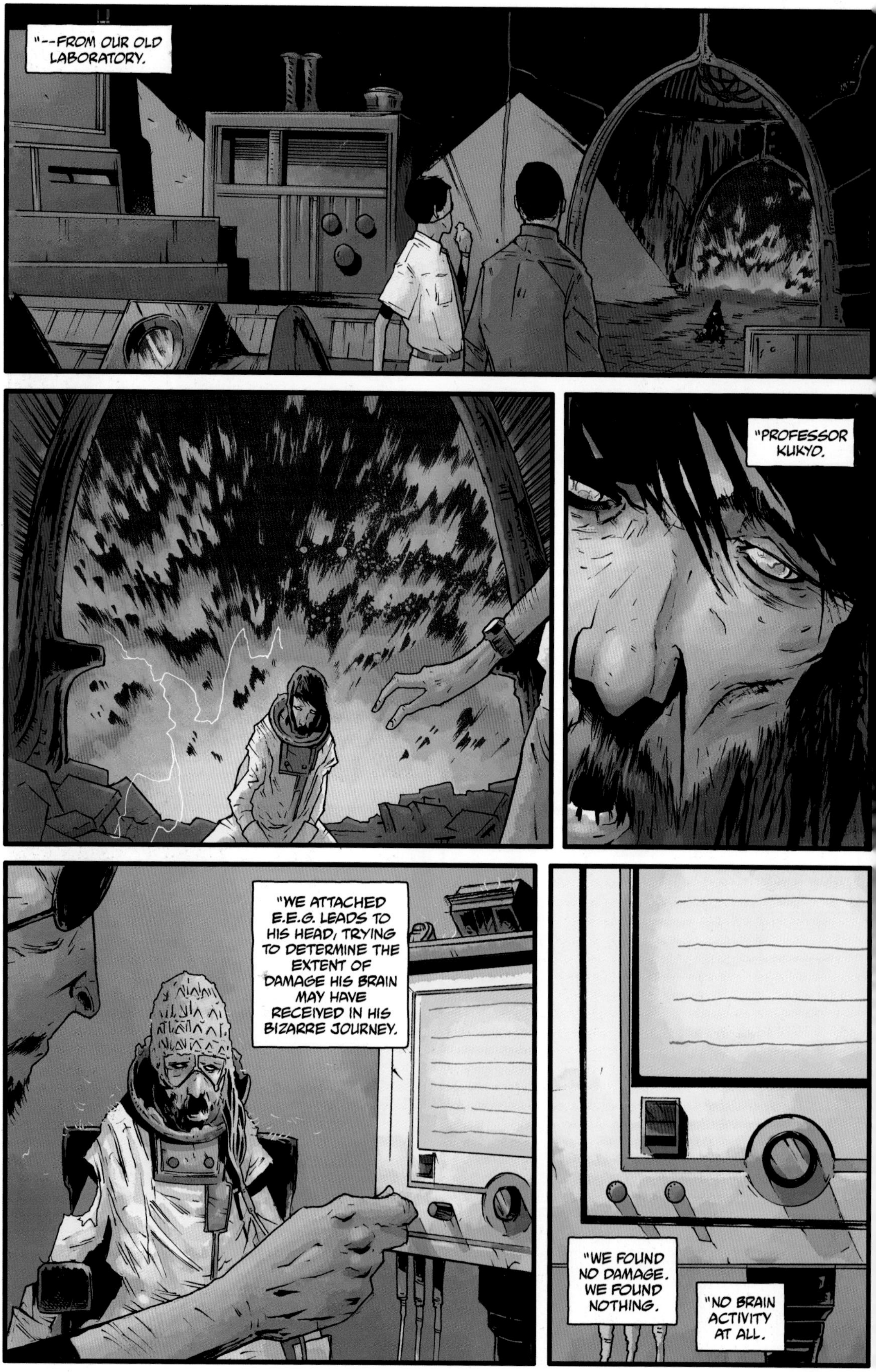
"--FROM OUR OLD LABORATORY.
"PROFESSOR KUKYO.
"WE ATTACHED E.E.G. LEADS TO HIS HEAD, TRYING TO DETERMINE THE EXTENT OF DAMAGE HIS BRAIN MAY HAVE RECEIVED IN HIS BIZARRE JOURNEY.
"WE FOUND NO DAMAGE. WE FOUND NOTHING.
"NO BRAIN ACTIVITY AT ALL.

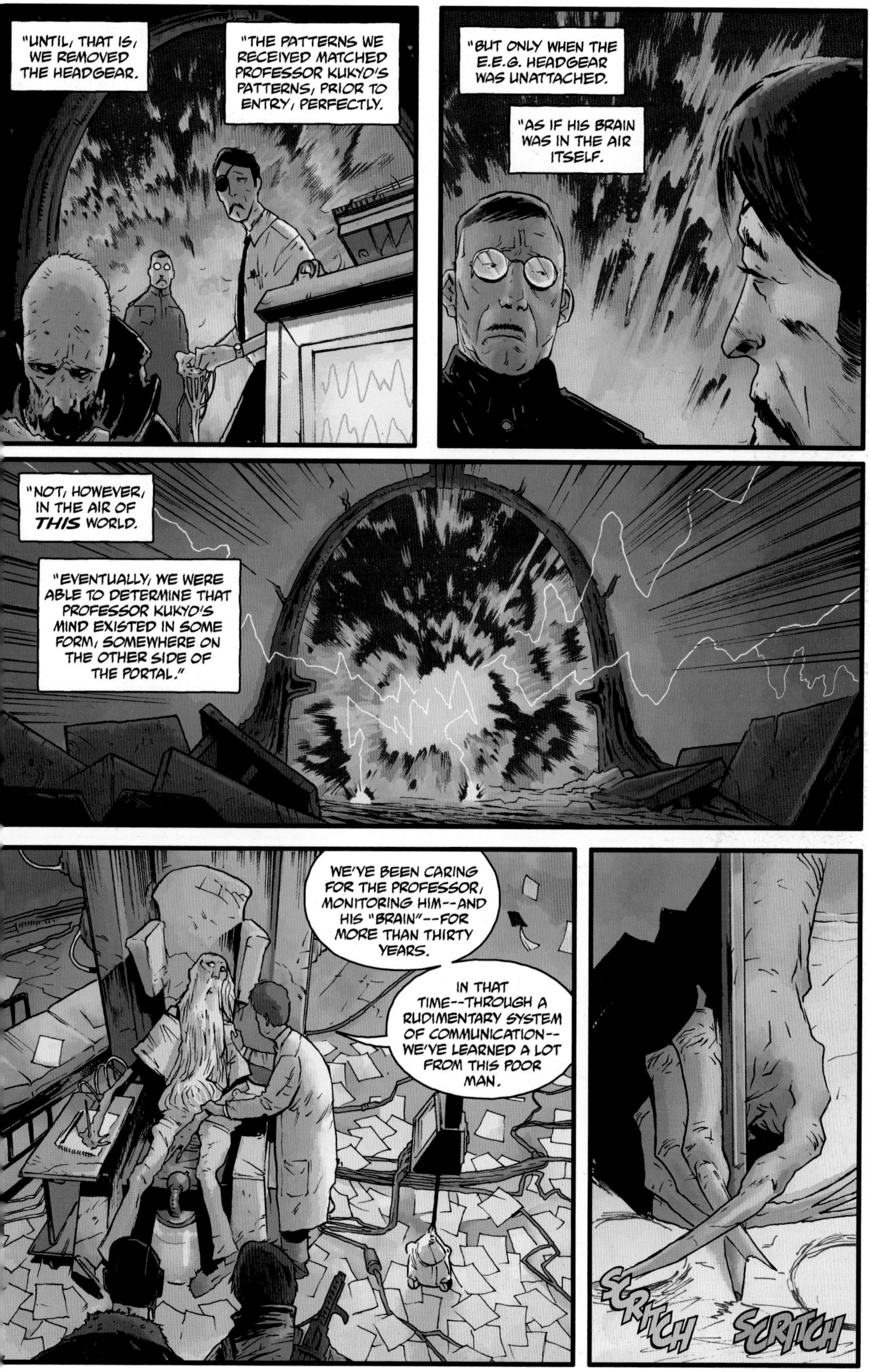
"UNTIL, THAT IS, WE REMOVED THE HEADGEAR.
"THE PATTERNS WE RECEIVED MATCHED PROFESSOR KUKYO'S PATTERNS, PRIOR TO ENTRY, PERFECTLY.
"BUT ONLY WHEN THE E.E.G. HEADGEAR WAS UNATTACHED.
"AS IF HIS BRAIN WAS IN THE AIR ITSELF.
"NOT, HOWEVER, IN THE AIR OF *THIS* WORLD.
"EVENTUALLY, WE WERE ABLE TO DETERMINE THAT PROFESSOR KUKYO'S MIND EXISTED IN SOME FORM, SOMEWHERE ON THE OTHER SIDE OF THE PORTAL."
WE'VE BEEN CARING FOR THE PROFESSOR, MONITORING HIM--AND HIS "BRAIN"--FOR MORE THAN THIRTY YEARS.
IN THAT TIME--THROUGH A RUDIMENTARY SYSTEM OF COMMUNICATION--WE'VE LEARNED A LOT FROM THIS POOR MAN.
SCRITCH
SCRITCH

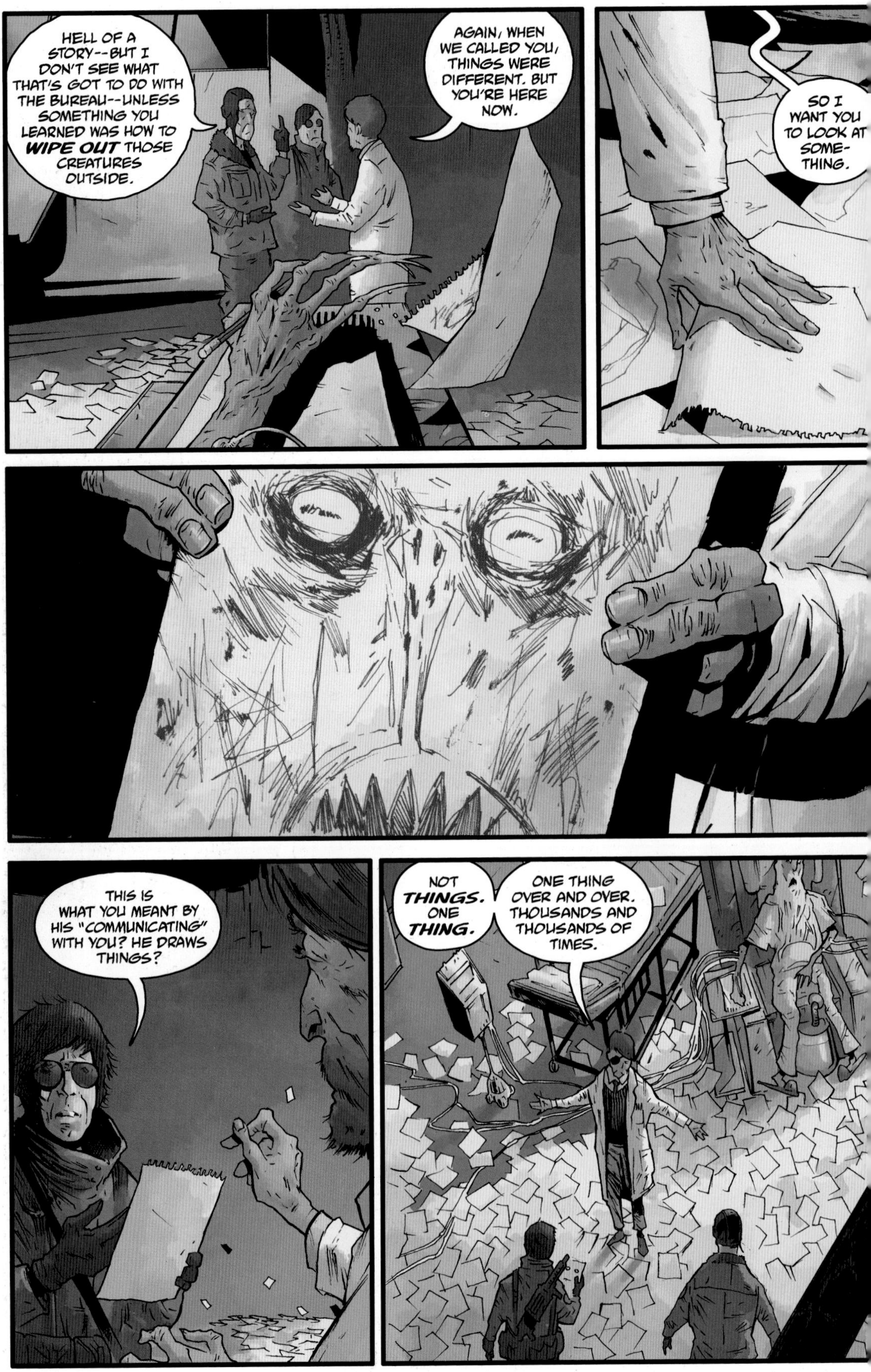
HELL OF A STORY--BUT I DON'T SEE WHAT THAT'S GOT TO DO WITH THE BUREAU--UNLESS SOMETHING YOU LEARNED WAS HOW TO **WIPE OUT** THOSE CREATURES OUTSIDE.
AGAIN, WHEN WE CALLED YOU, THINGS WERE DIFFERENT. BUT YOU'RE HERE NOW.
SO I WANT YOU TO LOOK AT SOME-THING.
THIS IS WHAT YOU MEANT BY HIS "COMMUNICATING" WITH YOU? HE DRAWS THINGS?
NOT ***THINGS.*** ONE ***THING.***
ONE THING OVER AND OVER. THOUSANDS AND THOUSANDS OF TIMES.

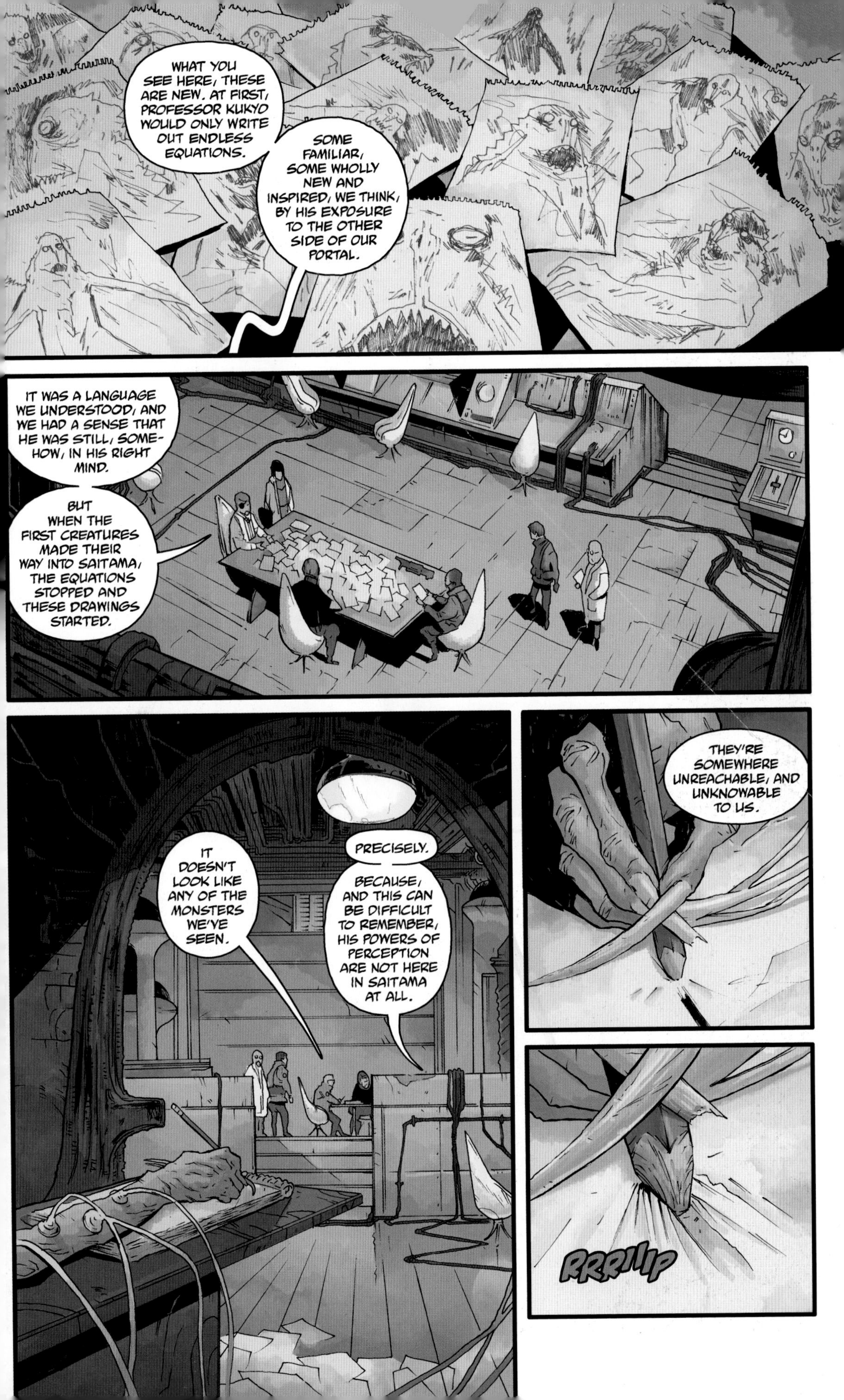
WHAT YOU SEE HERE, THESE ARE NEW. AT FIRST, PROFESSOR KUKYO WOULD ONLY WRITE OUT ENDLESS EQUATIONS.
SOME FAMILIAR, SOME WHOLLY NEW AND INSPIRED, WE THINK, BY HIS EXPOSURE TO THE OTHER SIDE OF OUR PORTAL.
IT WAS A LANGUAGE WE UNDERSTOOD, AND WE HAD A SENSE THAT HE WAS STILL, SOME-HOW, IN HIS RIGHT MIND.
BUT WHEN THE FIRST CREATURES MADE THEIR WAY INTO SAITAMA, THE EQUATIONS STOPPED AND THESE DRAWINGS STARTED.
IT DOESN'T LOOK LIKE ANY OF THE MONSTERS WE'VE SEEN.
PRECISELY.
BECAUSE, AND THIS CAN BE DIFFICULT TO REMEMBER, HIS POWERS OF PERCEPTION ARE NOT HERE IN SAITAMA AT ALL.
THEY'RE SOMEWHERE UNREACHABLE, AND UNKNOWABLE TO US.
RRRIIIP

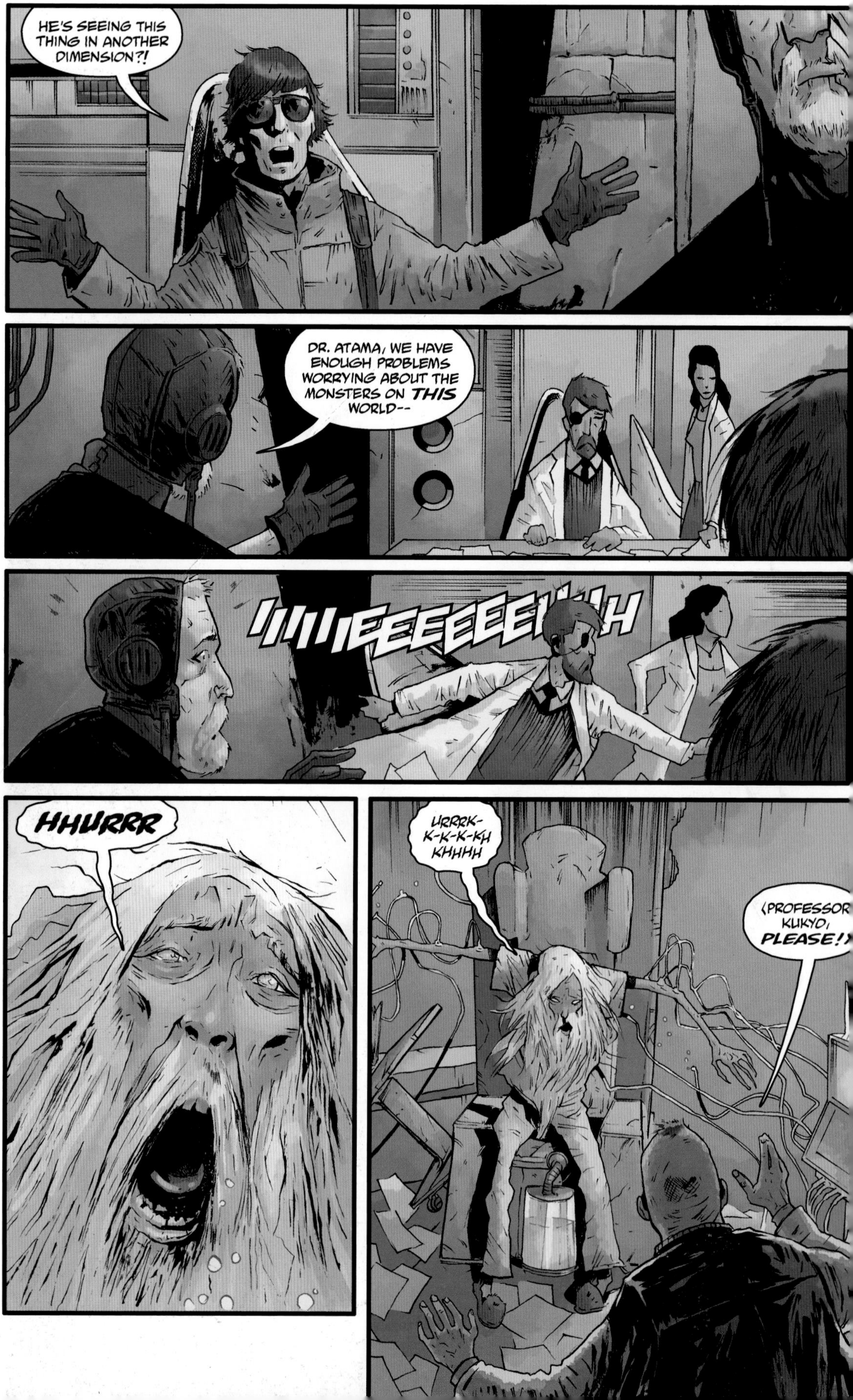
HE'S SEEING THIS THING IN ANOTHER DIMENSION?!
DR. ATAMA, WE HAVE ENOUGH PROBLEMS WORRYING ABOUT THE MONSTERS ON THIS WORLD--
IIIIIEEEEEEEEH
HHURRR
URRRK-K-K-K-KH KHHHH
‹PROFESSOR KUKYO, PLEASE!›

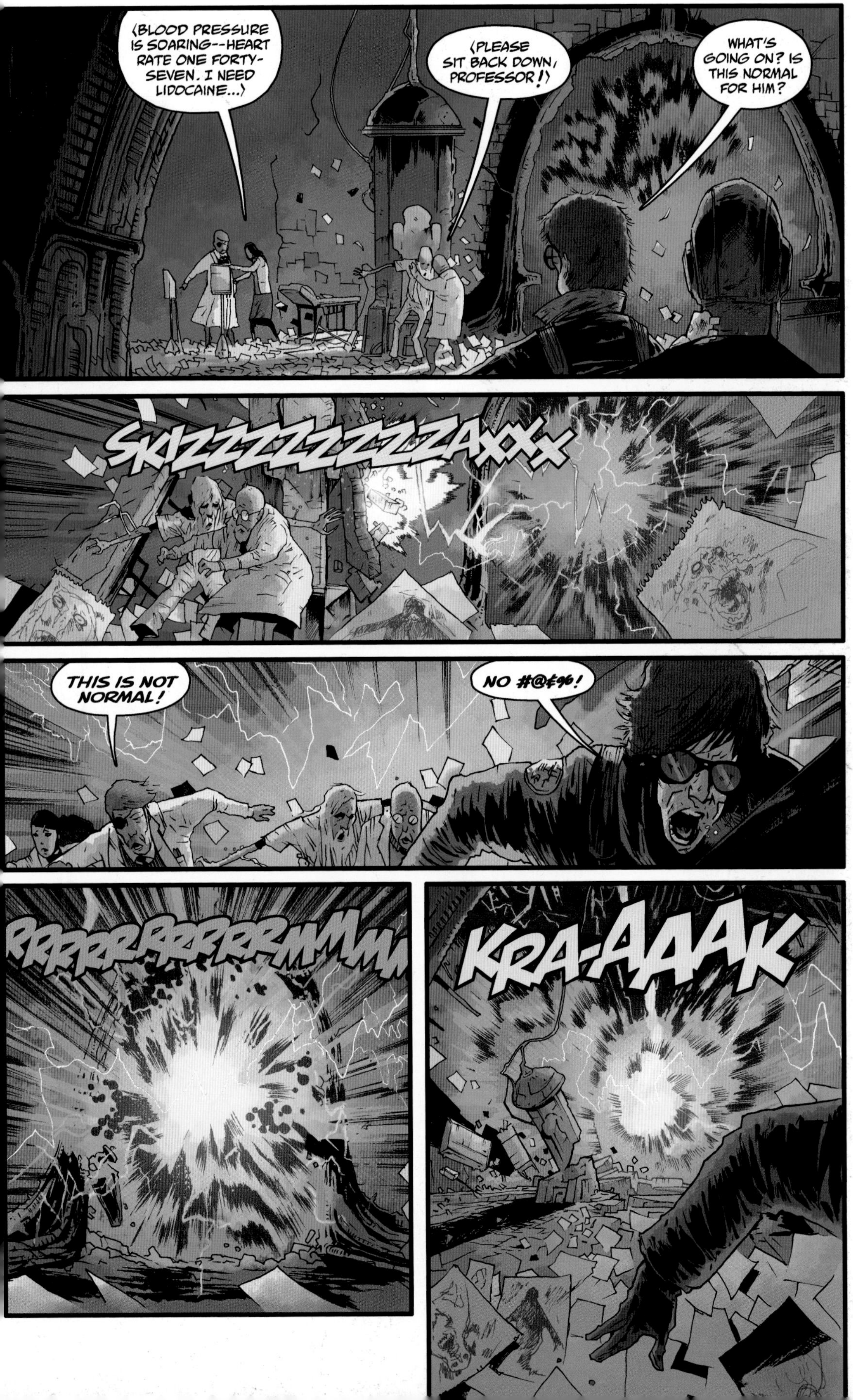
⟨BLOOD PRESSURE IS SOARING--HEART RATE ONE FORTY-SEVEN. I NEED LIDOCAINE...⟩
⟨PLEASE SIT BACK DOWN, PROFESSOR!⟩
WHAT'S GOING ON? IS THIS NORMAL FOR HIM?
SKIZZZZZZZZZAXXX
THIS IS NOT NORMAL!
NO #@&%!
RRRRRRRRRRMMMM
KRA-AAAK

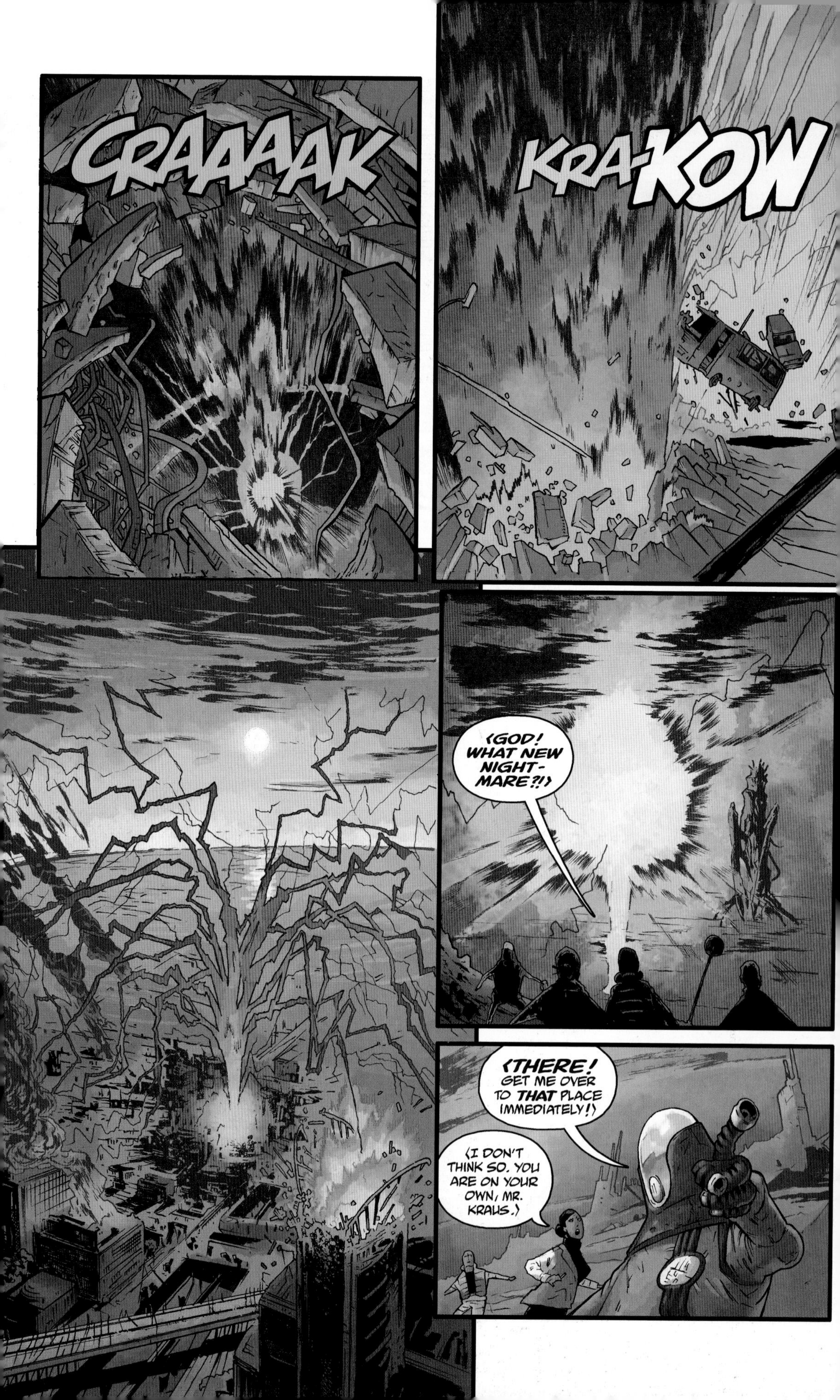
CRAAAAK
KRA-KOW
‹GOD! WHAT NEW NIGHT-MARE?!›
‹THERE! GET ME OVER TO THAT PLACE IMMEDIATELY!›
‹I DON'T THINK SO. YOU ARE ON YOUR OWN, MR. KRAUS.›

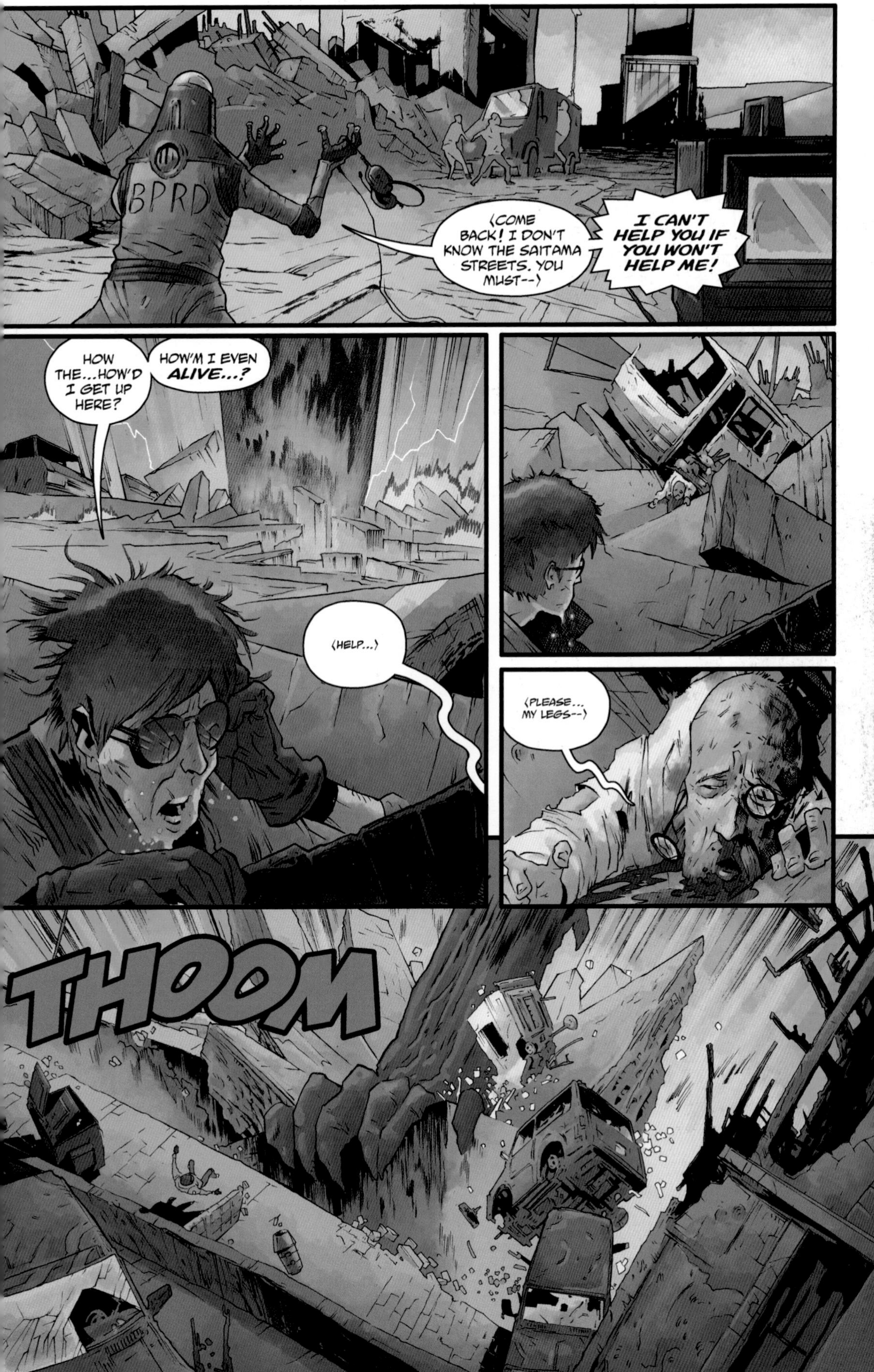
BPRD
⟨COME BACK! I DON'T KNOW THE SAITAMA STREETS. YOU MUST--⟩
I CAN'T HELP YOU IF YOU WON'T HELP ME!
HOW THE...HOW'D I GET UP HERE?
HOW'M I EVEN ALIVE...?
⟨HELP...⟩
⟨PLEASE... MY LEGS--⟩
THOOM

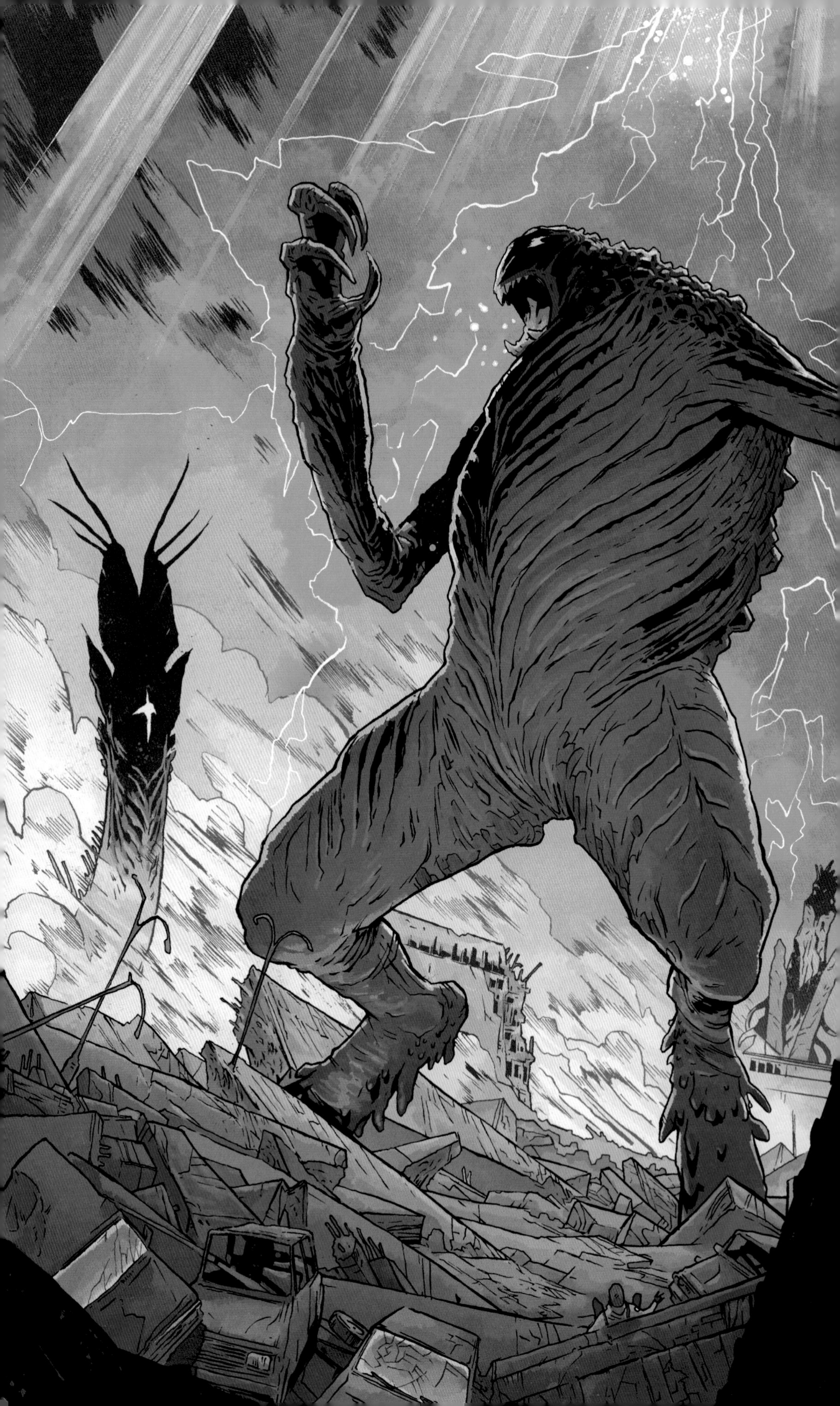

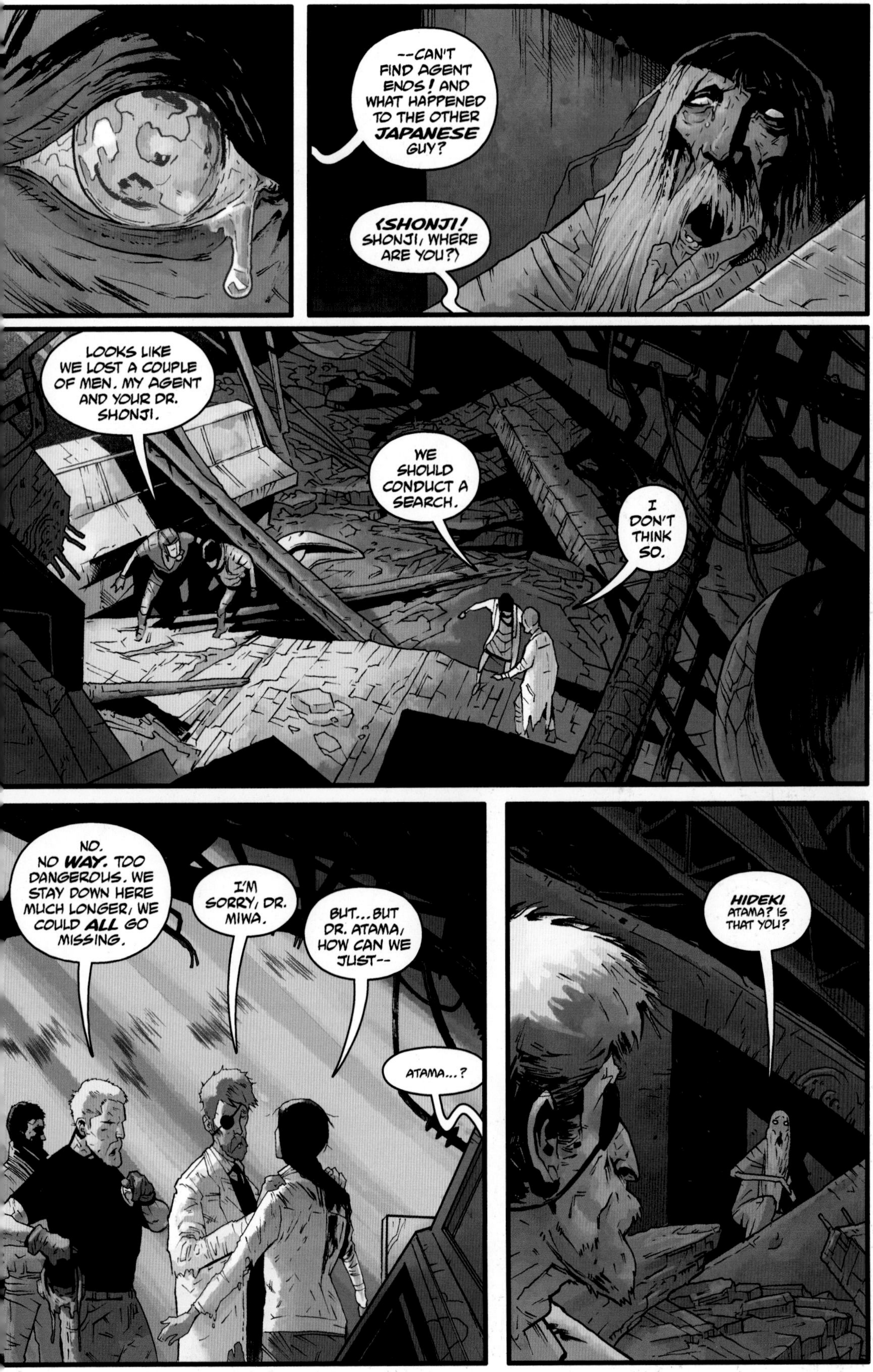
--CAN'T FIND AGENT ENOS! AND WHAT HAPPENED TO THE OTHER JAPANESE GUY?
‹SHONJI! SHONJI, WHERE ARE YOU?›
LOOKS LIKE WE LOST A COUPLE OF MEN. MY AGENT AND YOUR DR. SHONJI.
WE SHOULD CONDUCT A SEARCH.
I DON'T THINK SO.
NO. NO WAY. TOO DANGEROUS. WE STAY DOWN HERE MUCH LONGER, WE COULD ALL GO MISSING.
I'M SORRY, DR. MIWA.
BUT... BUT DR. ATAMA, HOW CAN WE JUST--
ATAMA...?
HIDEKI ATAMA? IS THAT YOU?

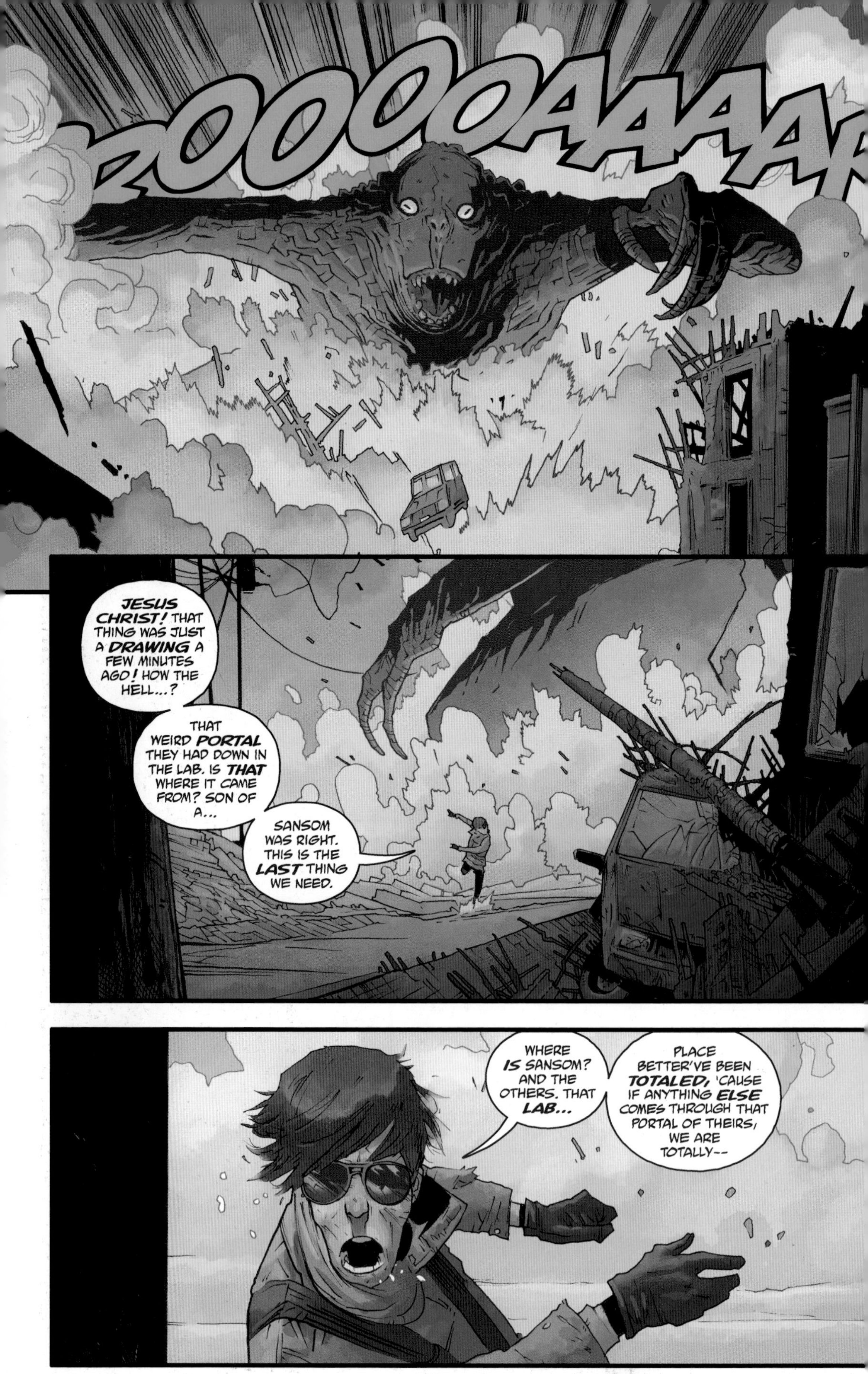
ROOOOAAAAR
JESUS CHRIST! THAT THING WAS JUST A DRAWING A FEW MINUTES AGO! HOW THE HELL...?
THAT WEIRD PORTAL THEY HAD DOWN IN THE LAB. IS THAT WHERE IT CAME FROM? SON OF A...
SANSOM WAS RIGHT. THIS IS THE LAST THING WE NEED.
WHERE IS SANSOM? AND THE OTHERS. THAT LAB...
PLACE BETTER'VE BEEN TOTALED, 'CAUSE IF ANYTHING ELSE COMES THROUGH THAT PORTAL OF THEIRS, WE ARE TOTALLY--

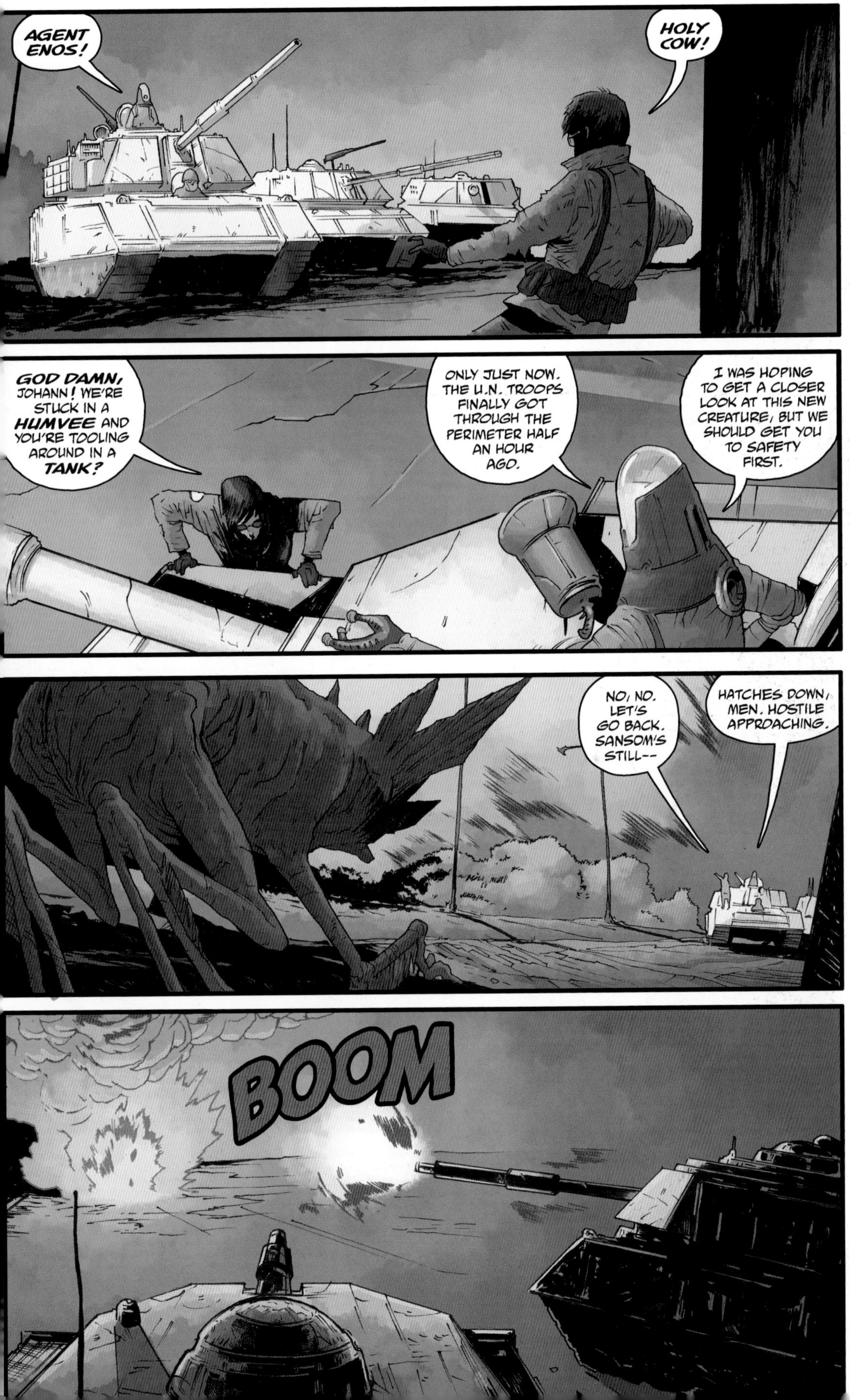
AGENT ENOS!
HOLY COW!
GOD DAMN, JOHANN! WE'RE STUCK IN A HUMVEE AND YOU'RE TOOLING AROUND IN A TANK?
ONLY JUST NOW. THE U.N. TROOPS FINALLY GOT THROUGH THE PERIMETER HALF AN HOUR AGO.
I WAS HOPING TO GET A CLOSER LOOK AT THIS NEW CREATURE, BUT WE SHOULD GET YOU TO SAFETY FIRST.
NO, NO. LET'S GO BACK. SANSOM'S STILL--
HATCHES DOWN, MEN. HOSTILE APPROACHING.
BOOM

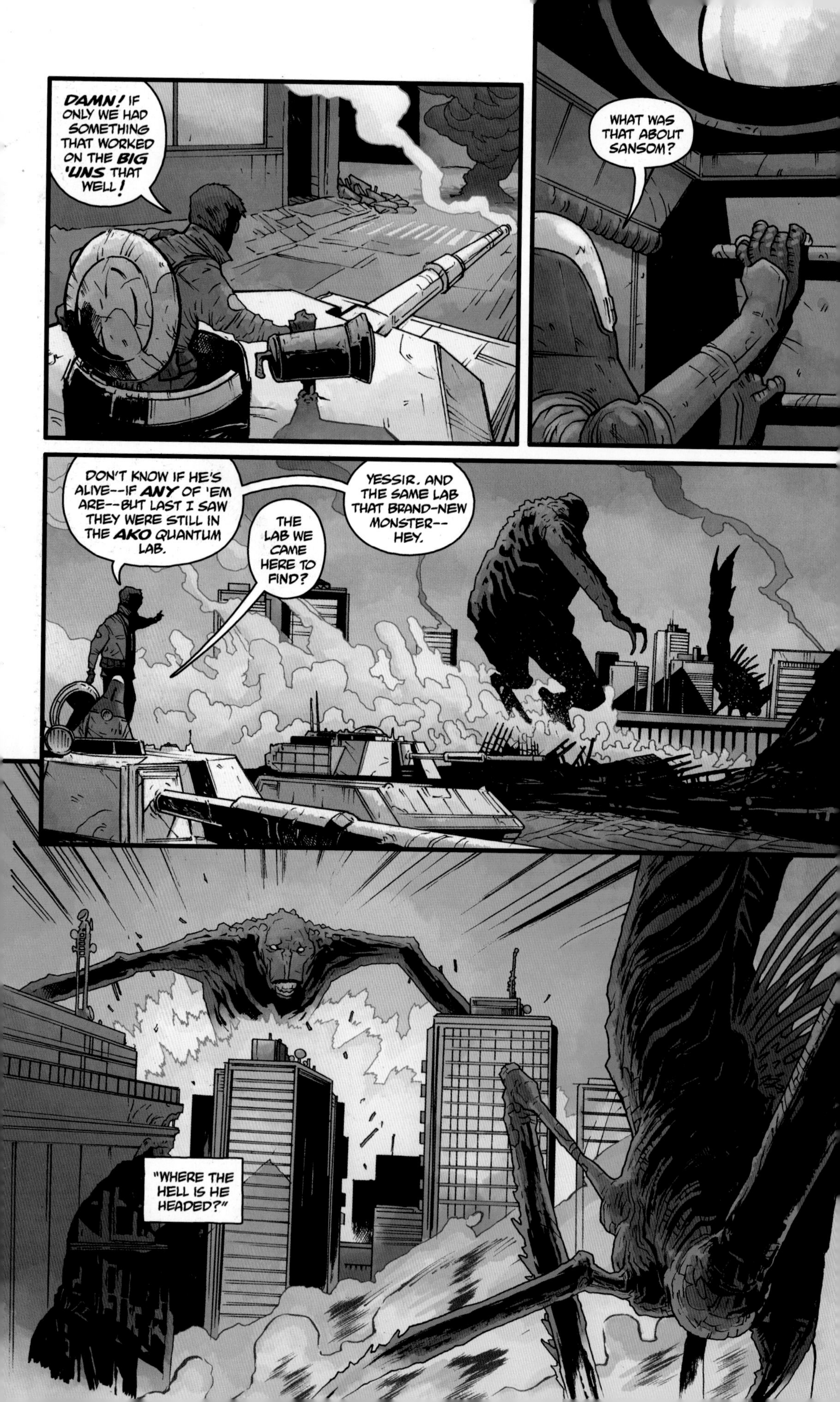
DAMN! IF ONLY WE HAD SOMETHING THAT WORKED ON THE BIG 'UNS THAT WELL!
WHAT WAS THAT ABOUT SANSOM?
DON'T KNOW IF HE'S ALIVE--IF ANY OF 'EM ARE--BUT LAST I SAW THEY WERE STILL IN THE AKO QUANTUM LAB.
THE LAB WE CAME HERE TO FIND?
YESSIR. AND THE SAME LAB THAT BRAND-NEW MONSTER--HEY.
"WHERE THE HELL IS HE HEADED?"

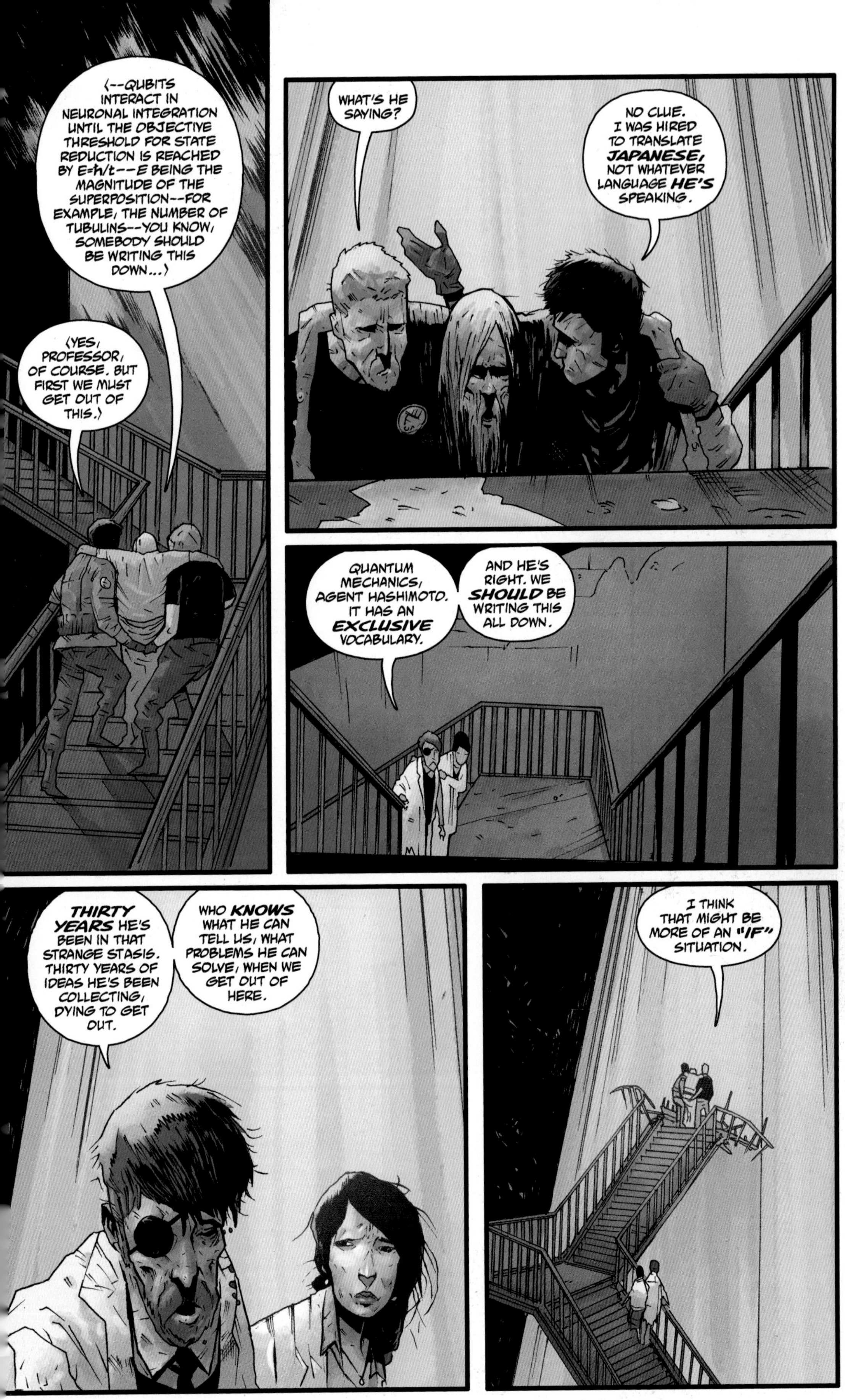

‹--QUBITS INTERACT IN NEURONAL INTEGRATION UNTIL THE OBJECTIVE THRESHOLD FOR STATE REDUCTION IS REACHED BY E=ℏ/t--E BEING THE MAGNITUDE OF THE SUPERPOSITION--FOR EXAMPLE, THE NUMBER OF TUBULINS--YOU KNOW, SOMEBODY SHOULD BE WRITING THIS DOWN...›
‹YES, PROFESSOR, OF COURSE. BUT FIRST WE MUST GET OUT OF THIS.›
WHAT'S HE SAYING?
NO CLUE. I WAS HIRED TO TRANSLATE JAPANESE, NOT WHATEVER LANGUAGE HE'S SPEAKING.
QUANTUM MECHANICS, AGENT HASHIMOTO. IT HAS AN EXCLUSIVE VOCABULARY.
AND HE'S RIGHT. WE SHOULD BE WRITING THIS ALL DOWN.
THIRTY YEARS HE'S BEEN IN THAT STRANGE STASIS. THIRTY YEARS OF IDEAS HE'S BEEN COLLECTING, DYING TO GET OUT.
WHO KNOWS WHAT HE CAN TELL US, WHAT PROBLEMS HE CAN SOLVE, WHEN WE GET OUT OF HERE.
I THINK THAT MIGHT BE MORE OF AN "IF" SITUATION.

SANSOM? OSCAR? THAT YOU?

YEAH! ATAMA AND MIWA ARE WITH US. *KUKYO*, TOO. WE DON'T KNOW WHAT HAPPENED TO SHONJI.

I'M GUESSING THERE'S A LOT YOU DON'T KNOW, BUT YOU'LL FIND OUT SOON ENOUGH.

"LET'S GET YOU OUT FIRST."

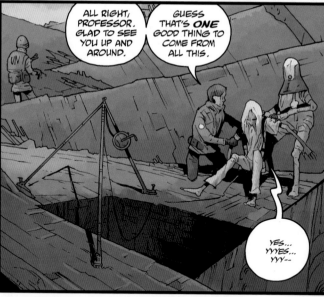

ALL RIGHT, PROFESSOR. GLAD TO SEE YOU UP AND AROUND.

GUESS THAT'S **ONE** GOOD THING TO COME FROM ALL THIS.

YES... YYYES... YYY--

YAAA!!

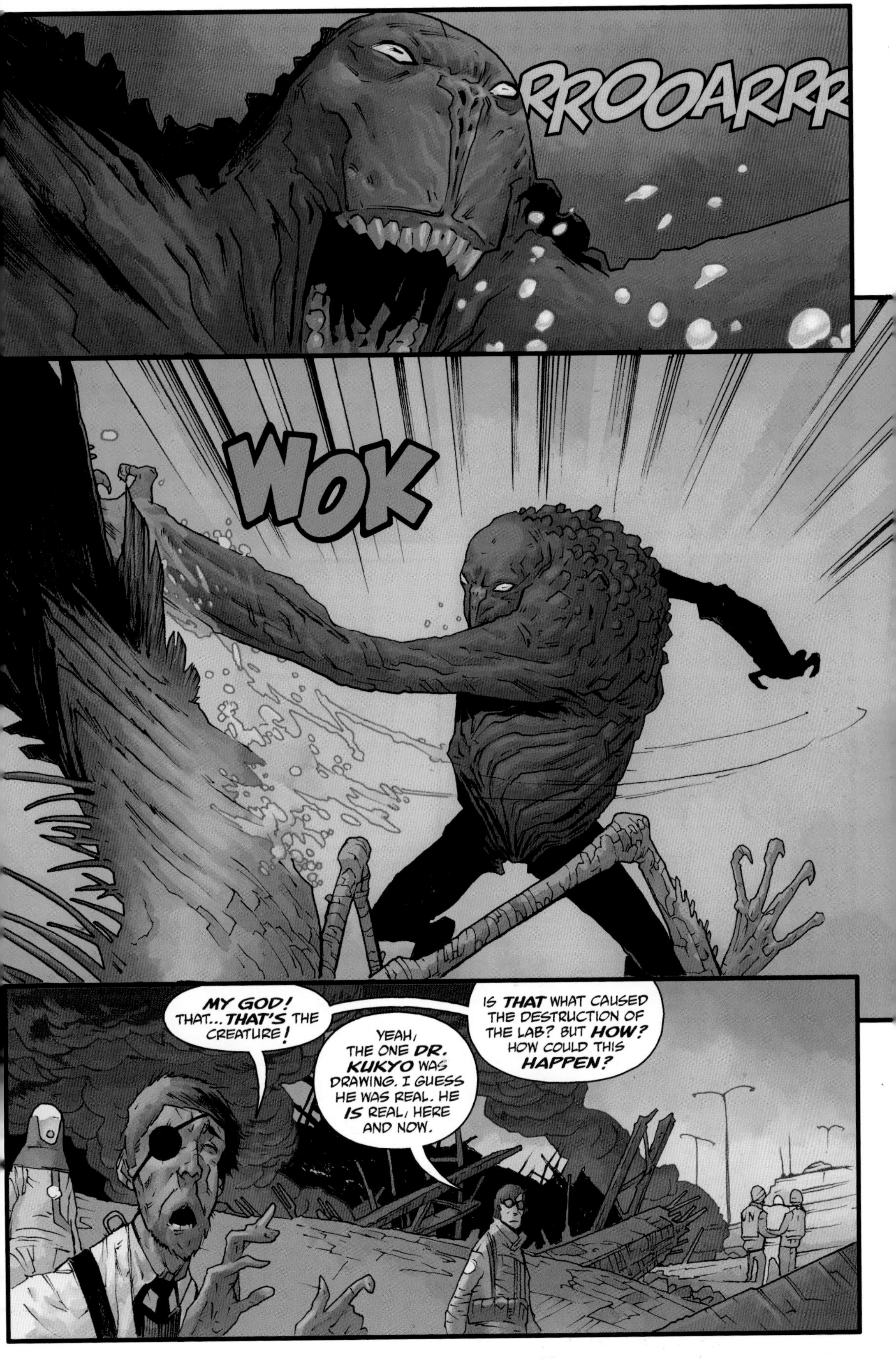
RROOARRR
WOK
MY GOD! THAT... THAT'S THE CREATURE!
IS THAT WHAT CAUSED THE DESTRUCTION OF THE LAB? BUT HOW? HOW COULD THIS HAPPEN?
YEAH, THE ONE DR. KUKYO WAS DRAWING. I GUESS HE WAS REAL. HE IS REAL, HERE AND NOW.

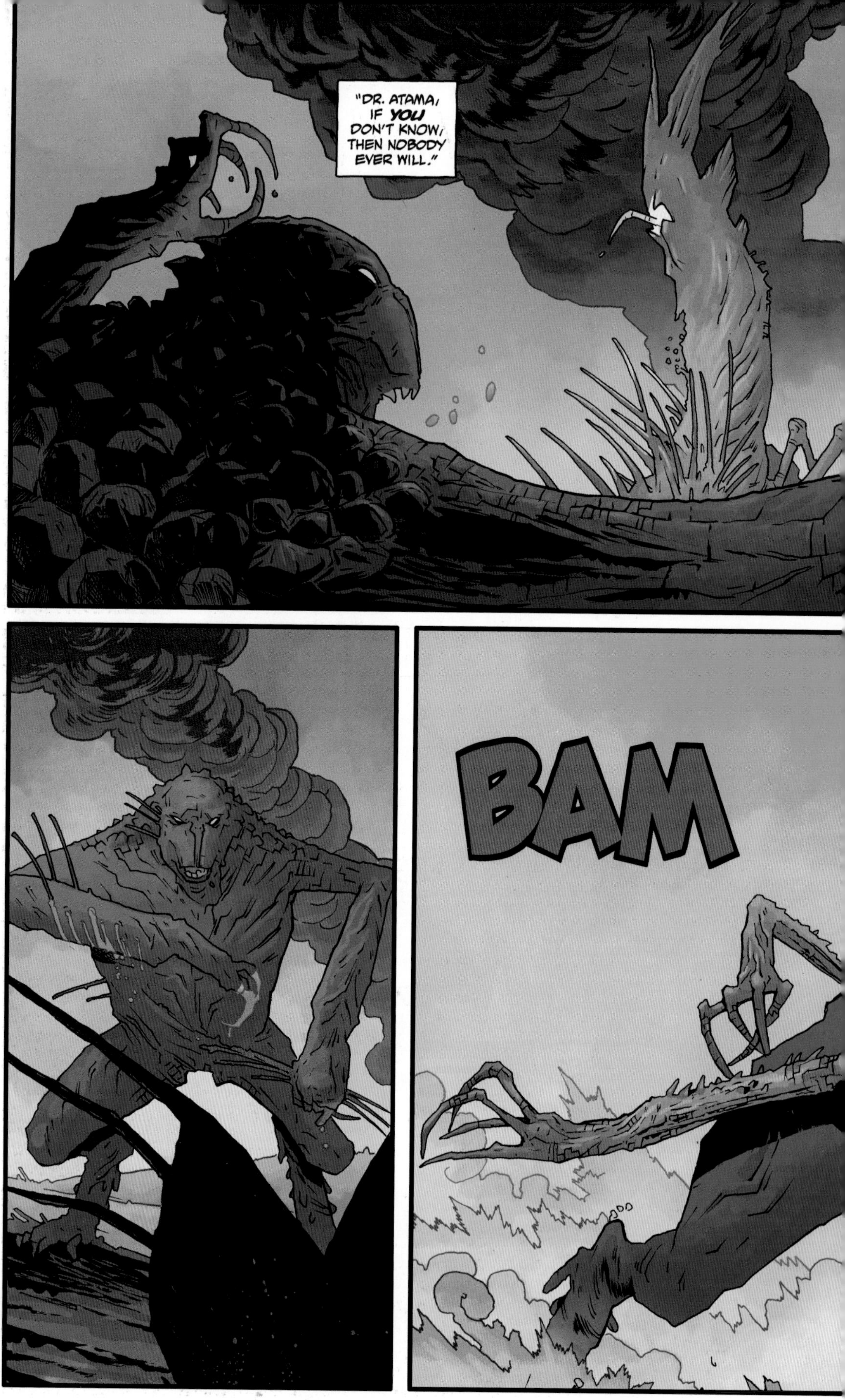
"DR. ATAMA, IF YOU DON'T KNOW, THEN NOBODY EVER WILL."
BAM

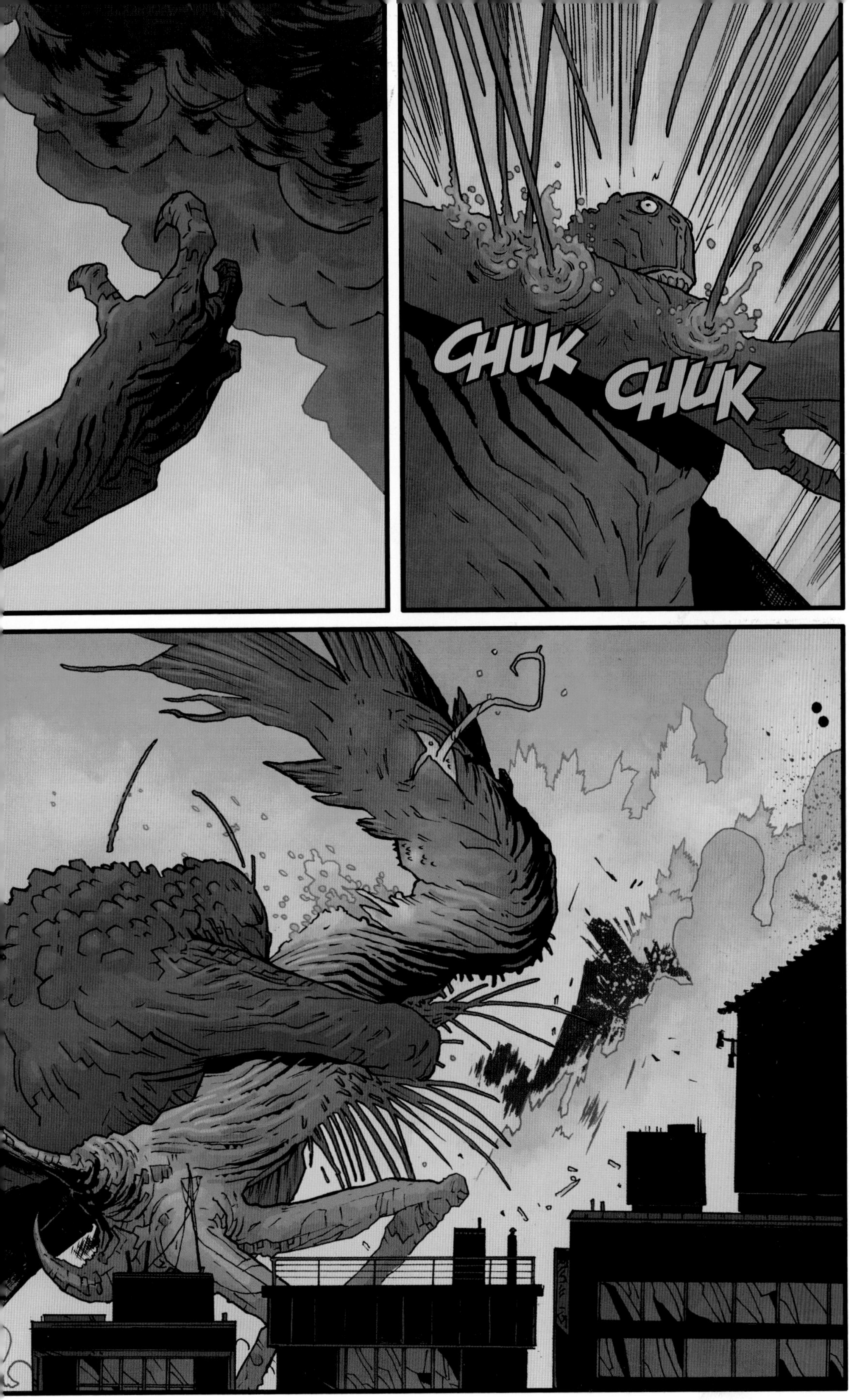
CHUK
CHUK

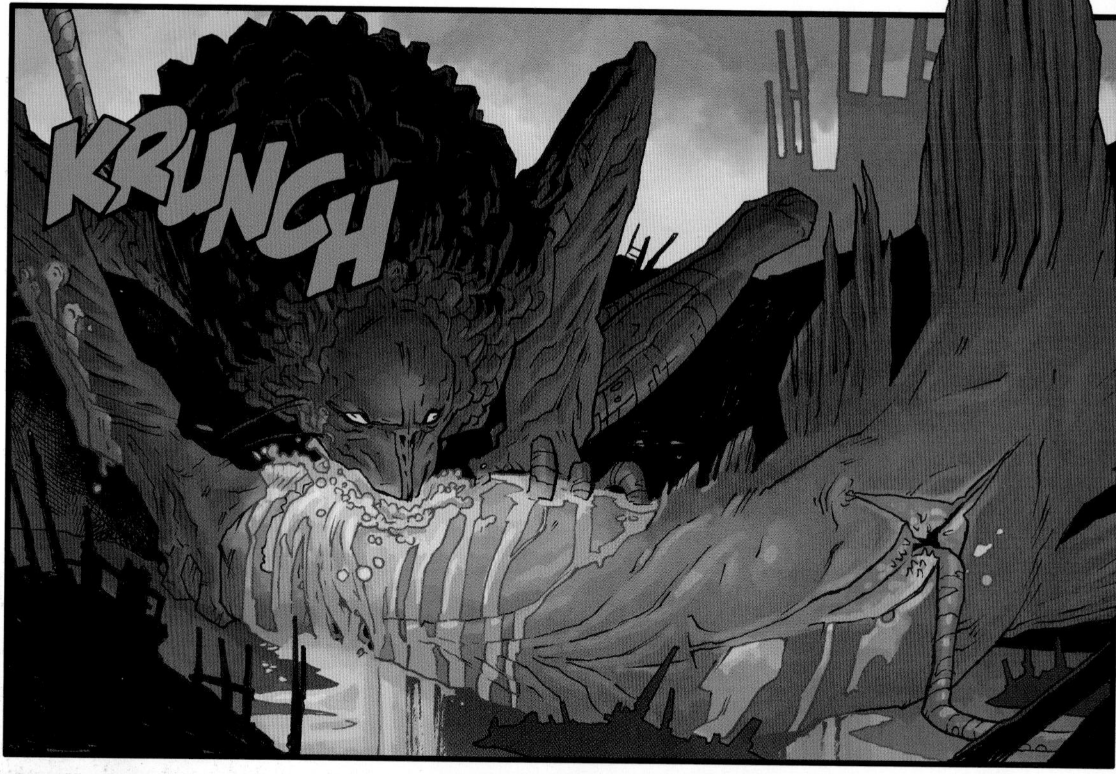
KRUNCH

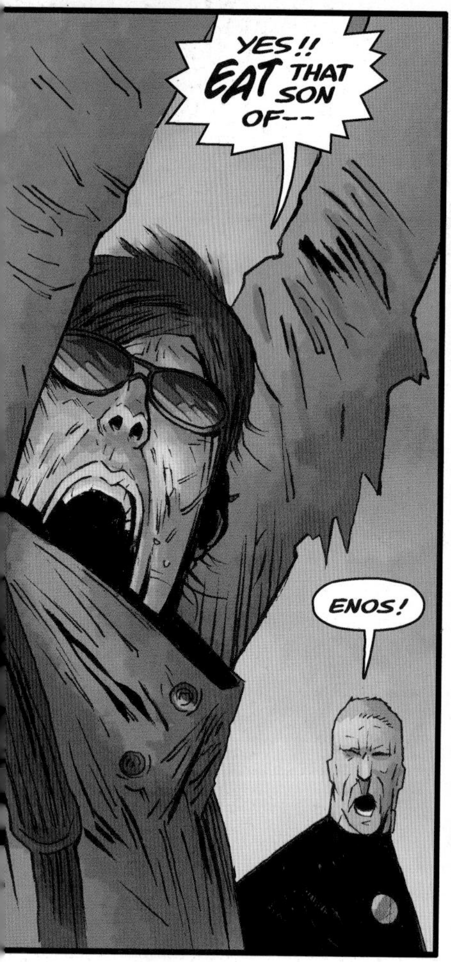
YES!! EAT THAT SON OF--
ENOS!

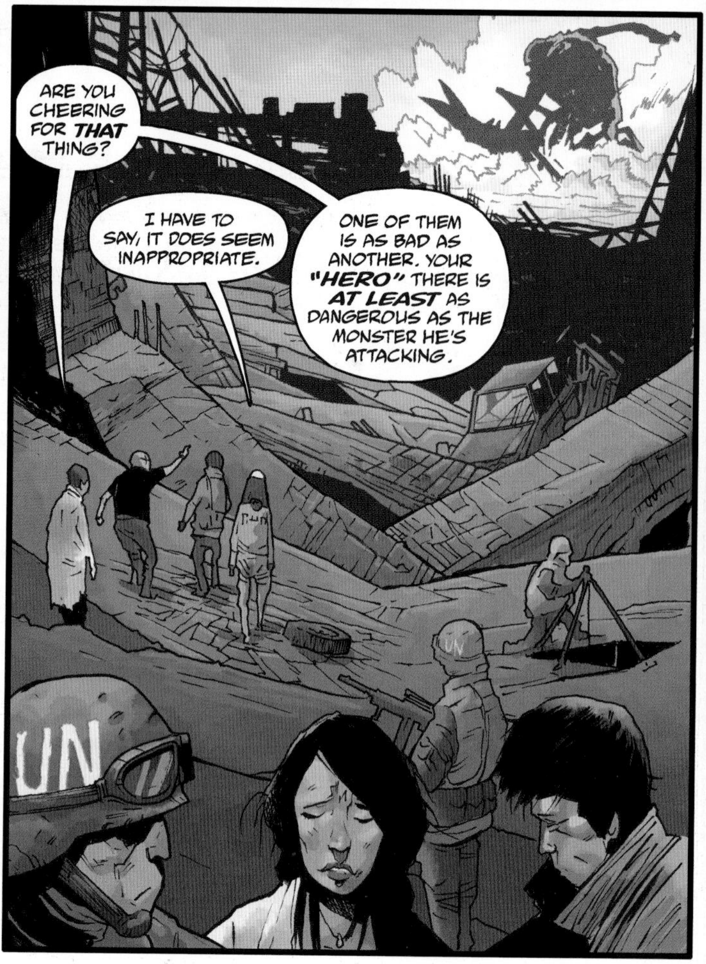
ARE YOU CHEERING FOR THAT THING?
I HAVE TO SAY, IT DOES SEEM INAPPROPRIATE.
ONE OF THEM IS AS BAD AS ANOTHER. YOUR "HERO" THERE IS AT LEAST AS DANGEROUS AS THE MONSTER HE'S ATTACKING.
UN

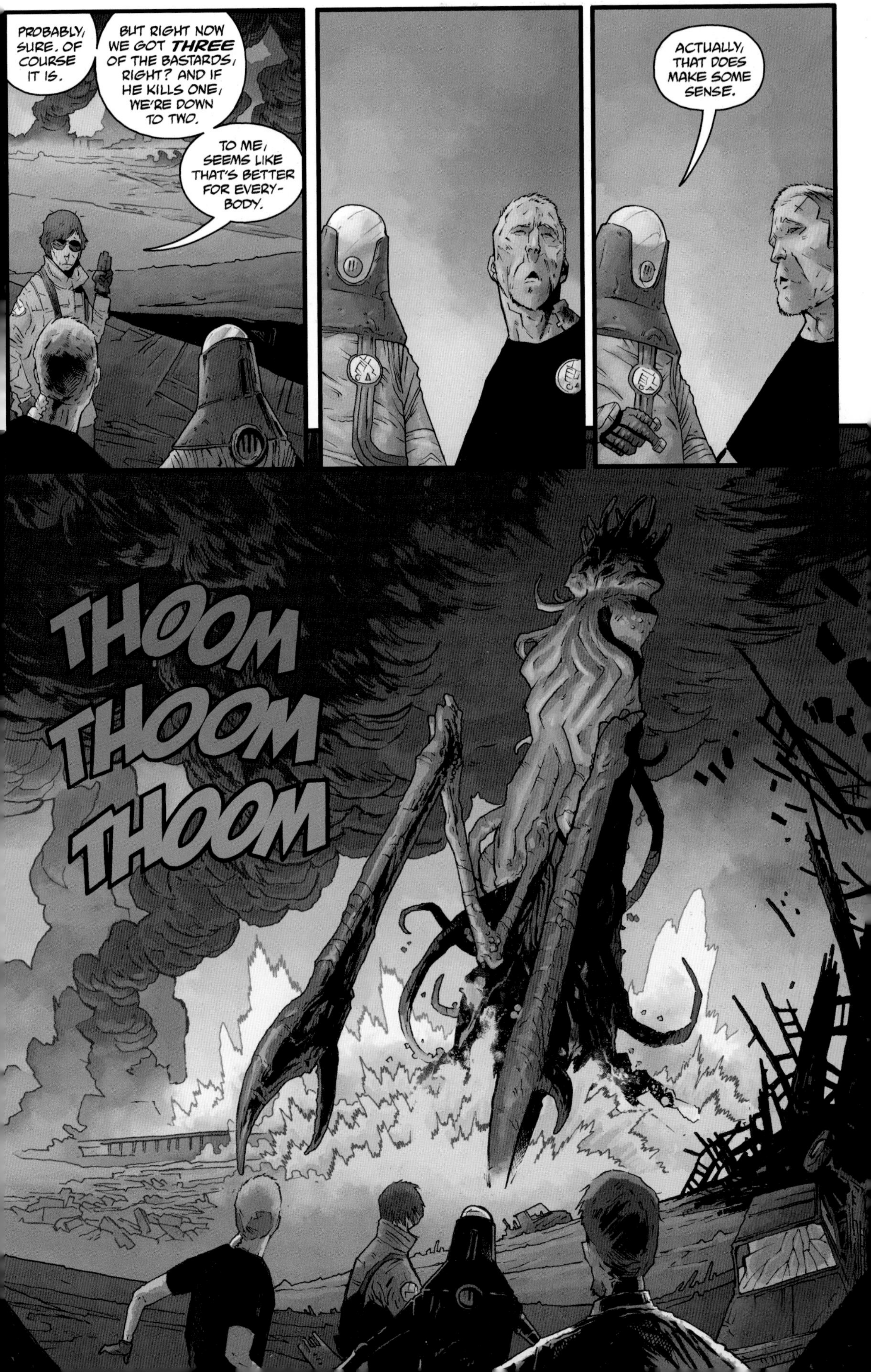
PROBABLY, SURE. OF COURSE IT IS.
BUT RIGHT NOW WE GOT THREE OF THE BASTARDS, RIGHT? AND IF HE KILLS ONE, WE'RE DOWN TO TWO.
TO ME, SEEMS LIKE THAT'S BETTER FOR EVERY-BODY.
ACTUALLY, THAT DOES MAKE SOME SENSE.
THOOM
THOOM
THOOM

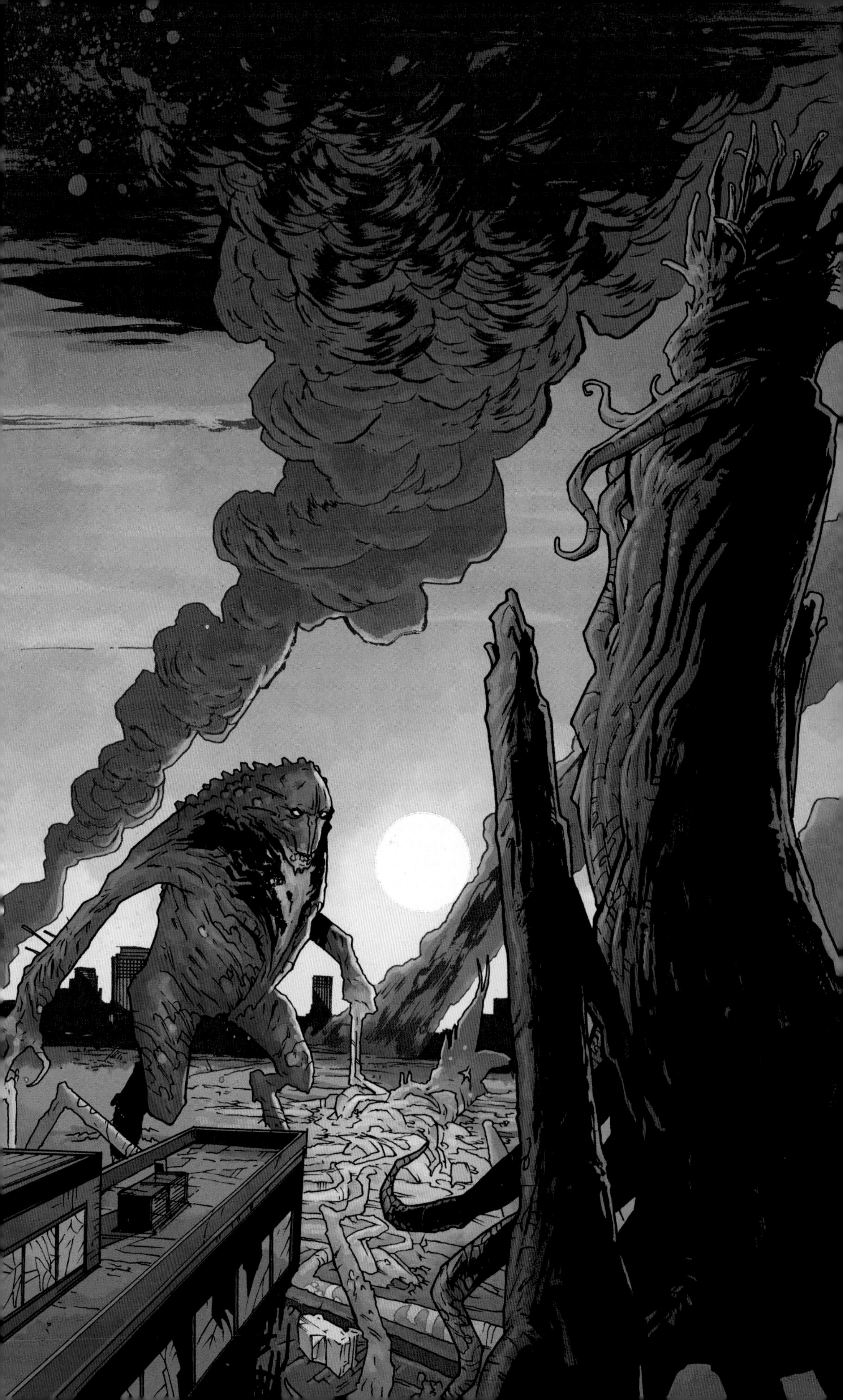

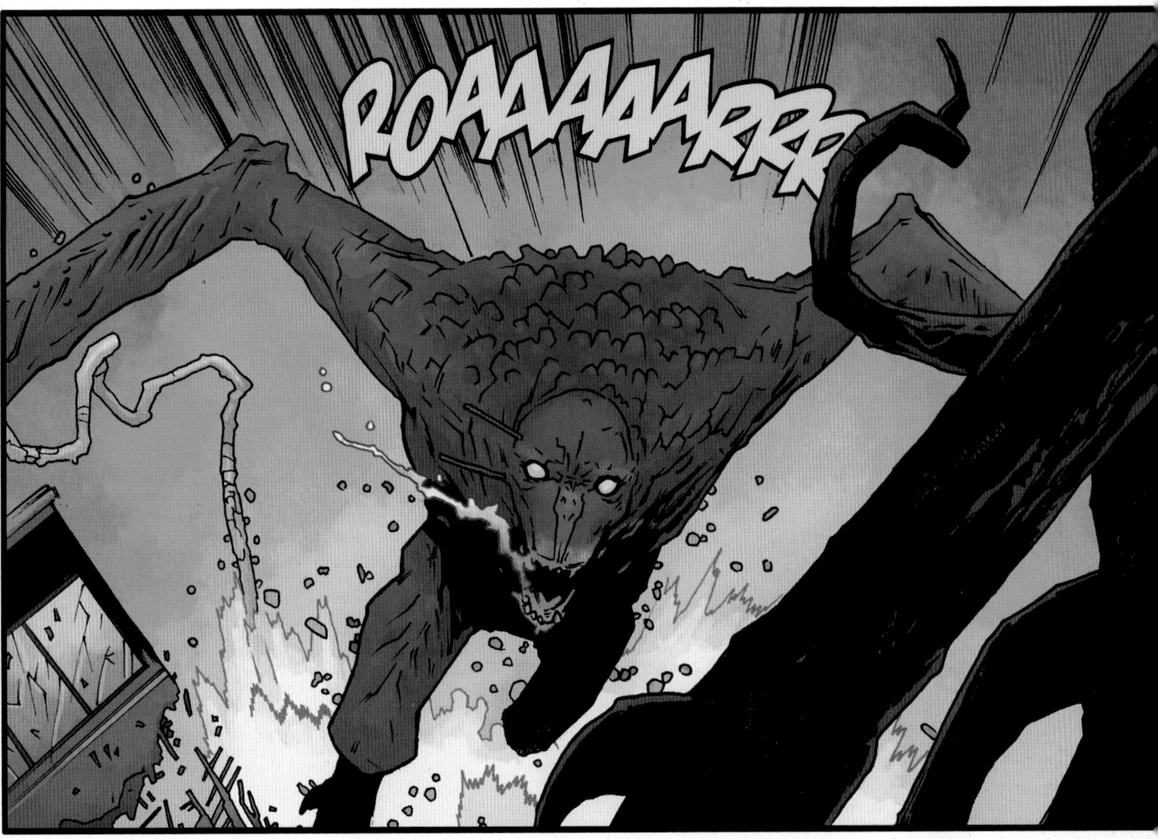
ROAAAAARRR

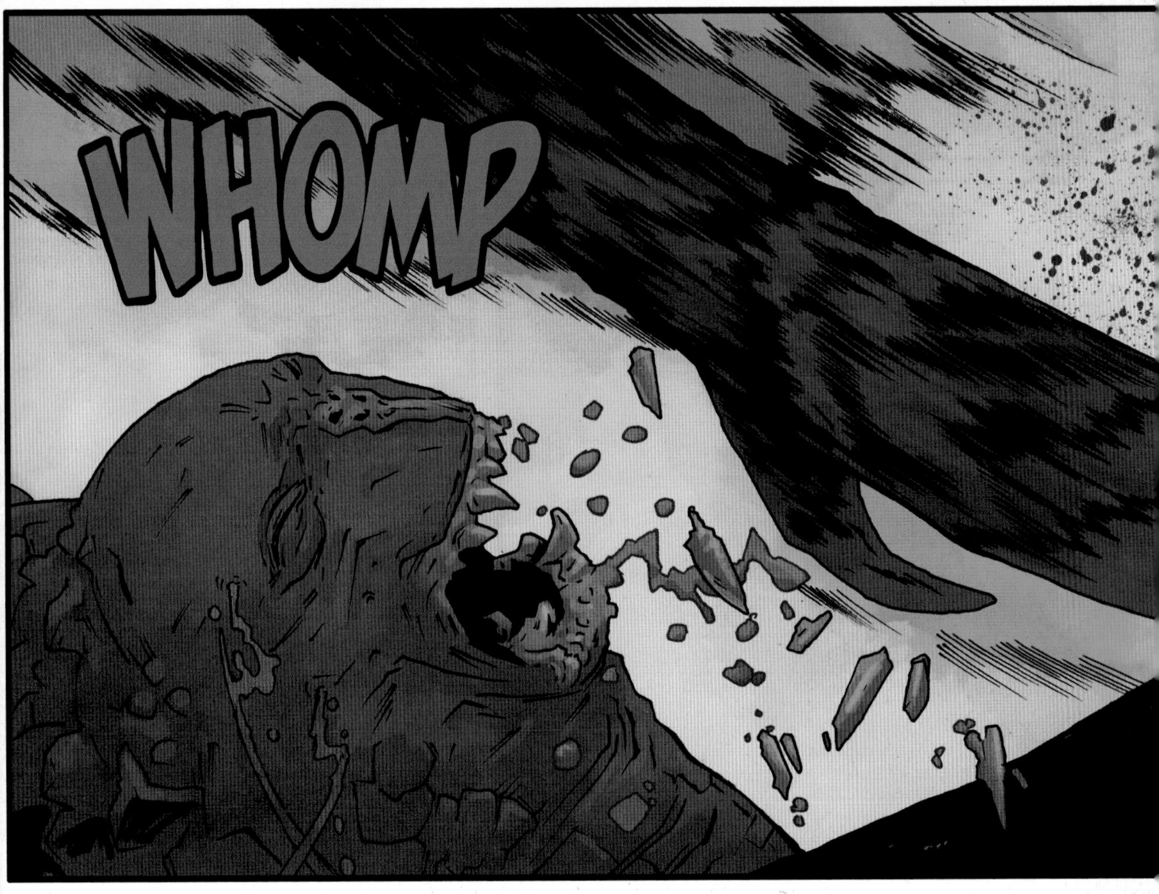
WHOMP

BOOM

...DAMN.

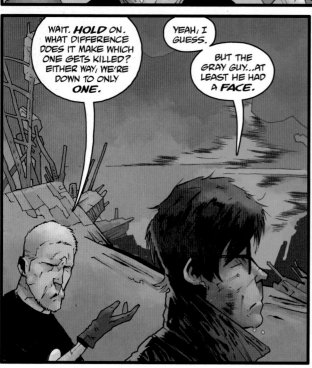

WAIT. *HOLD* ON. WHAT DIFFERENCE DOES IT MAKE WHICH ONE GETS KILLED? EITHER WAY, WE'RE DOWN TO ONLY *ONE.*

YEAH, I GUESS.

BUT THE GRAY GUY...AT LEAST HE HAD A *FACE.*

COME.

WE SHOULD NOT JUST BE STANDING AROUND HERE ANYWAY.

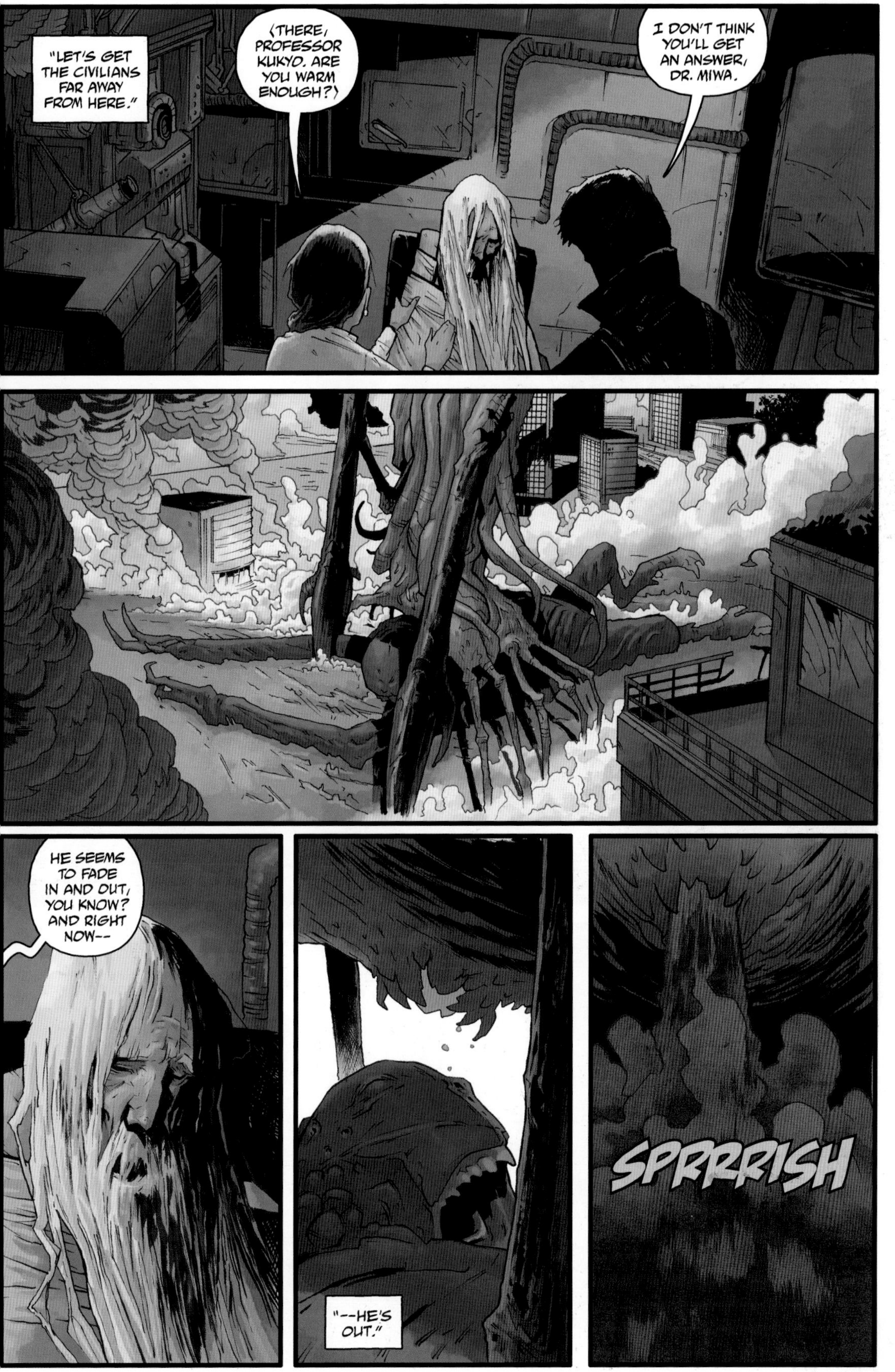
"LET'S GET THE CIVILIANS FAR AWAY FROM HERE."
⟨THERE, PROFESSOR KUKYO. ARE YOU WARM ENOUGH?⟩
I DON'T THINK YOU'LL GET AN ANSWER, DR. MIWA.
HE SEEMS TO FADE IN AND OUT, YOU KNOW? AND RIGHT NOW--
"--HE'S OUT."
SPRRRISH

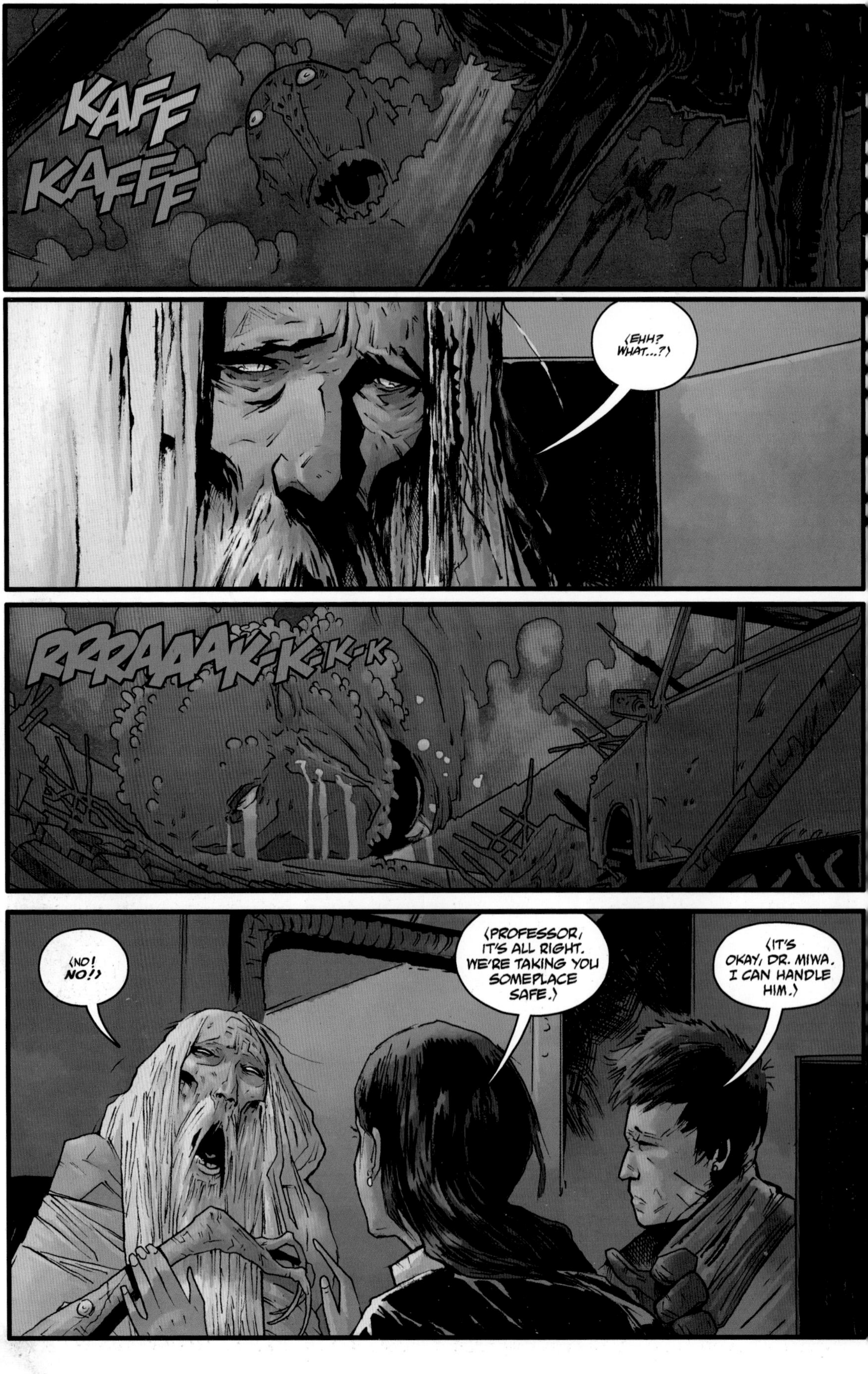
KAFF KAFFF
⟨EHH? WHAT...?⟩
RRRAAAK-K-K-K
⟨NO! NO!⟩
⟨PROFESSOR, IT'S ALL RIGHT. WE'RE TAKING YOU SOMEPLACE SAFE.⟩
⟨IT'S OKAY, DR. MIWA. I CAN HANDLE HIM.⟩

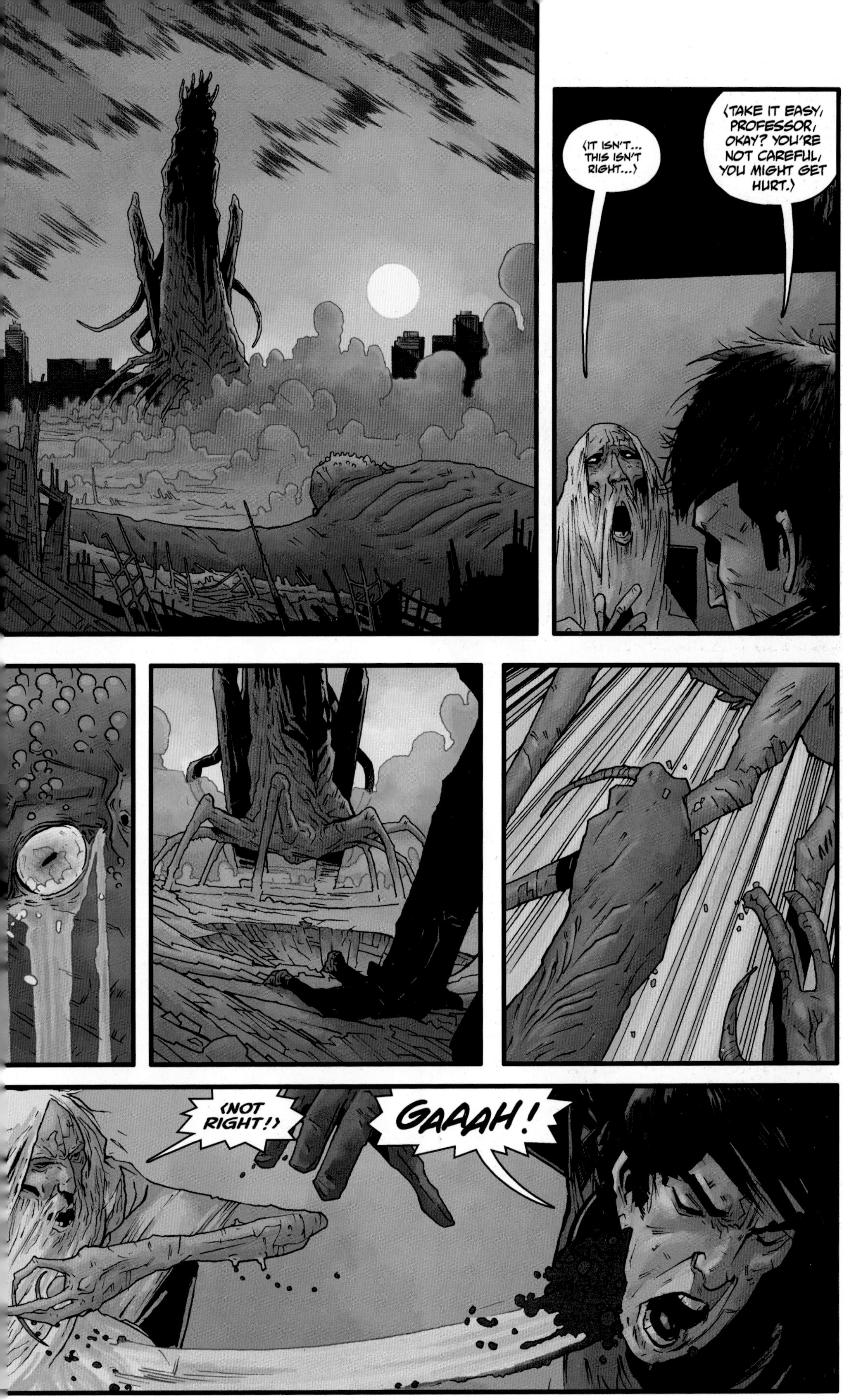
⟨IT ISN'T... THIS ISN'T RIGHT...⟩
⟨TAKE IT EASY, PROFESSOR, OKAY? YOU'RE NOT CAREFUL, YOU MIGHT GET HURT.⟩
⟨NOT RIGHT!⟩
GAAAH!

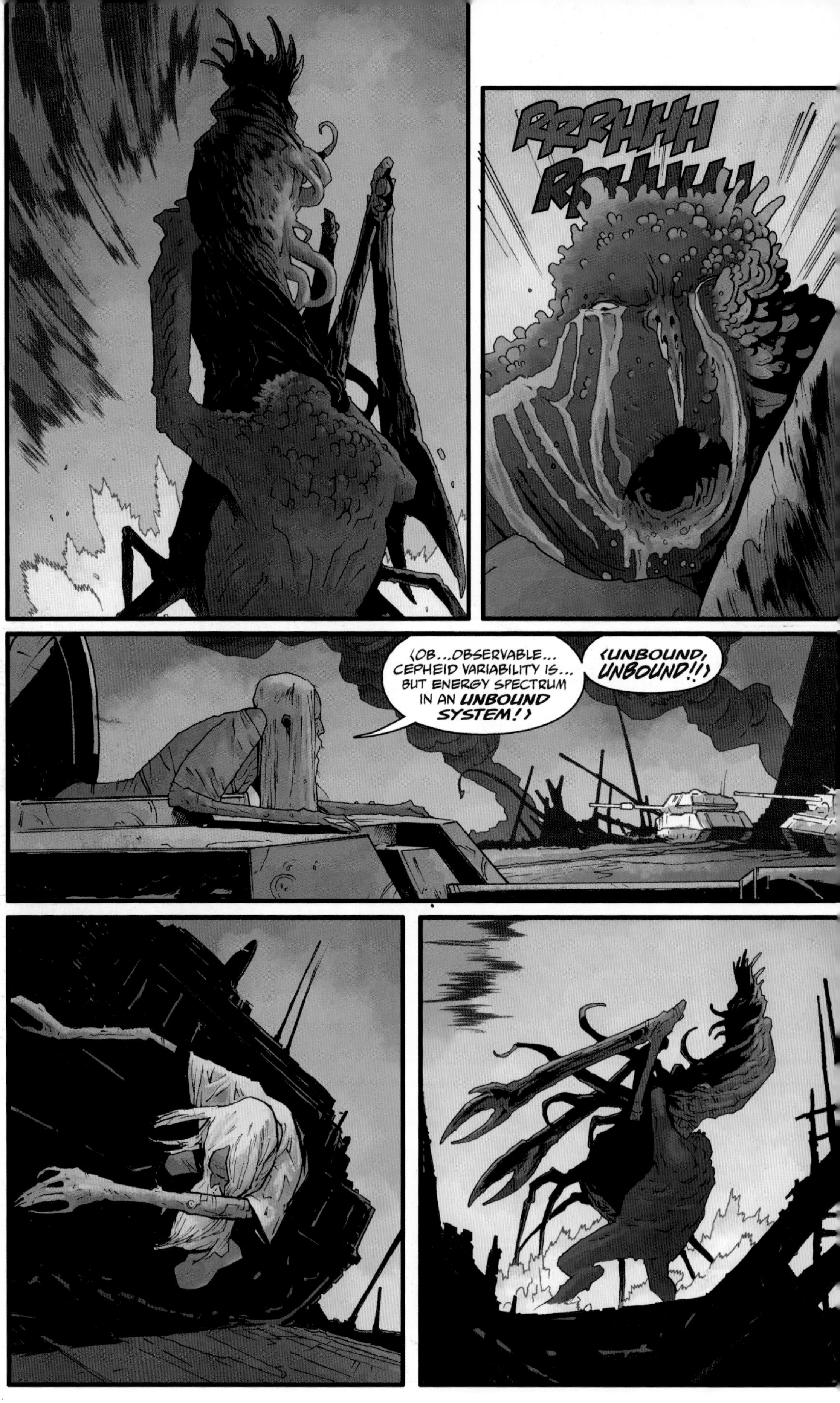
RRRHHH
‹OB...OBSERVABLE... CEPHEID VARIABILITY IS... BUT ENERGY SPECTRUM IN AN UNBOUND SYSTEM!›
‹UNBOUND, UNBOUND!!›

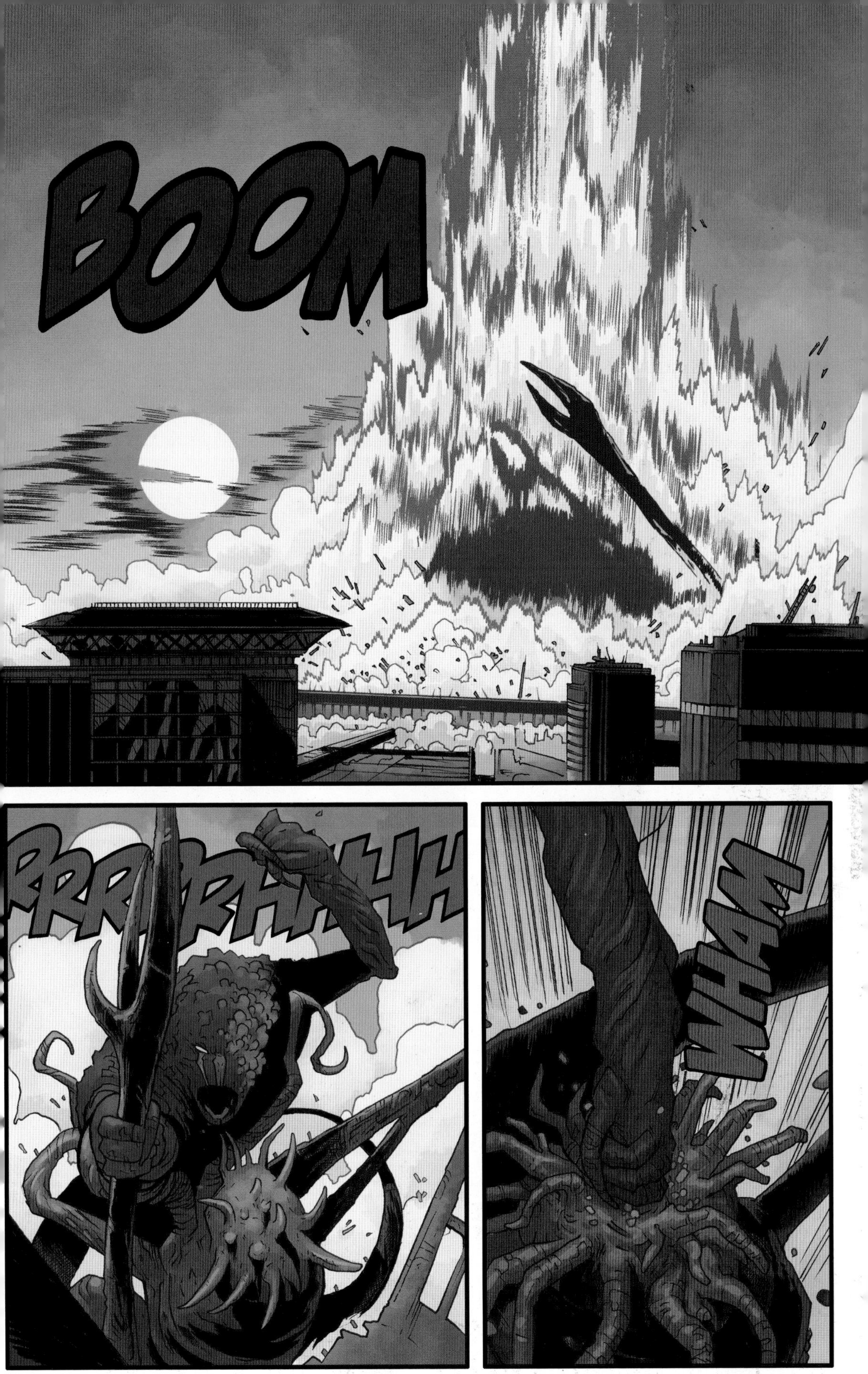
BOOM
RRRRAHHHH
WHAM

KRONCH

UNBOUND...

KRO

SPLUNSSHH

KROLCH

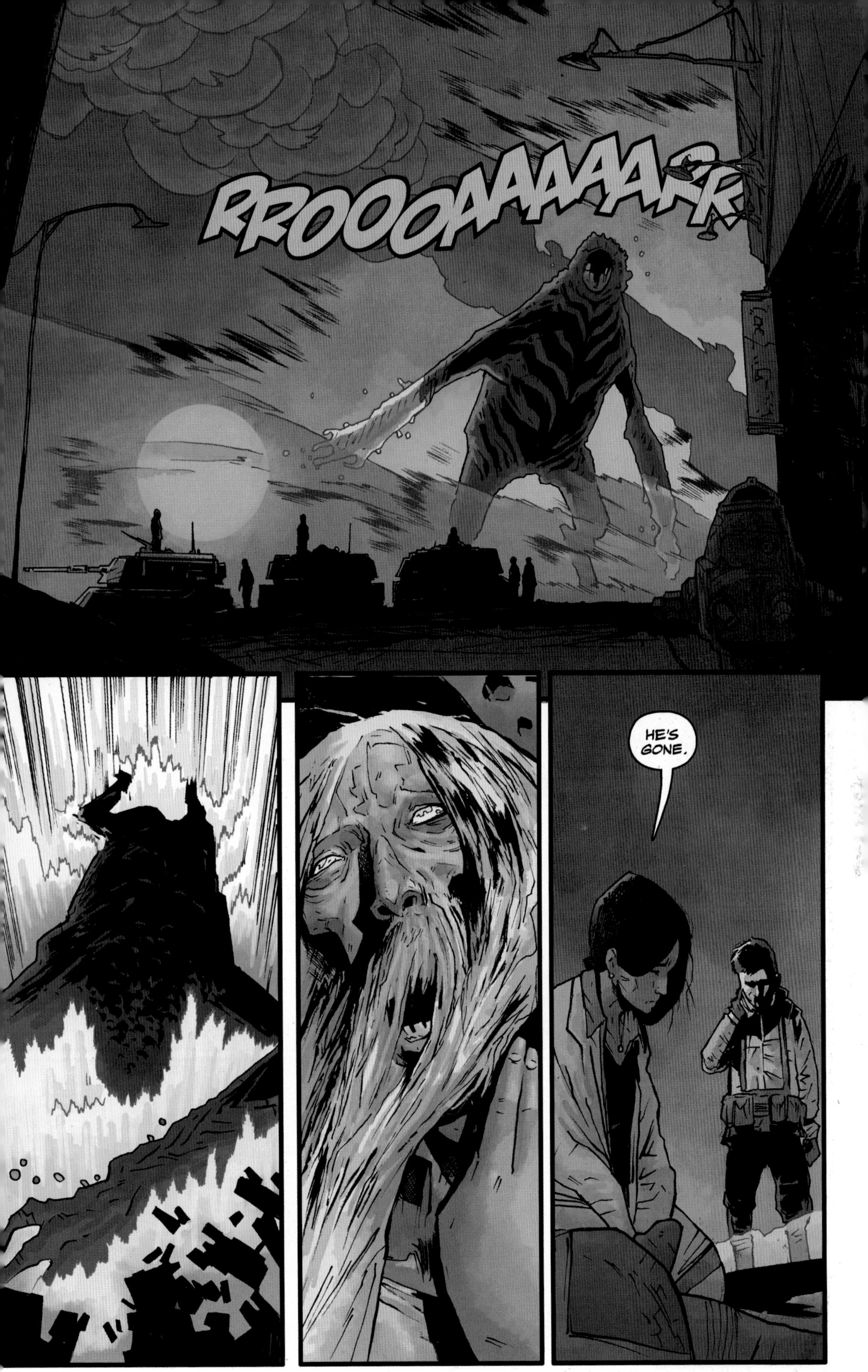
RROOOAAAAARR
HE'S GONE.

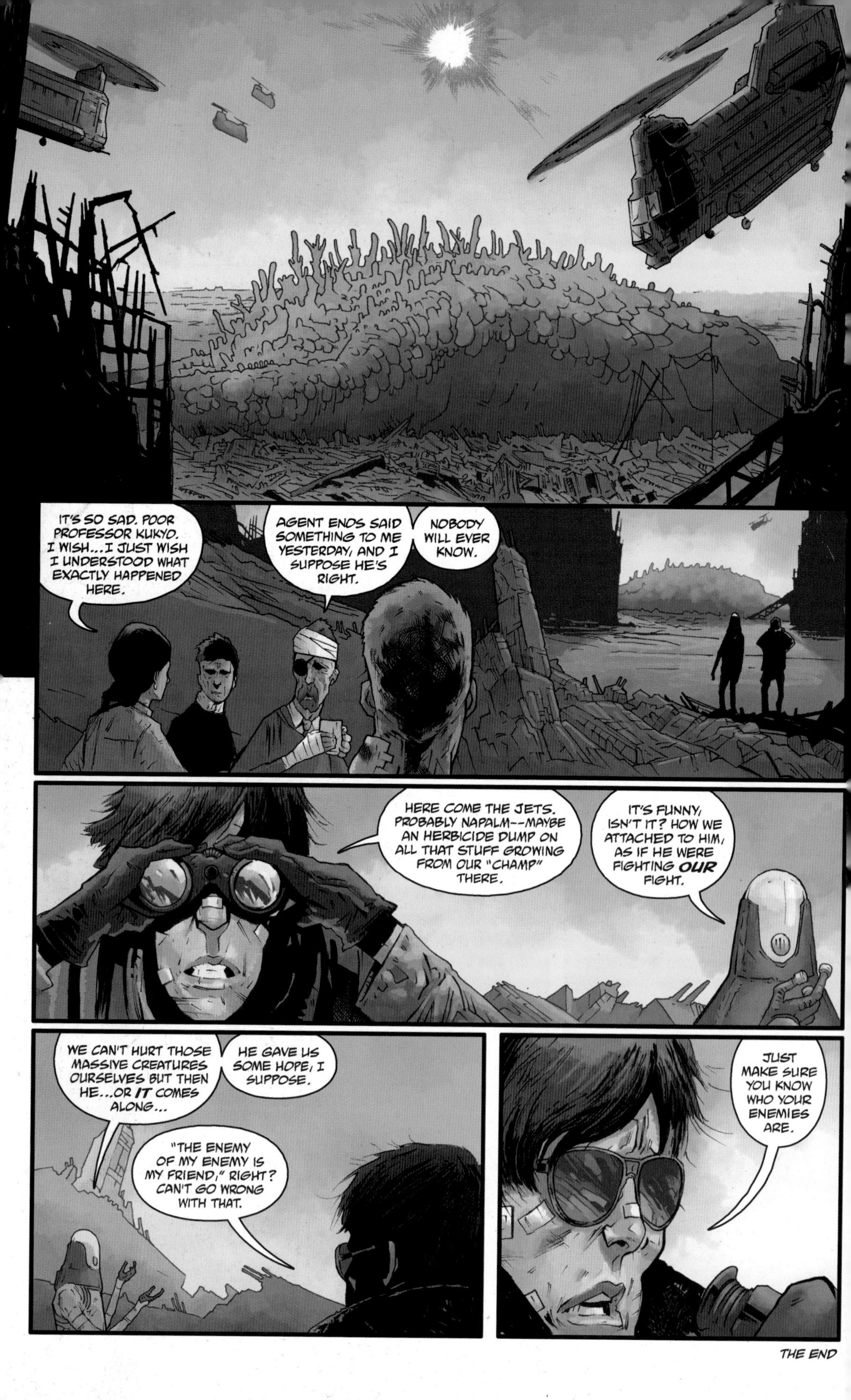
IT'S SO SAD. POOR PROFESSOR KUKYO. I WISH... I JUST WISH I UNDERSTOOD WHAT EXACTLY HAPPENED HERE.
AGENT ENDS SAID SOMETHING TO ME YESTERDAY, AND I SUPPOSE HE'S RIGHT.
NOBODY WILL EVER KNOW.
HERE COME THE JETS. PROBABLY NAPALM--MAYBE AN HERBICIDE DUMP ON ALL THAT STUFF GROWING FROM OUR "CHAMP" THERE.
IT'S FUNNY, ISN'T IT? HOW WE ATTACHED TO HIM, AS IF HE WERE FIGHTING OUR FIGHT.
WE CAN'T HURT THOSE MASSIVE CREATURES OURSELVES BUT THEN HE...OR IT COMES ALONG...
HE GAVE US SOME HOPE, I SUPPOSE.
"THE ENEMY OF MY ENEMY IS MY FRIEND," RIGHT? CAN'T GO WRONG WITH THAT.
JUST MAKE SURE YOU KNOW WHO YOUR ENEMIES ARE.

THE END

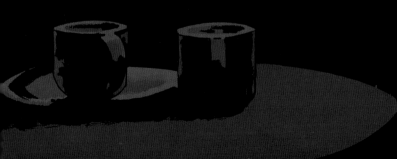

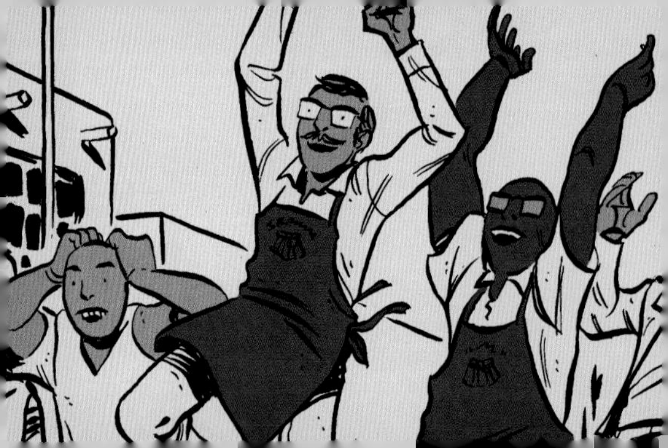

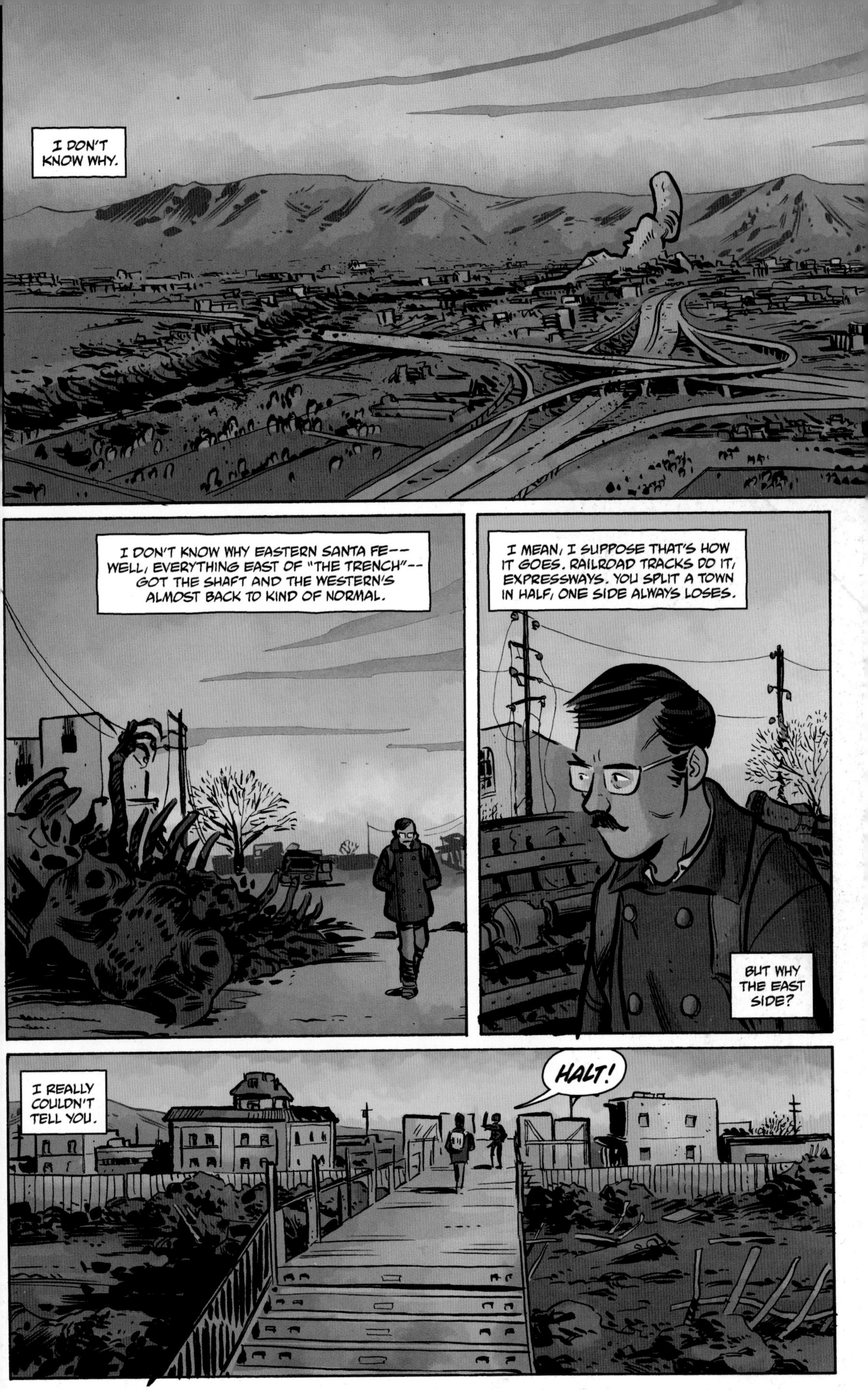

I DON'T KNOW WHY.
I DON'T KNOW WHY EASTERN SANTA FE-- WELL, EVERYTHING EAST OF "THE TRENCH"-- GOT THE SHAFT AND THE WESTERN'S ALMOST BACK TO KIND OF NORMAL.
I MEAN, I SUPPOSE THAT'S HOW IT GOES. RAILROAD TRACKS DO IT, EXPRESSWAYS. YOU SPLIT A TOWN IN HALF, ONE SIDE ALWAYS LOSES.
BUT WHY THE EAST SIDE?
I REALLY COULDN'T TELL YOU.
HALT!

I.D.

COME ON, MAN! WE JUST DID THIS YESTERDAY.

WHY DO YOU DO THIS, ANYWAY? HOW DOES IT STOP THE MONSTERS, HUH?

Y'KNOW, INSTEAD OF TRYING TO KEEP FOLKS OUT OF THE WESTERN, WHY DON'T YOU PUT SOME EFFORT IN CLEANING UP THE EASTERN? LIKE, DO SOMETHING ABOUT *MY* NEIGHBORHOOD.

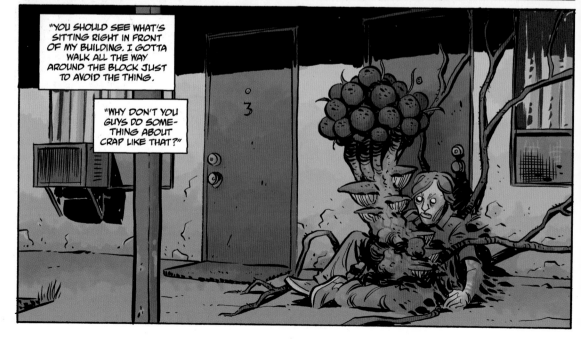

"YOU SHOULD SEE WHAT'S SITTING RIGHT IN FRONT OF MY BUILDING. I GOTTA WALK ALL THE WAY AROUND THE BLOCK JUST TO AVOID THE THING.

"WHY DON'T YOU GUYS DO SOMETHING ABOUT CRAP LIKE THAT?"

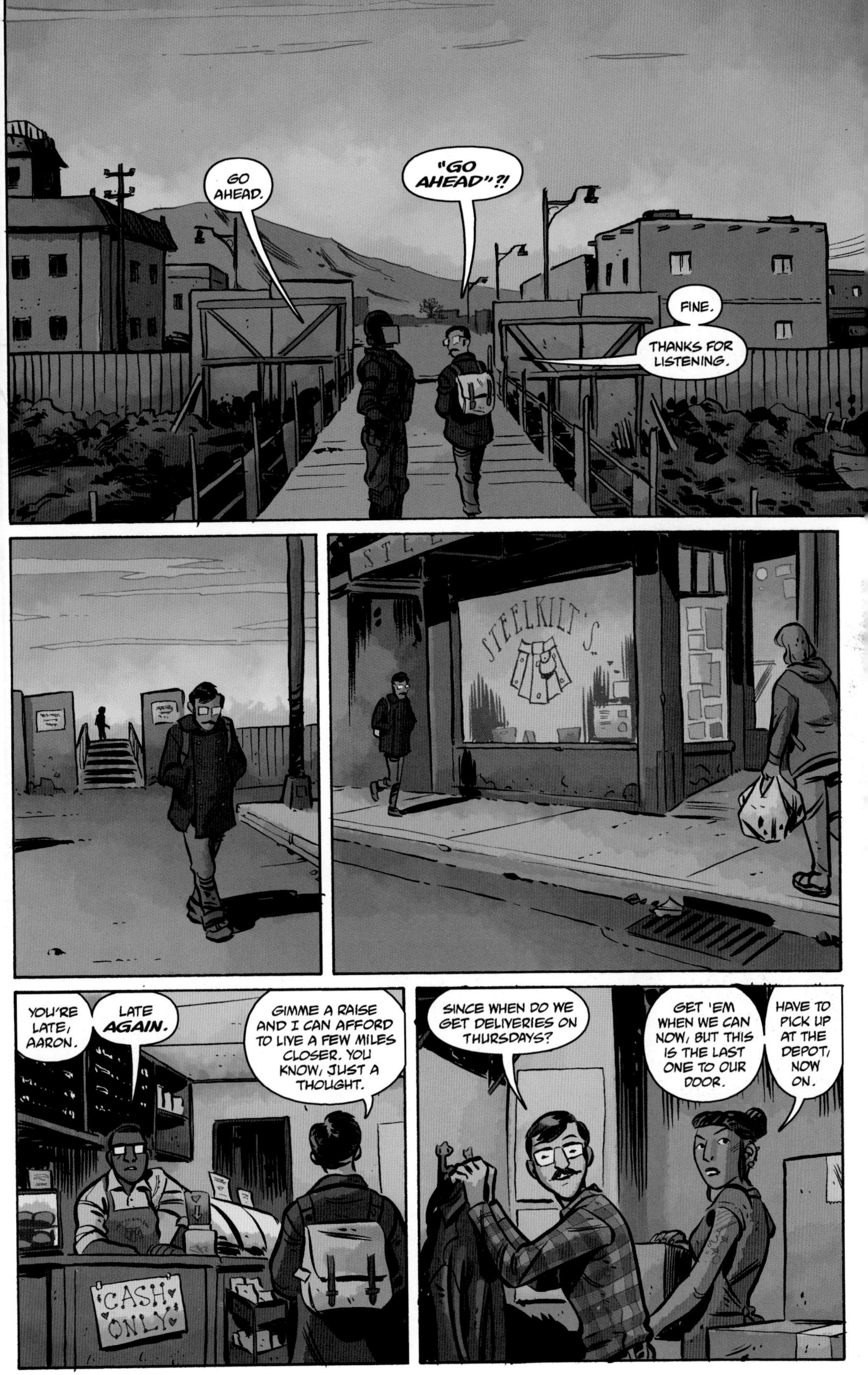
GO AHEAD.
"GO AHEAD"?!
FINE.
THANKS FOR LISTENING.
STEELKILT'S
YOU'RE LATE, AARON.
LATE AGAIN.
GIMME A RAISE AND I CAN AFFORD TO LIVE A FEW MILES CLOSER. YOU KNOW, JUST A THOUGHT.
CASH ONLY
SINCE WHEN DO WE GET DELIVERIES ON THURSDAYS?
GET 'EM WHEN WE CAN NOW, BUT THIS IS THE LAST ONE TO OUR DOOR.
HAVE TO PICK UP AT THE DEPOT, NOW ON.

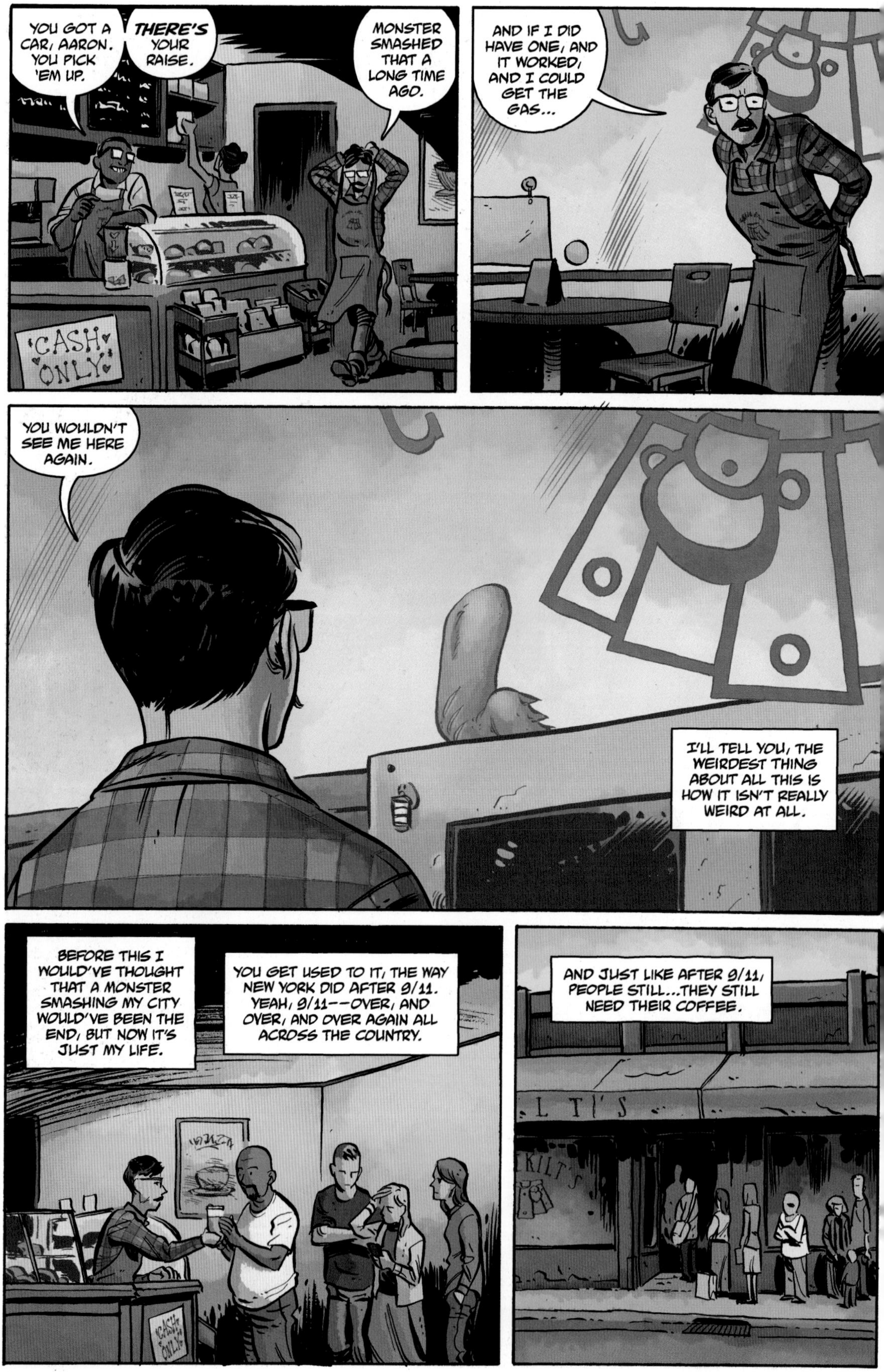

YOU GOT A CAR, AARON. YOU PICK 'EM UP.
THERE'S YOUR RAISE.
MONSTER SMASHED THAT A LONG TIME AGO.
CASH ONLY
AND IF I DID HAVE ONE, AND IT WORKED, AND I COULD GET THE GAS...
YOU WOULDN'T SEE ME HERE AGAIN.
I'LL TELL YOU, THE WEIRDEST THING ABOUT ALL THIS IS HOW IT ISN'T REALLY WEIRD AT ALL.
BEFORE THIS I WOULD'VE THOUGHT THAT A MONSTER SMASHING MY CITY WOULD'VE BEEN THE END, BUT NOW IT'S JUST MY LIFE.
YOU GET USED TO IT, THE WAY NEW YORK DID AFTER 9/11. YEAH, 9/11--OVER, AND OVER, AND OVER AGAIN ALL ACROSS THE COUNTRY.
CASH ONLY
AND JUST LIKE AFTER 9/11, PEOPLE STILL...THEY STILL NEED THEIR COFFEE.

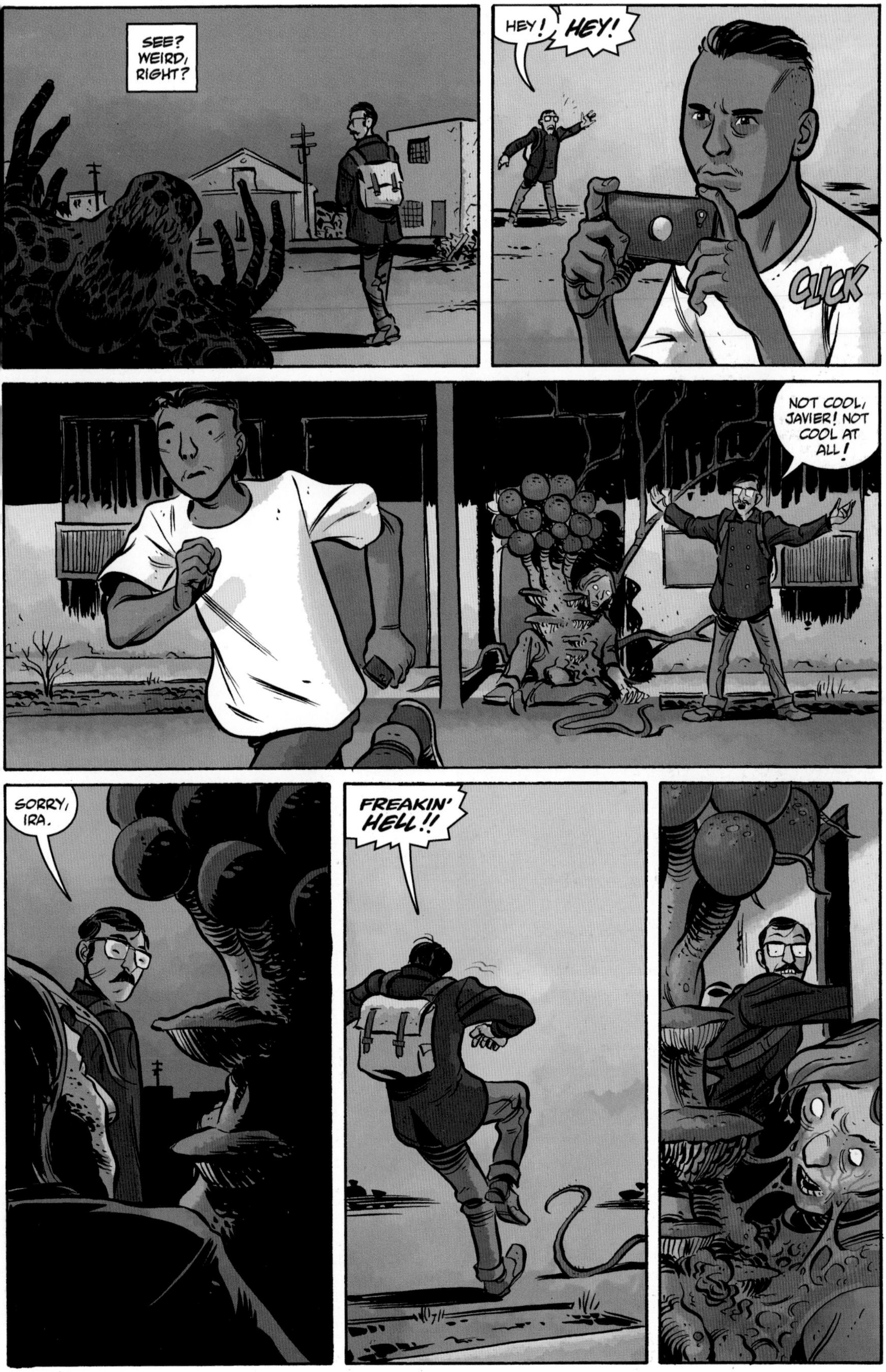

SEE? WEIRD, RIGHT?
HEY!
HEY!
CLICK
NOT COOL, JAVIER! NOT COOL AT ALL!
SORRY, IRA.
FREAKIN' HELL!!

NO, I GUESS YOU DON'T EVER REALLY GET USED TO IT.

OR I DON'T. NOT AT NIGHT.

BECAUSE IT'S NOT BUILDINGS FALLING AND THEN REBUILDING.

THE THINGS THAT KNOCKED DOWN THE BUILDINGS, THAT KILLED MY FRIENDS, THEY'RE STILL HERE.

SLISSSSS SLISSSSS SLISSSSS

I HEAR THEM AT NIGHT, SOMETIMES FAR AWAY, SOMETIMES CLOSER.

HOW CAN ANYBODY SLEEP? YOU CAN'T. NOT FOR DAYS ON END.

BUT THE ANXIETY, IT'S EXHAUSTING, AND EVENTUALLY, YOU FINALLY JUST...

SLISSSSSSS SLISSSSSSS SLISSSSSS

WHUP WHUP WHUP WHUP

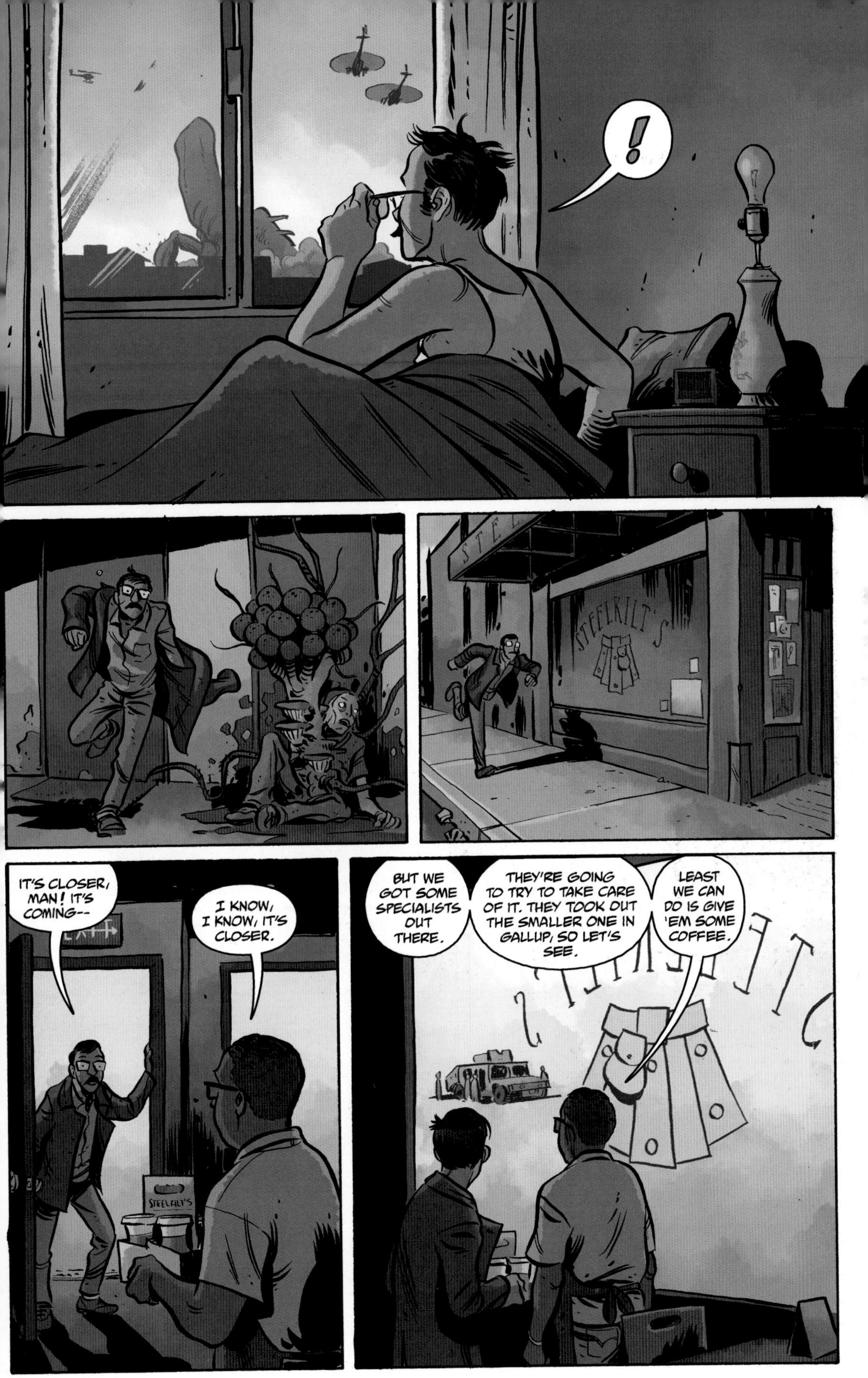
!
STEELKILT'S
IT'S CLOSER, MAN! IT'S COMING--
I KNOW, I KNOW, IT'S CLOSER.
STEELKILT'S
BUT WE GOT SOME SPECIALISTS OUT THERE.
THEY'RE GOING TO TRY TO TAKE CARE OF IT. THEY TOOK OUT THE SMALLER ONE IN GALLUP, SO LET'S SEE.
LEAST WE CAN DO IS GIVE 'EM SOME COFFEE.

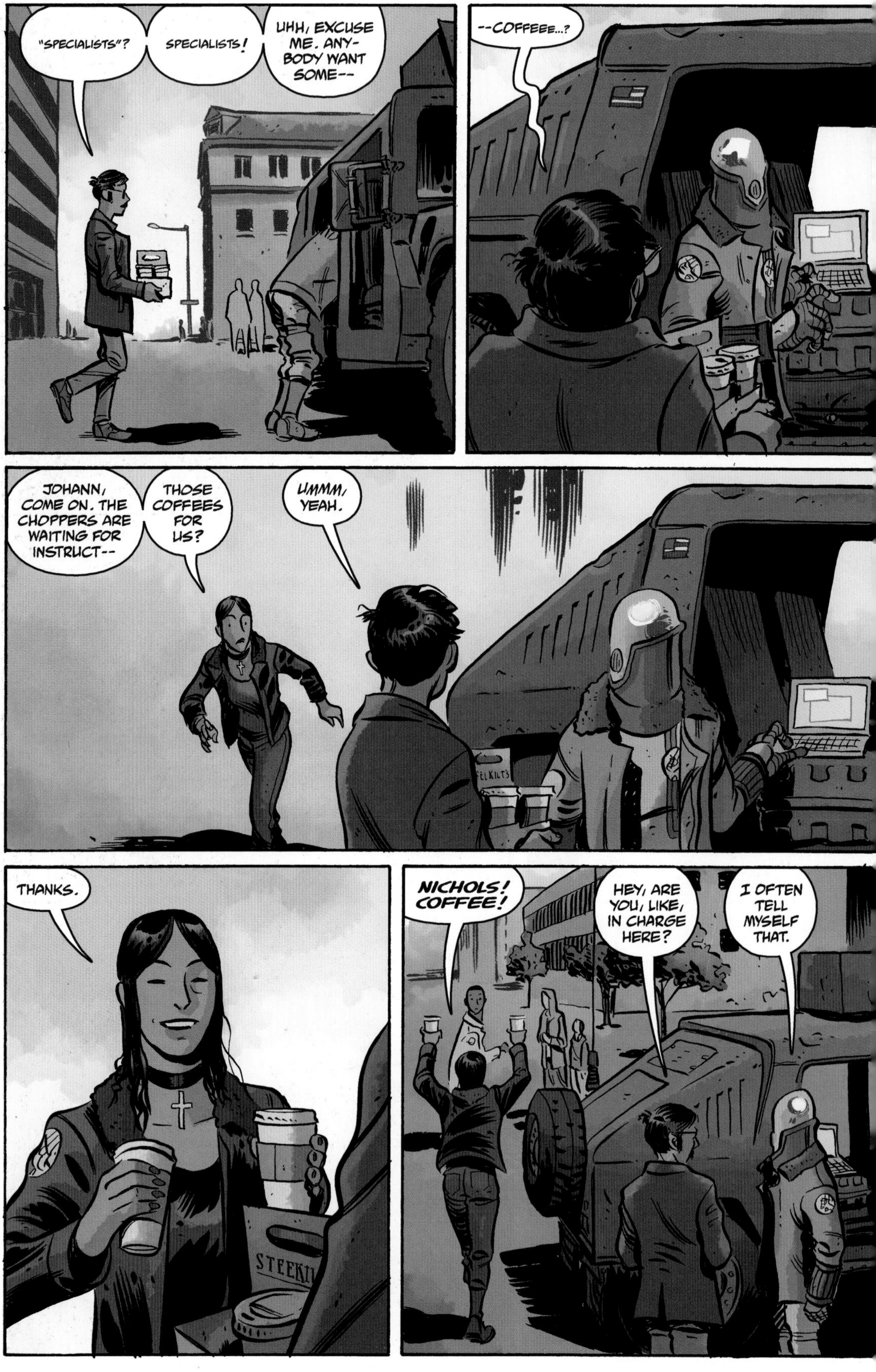
"SPECIALISTS"?
SPECIALISTS!
UHH, EXCUSE ME. ANY-BODY WANT SOME--
--COFFEEE...?
JOHANN, COME ON. THE CHOPPERS ARE WAITING FOR INSTRUCT--
THOSE COFFEES FOR US?
UMMM, YEAH.
THANKS.
STEEKIL
NICHOLS! COFFEE!
HEY, ARE YOU, LIKE, IN CHARGE HERE?
I OFTEN TELL MYSELF THAT.

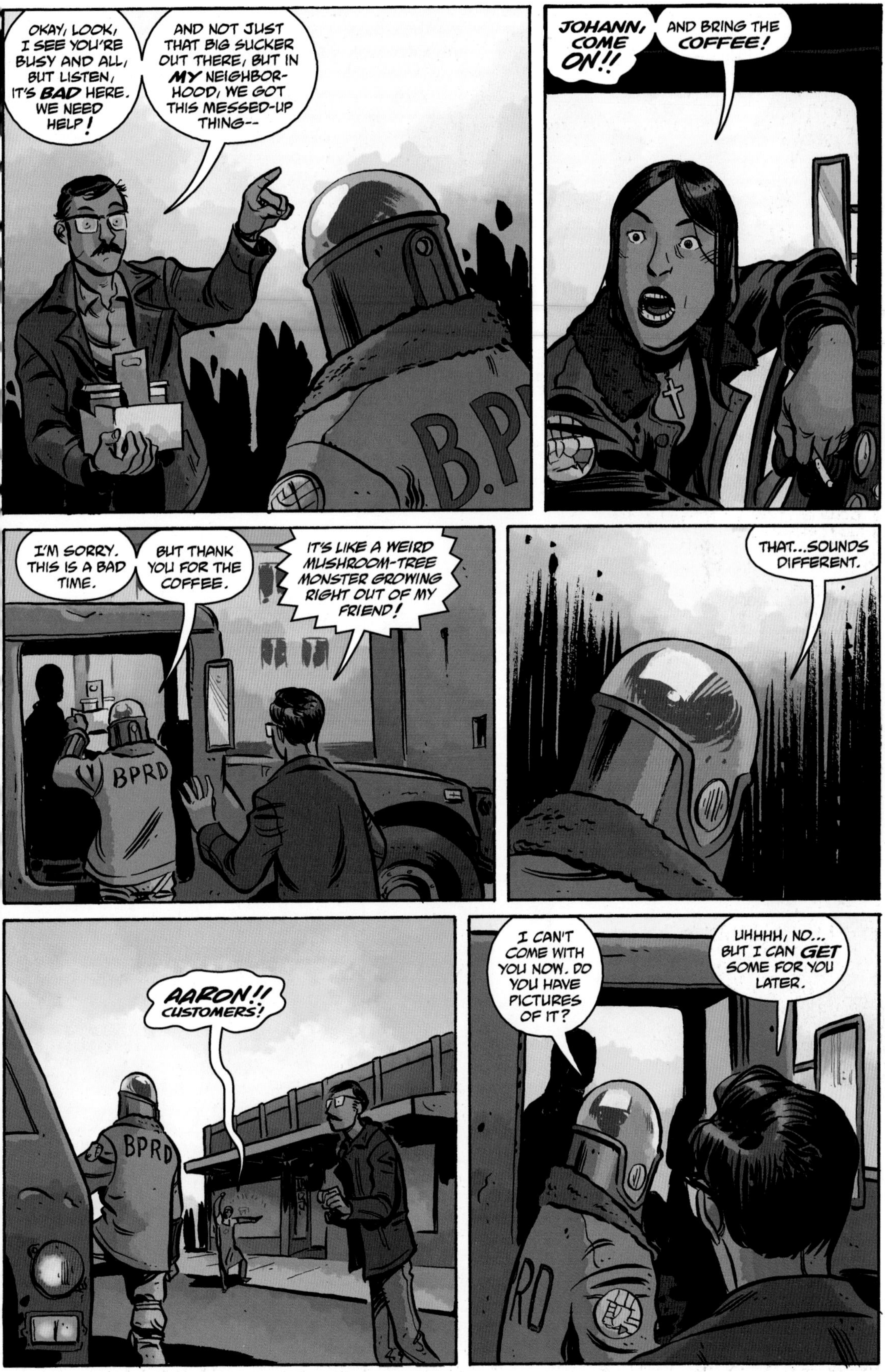
OKAY, LOOK, I SEE YOU'RE BUSY AND ALL, BUT LISTEN, IT'S BAD HERE. WE NEED HELP!
AND NOT JUST THAT BIG SUCKER OUT THERE, BUT IN MY NEIGHBORHOOD, WE GOT THIS MESSED-UP THING--
JOHANN, COME ON!!
AND BRING THE COFFEE!
I'M SORRY. THIS IS A BAD TIME.
BUT THANK YOU FOR THE COFFEE.
IT'S LIKE A WEIRD MUSHROOM-TREE MONSTER GROWING RIGHT OUT OF MY FRIEND!
THAT...SOUNDS DIFFERENT.
AARON!! CUSTOMERS!
I CAN'T COME WITH YOU NOW. DO YOU HAVE PICTURES OF IT?
UHHHH, NO... BUT I CAN GET SOME FOR YOU LATER.

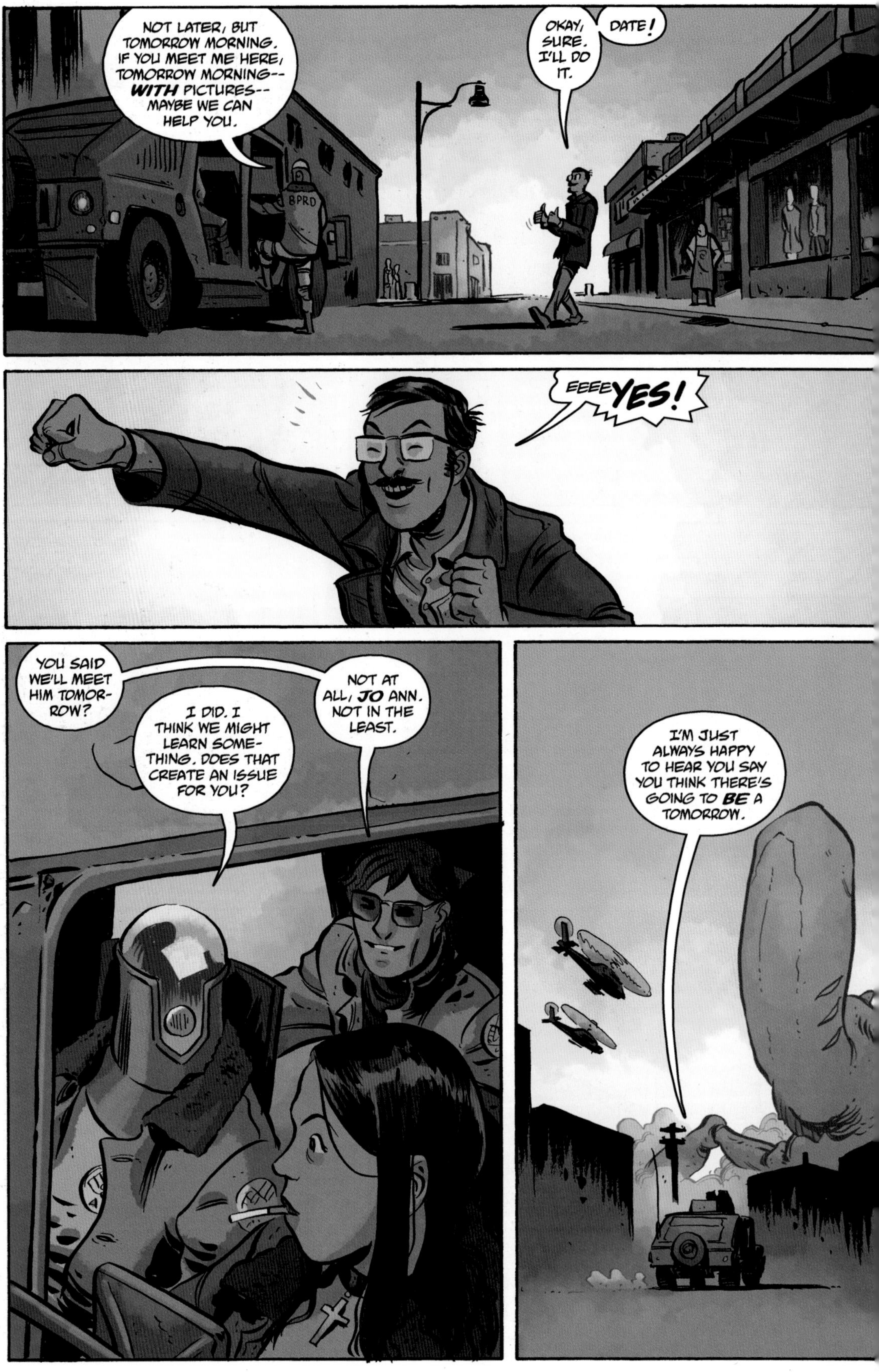

NOT LATER, BUT TOMORROW MORNING. IF YOU MEET ME HERE, TOMORROW MORNING-- WITH PICTURES-- MAYBE WE CAN HELP YOU.
OKAY, SURE. I'LL DO IT.
DATE!
BPRD
EEEEYES!
YOU SAID WE'LL MEET HIM TOMOR-ROW?
I DID. I THINK WE MIGHT LEARN SOME-THING. DOES THAT CREATE AN ISSUE FOR YOU?
NOT AT ALL, JO ANN. NOT IN THE LEAST.
I'M JUST ALWAYS HAPPY TO HEAR YOU SAY YOU THINK THERE'S GOING TO BE A TOMORROW.

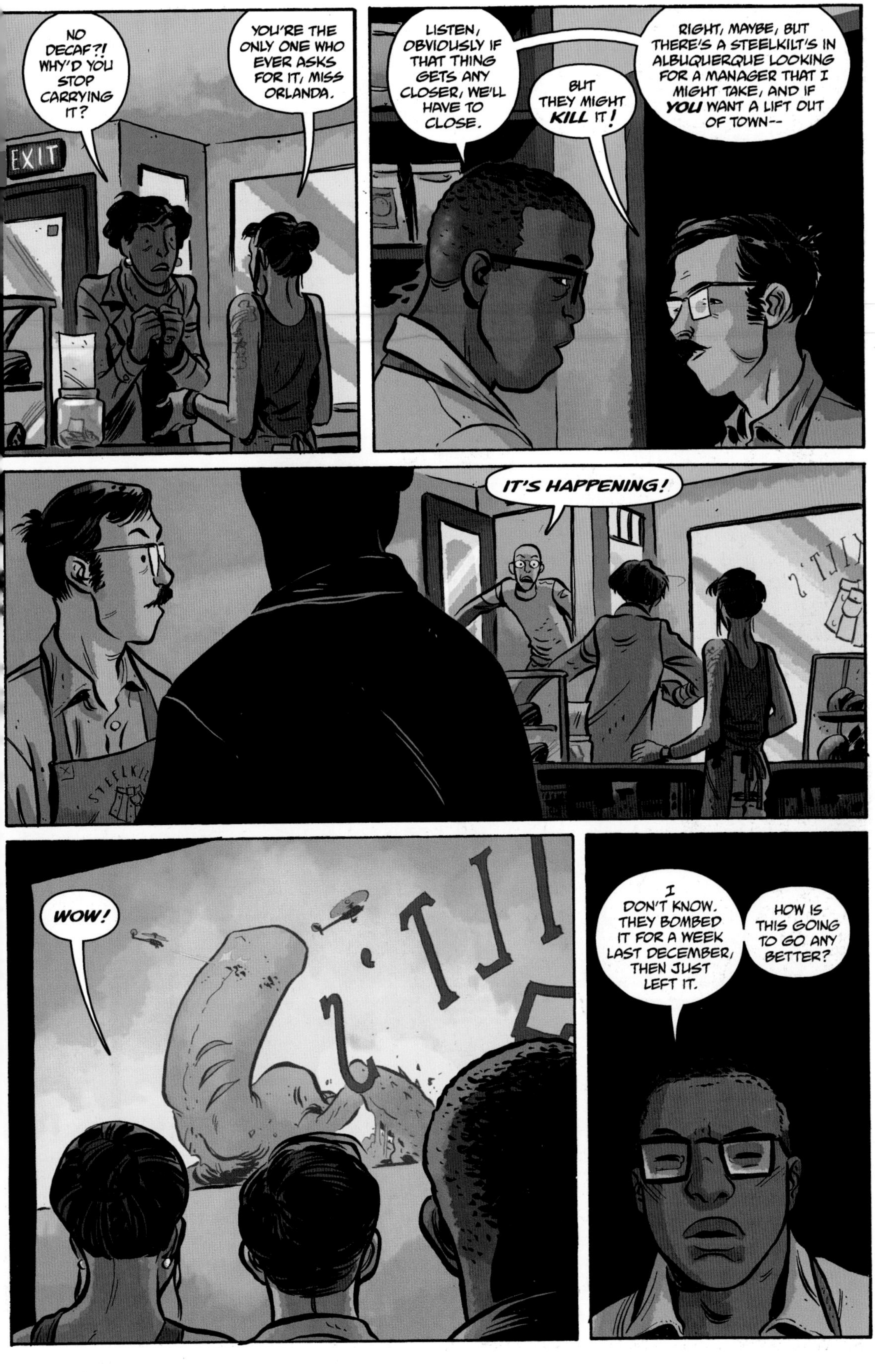
NO DECAF?! WHY'D YOU STOP CARRYING IT?
YOU'RE THE ONLY ONE WHO EVER ASKS FOR IT, MISS ORLANDA.
EXIT
LISTEN, OBVIOUSLY IF THAT THING GETS ANY CLOSER, WE'LL HAVE TO CLOSE.
BUT THEY MIGHT KILL IT!
RIGHT, MAYBE, BUT THERE'S A STEELKILT'S IN ALBUQUERQUE LOOKING FOR A MANAGER THAT I MIGHT TAKE, AND IF YOU WANT A LIFT OUT OF TOWN--
IT'S HAPPENING!
STEELKILT
WOW!
I DON'T KNOW. THEY BOMBED IT FOR A WEEK LAST DECEMBER, THEN JUST LEFT IT.
HOW IS THIS GOING TO GO ANY BETTER?

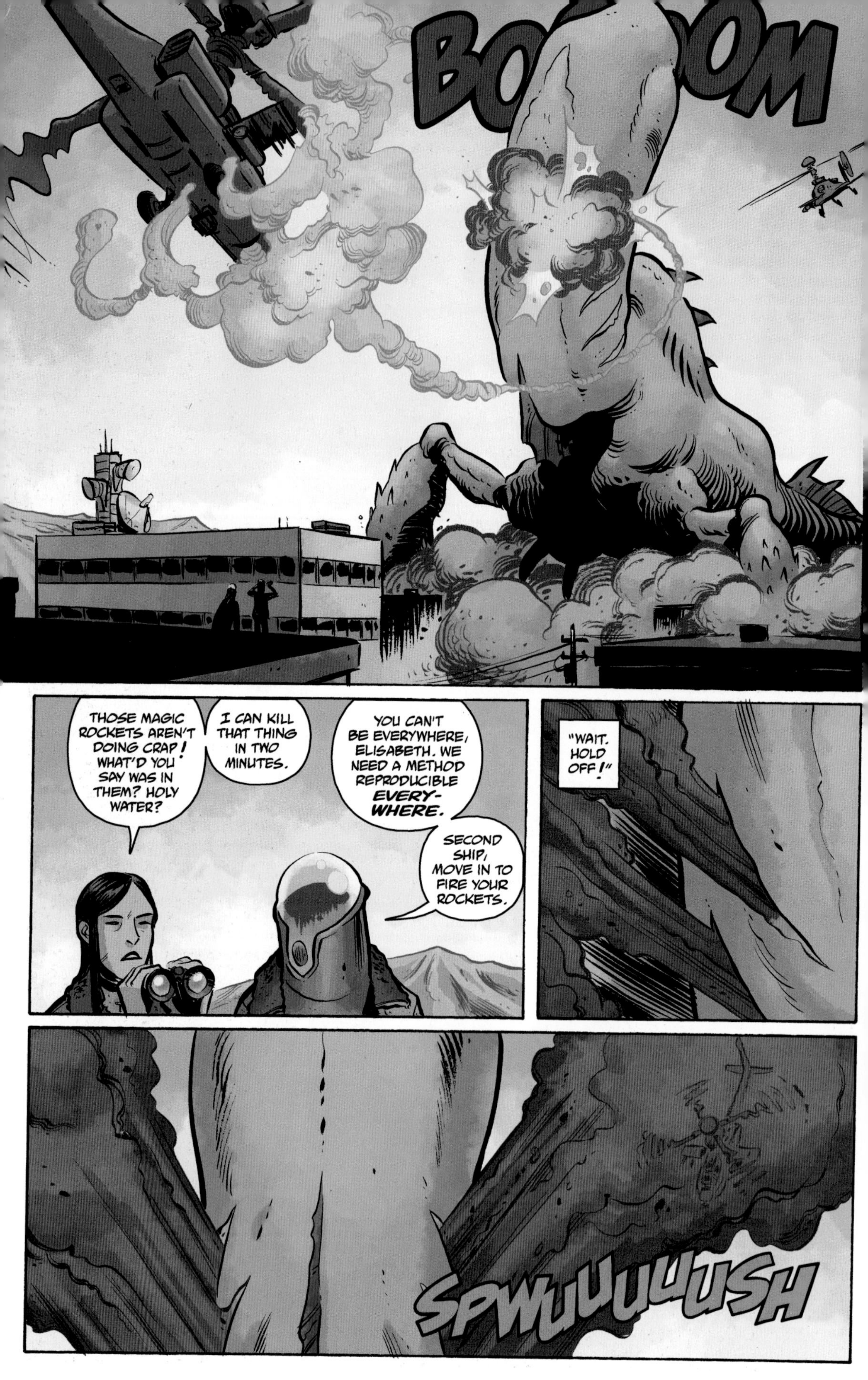
BOOOOM
THOSE MAGIC ROCKETS AREN'T DOING CRAP! WHAT'D YOU SAY WAS IN THEM? HOLY WATER?
I CAN KILL THAT THING IN TWO MINUTES.
YOU CAN'T BE EVERYWHERE, ELISABETH. WE NEED A METHOD REPRODUCIBLE EVERY-WHERE.
SECOND SHIP, MOVE IN TO FIRE YOUR ROCKETS.
"WAIT. HOLD OFF!"
SPWUUUUUSH

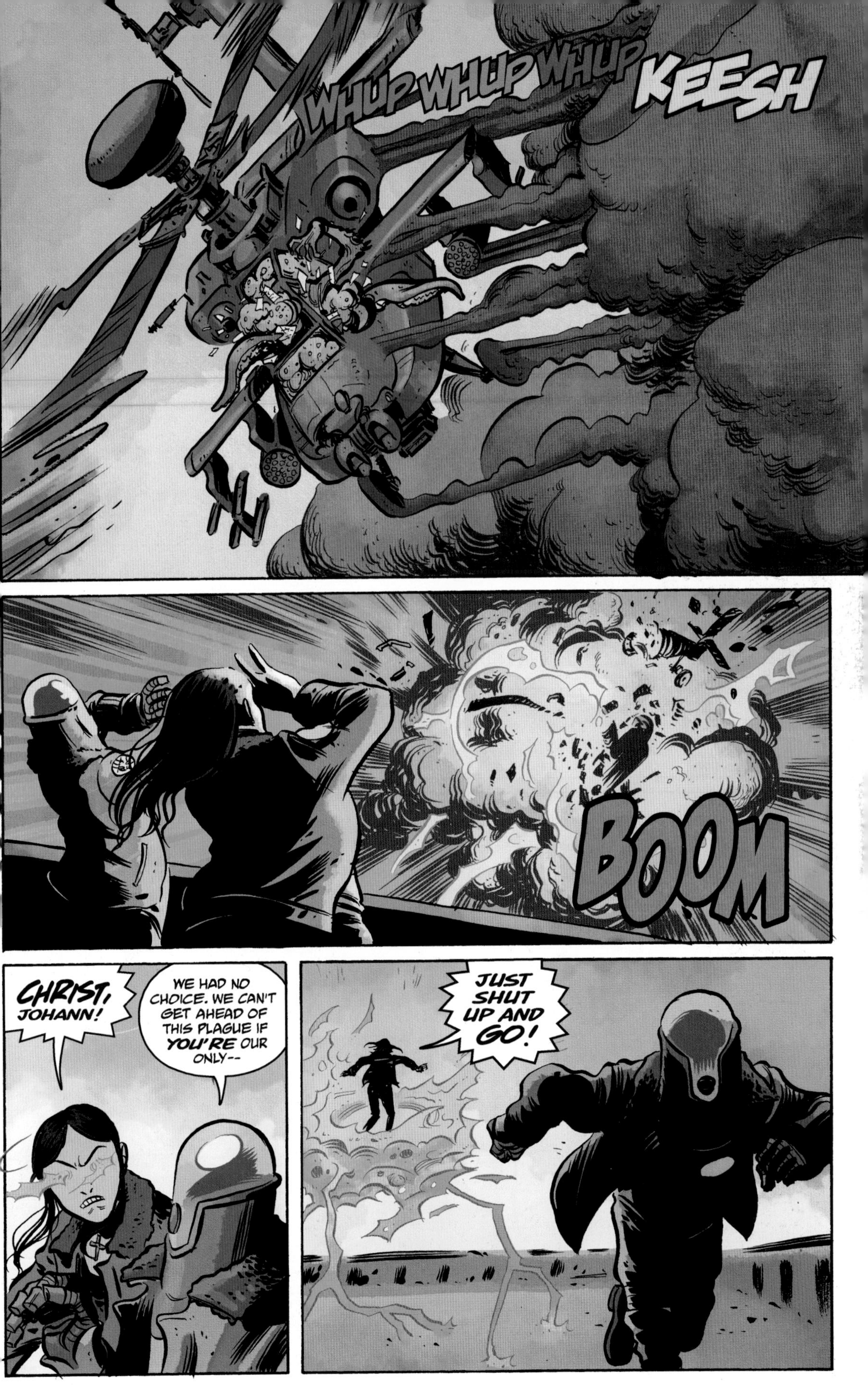
WHUP WHUP WHUP
KEESH
BOOM
CHRIST, JOHANN!
WE HAD NO CHOICE. WE CAN'T GET AHEAD OF THIS PLAGUE IF YOU'RE OUR ONLY--
JUST SHUT UP AND GO!

MOTHER... IT'S SPITTING OUT **MORE** OF THAT STUFF!!

NO. IT'S NOT **SPRAYING!**--

THAT'S **SMOKE!**

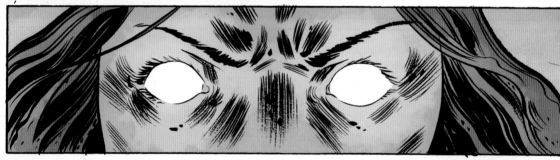

ZAP

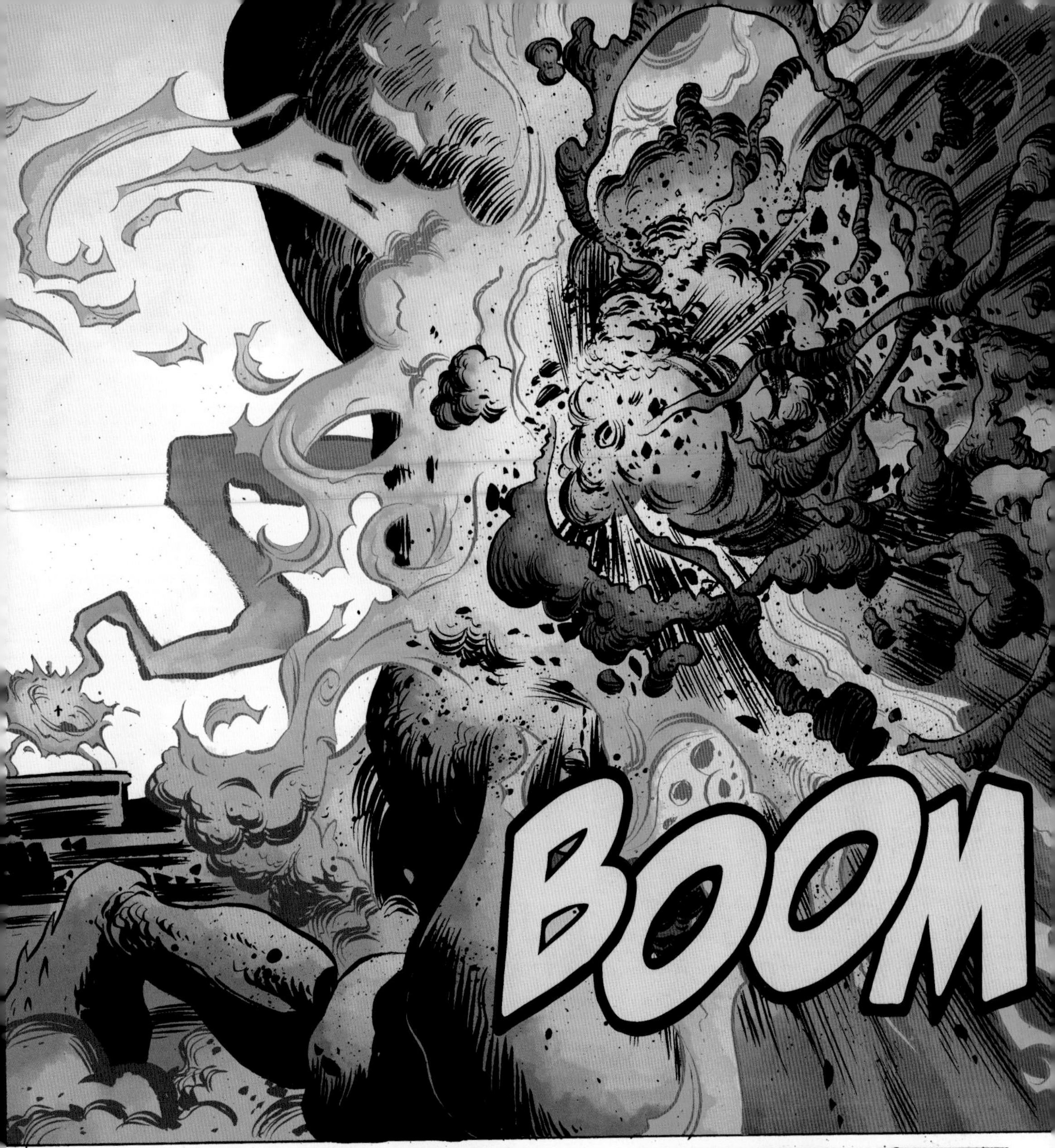
BOOM
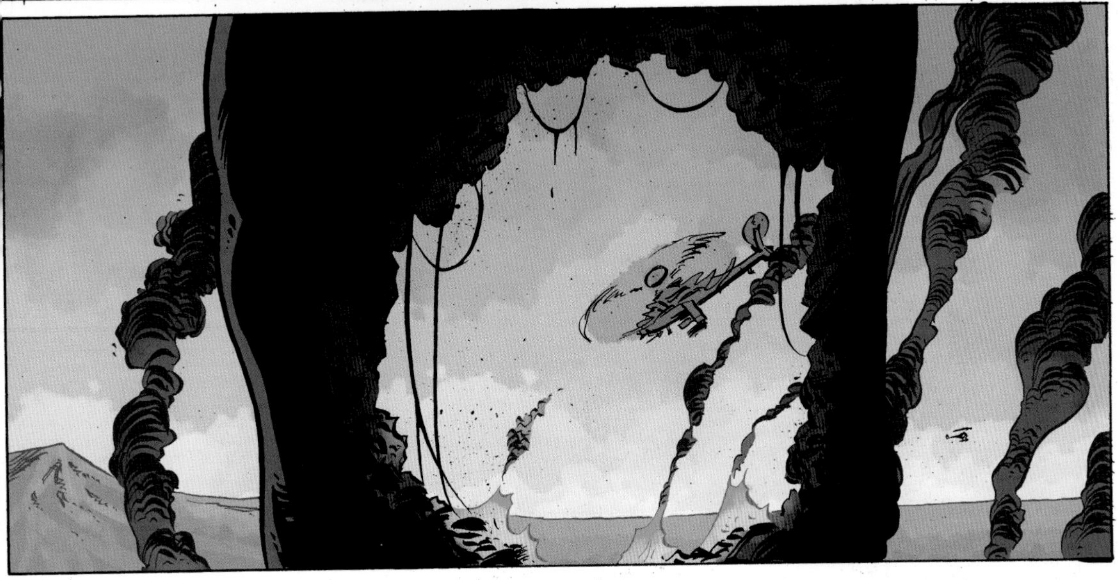

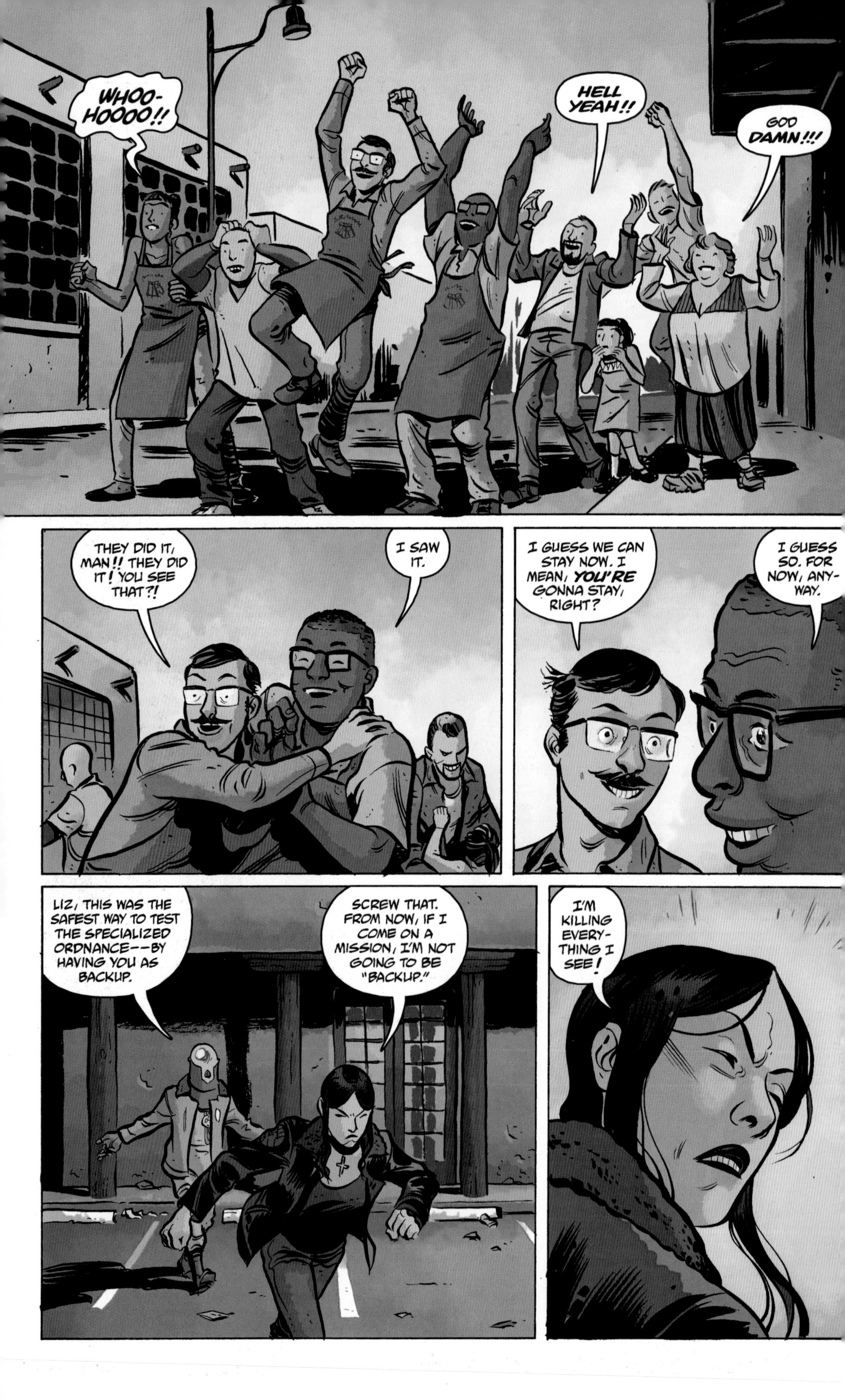
WHOO-HOOOO!!
HELL YEAH!!
GOD DAMN!!!
THEY DID IT, MAN!! THEY DID IT! YOU SEE THAT?!
I SAW IT.
I GUESS WE CAN STAY NOW. I MEAN, YOU'RE GONNA STAY, RIGHT?
I GUESS SO. FOR NOW, ANYWAY.
LIZ, THIS WAS THE SAFEST WAY TO TEST THE SPECIALIZED ORDNANCE--BY HAVING YOU AS BACKUP.
SCREW THAT. FROM NOW, IF I COME ON A MISSION, I'M NOT GOING TO BE "BACKUP."
I'M KILLING EVERYTHING I SEE!

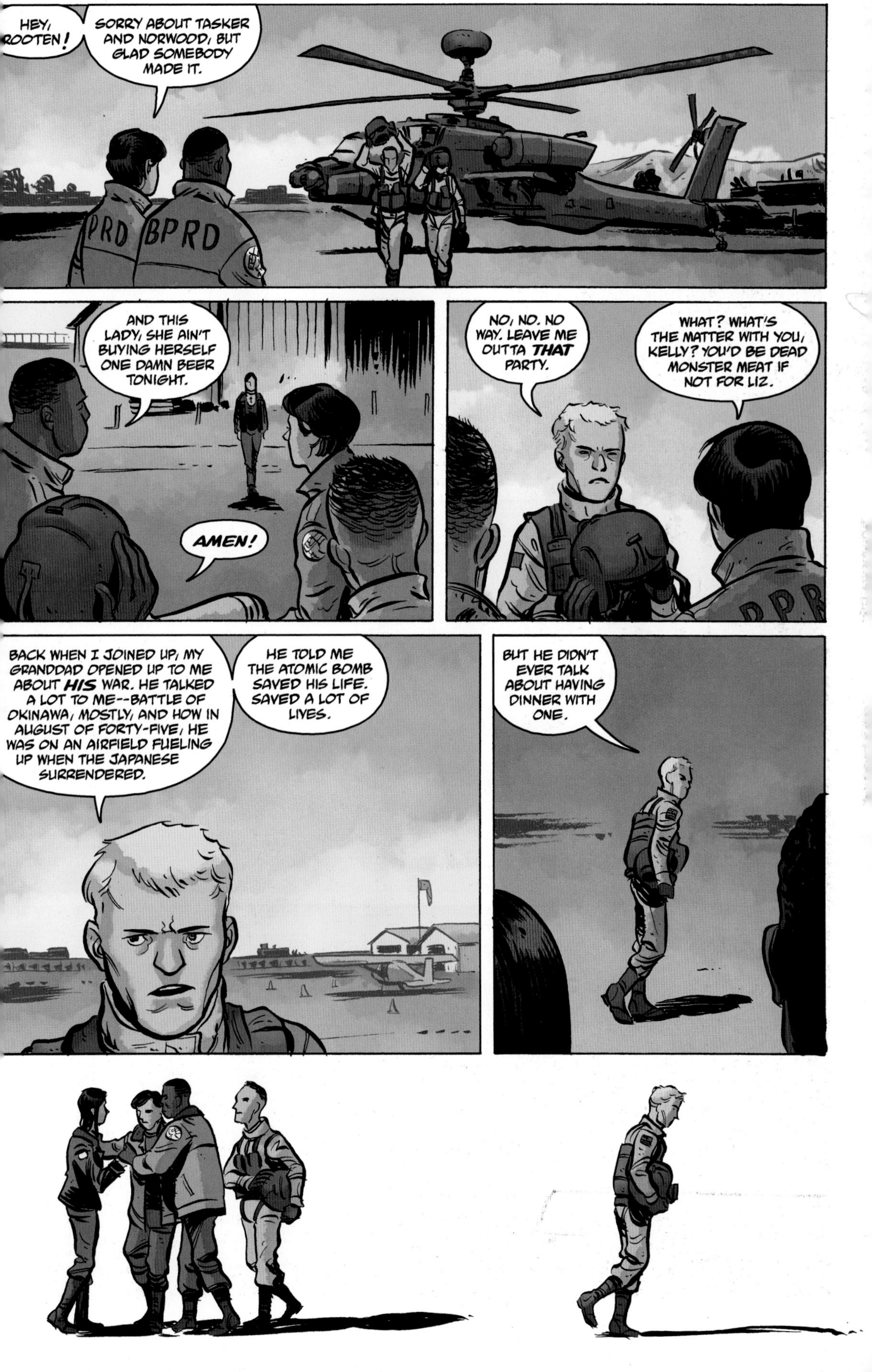
HEY, ROOTEN!
SORRY ABOUT TASKER AND NORWOOD, BUT GLAD SOMEBODY MADE IT.
PRD
BPRD
AND THIS LADY, SHE AIN'T BUYING HERSELF ONE DAMN BEER TONIGHT.
AMEN!
NO, NO. NO WAY. LEAVE ME OUTTA THAT PARTY.
WHAT? WHAT'S THE MATTER WITH YOU, KELLY? YOU'D BE DEAD MONSTER MEAT IF NOT FOR LIZ.
BACK WHEN I JOINED UP, MY GRANDDAD OPENED UP TO ME ABOUT HIS WAR. HE TALKED A LOT TO ME--BATTLE OF OKINAWA, MOSTLY, AND HOW IN AUGUST OF FORTY-FIVE, HE WAS ON AN AIRFIELD FUELING UP WHEN THE JAPANESE SURRENDERED.
HE TOLD ME THE ATOMIC BOMB SAVED HIS LIFE. SAVED A LOT OF LIVES.
BUT HE DIDN'T EVER TALK ABOUT HAVING DINNER WITH ONE.

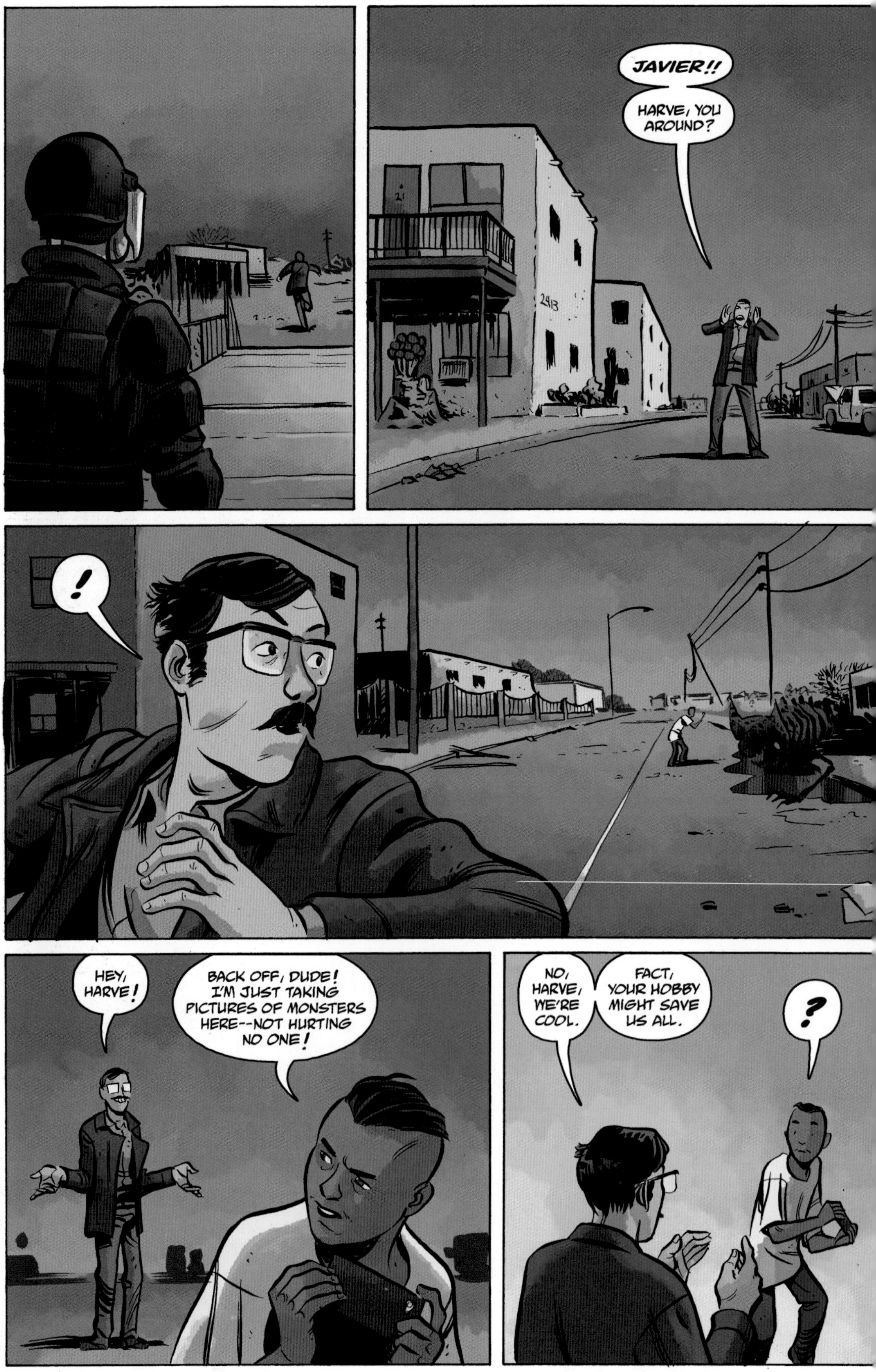
JAVIER!!
HARVE, YOU AROUND?
!
HEY, HARVE!
BACK OFF, DUDE! I'M JUST TAKING PICTURES OF MONSTERS HERE--NOT HURTING NO ONE!
NO, HARVE, WE'RE COOL.
FACT, YOUR HOBBY MIGHT SAVE US ALL.
?

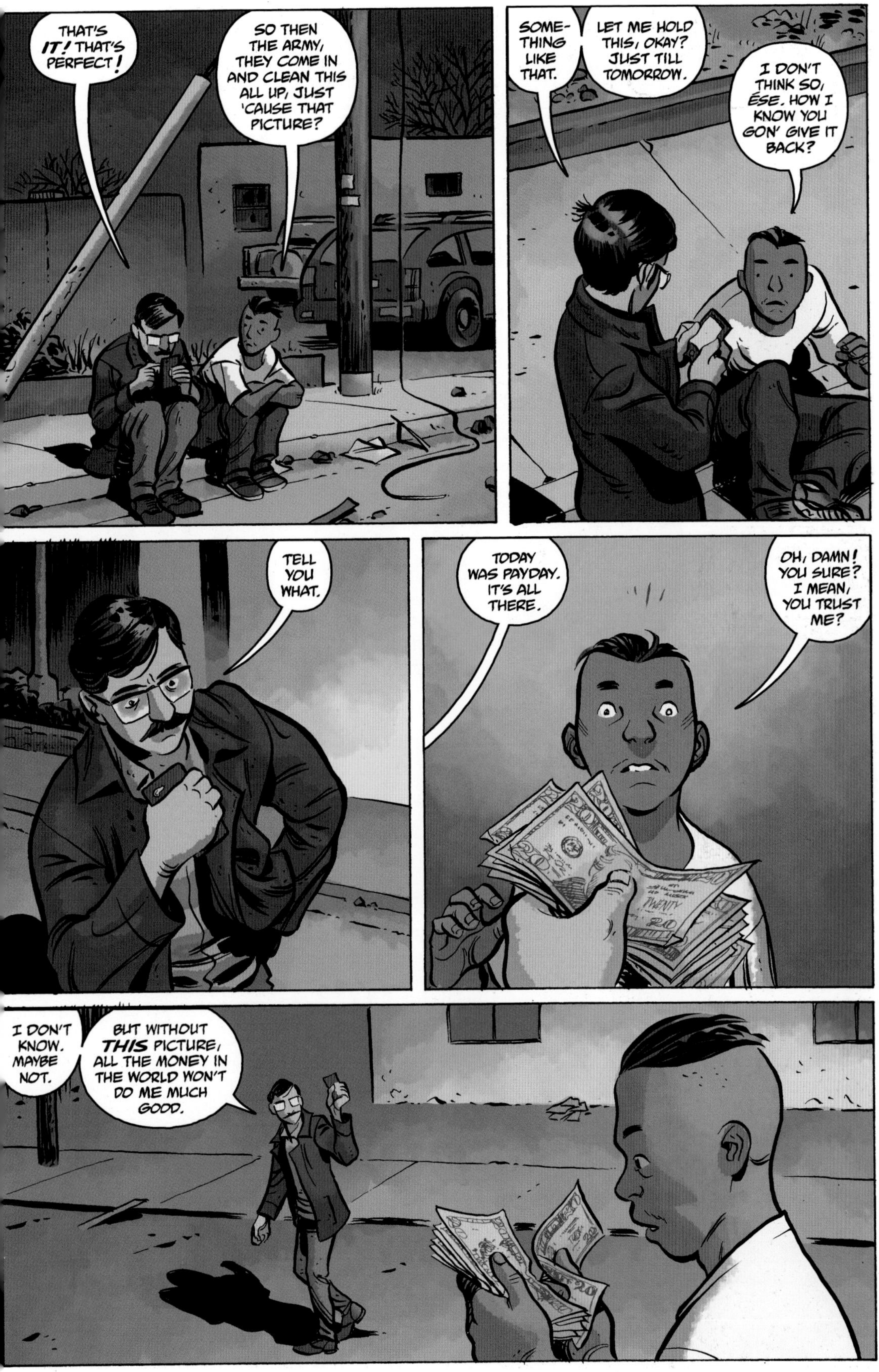
THAT'S IT! THAT'S PERFECT!
SO THEN THE ARMY, THEY COME IN AND CLEAN THIS ALL UP, JUST 'CAUSE THAT PICTURE?
SOMETHING LIKE THAT.
LET ME HOLD THIS, OKAY? JUST TILL TOMORROW.
I DON'T THINK SO, ÉSE. HOW I KNOW YOU GON' GIVE IT BACK?
TELL YOU WHAT.
TODAY WAS PAYDAY. IT'S ALL THERE.
OH, DAMN! YOU SURE? I MEAN, YOU TRUST ME?
I DON'T KNOW. MAYBE NOT.
BUT WITHOUT THIS PICTURE, ALL THE MONEY IN THE WORLD WON'T DO ME MUCH GOOD.

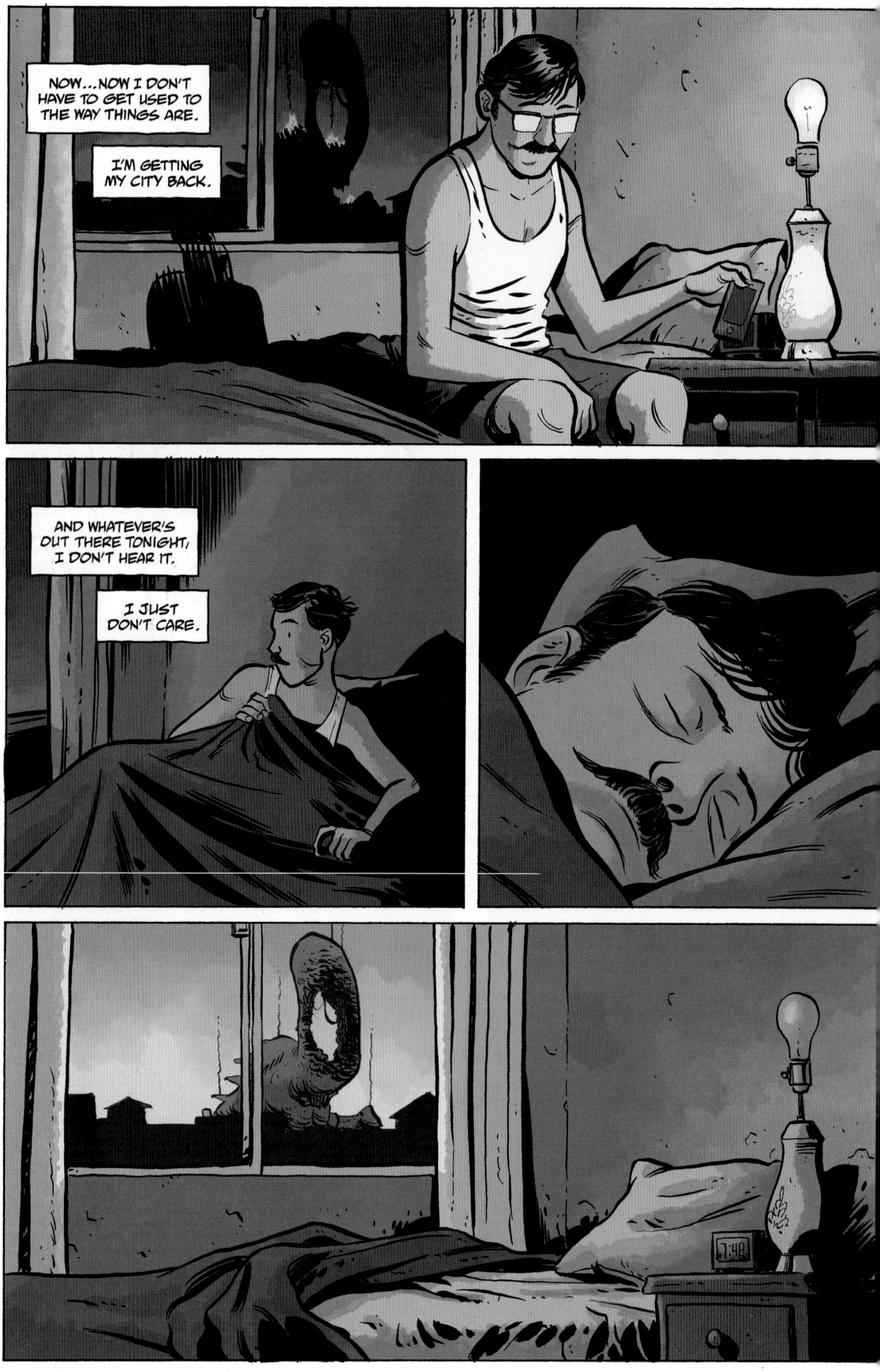
NOW...NOW I DON'T HAVE TO GET USED TO THE WAY THINGS ARE.
I'M GETTING MY CITY BACK.
AND WHATEVER'S OUT THERE TONIGHT, I DON'T HEAR IT.
I JUST DON'T CARE.

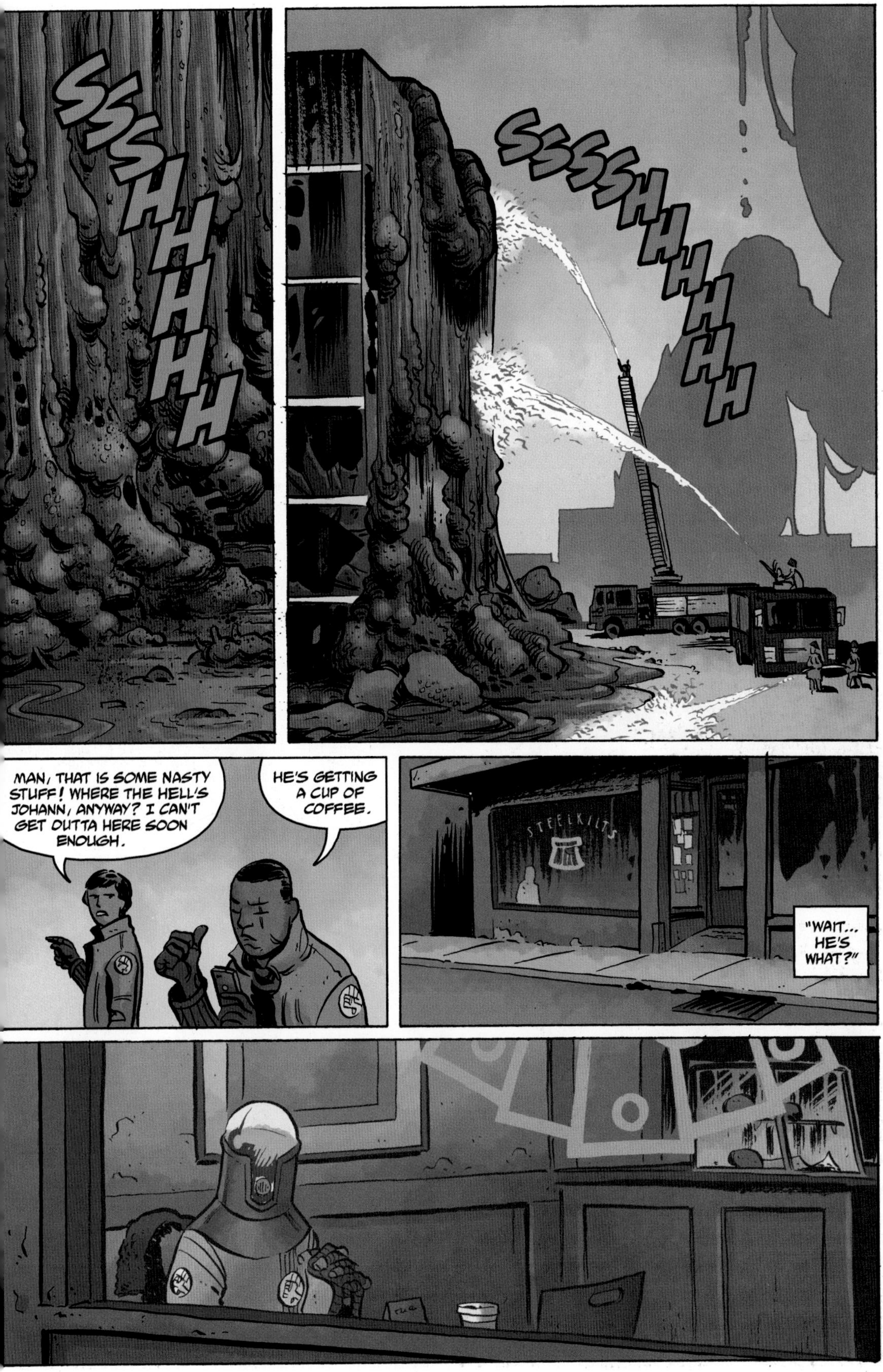
SSSHHHHHH
SSSSHHHHHHH
MAN, THAT IS SOME NASTY STUFF! WHERE THE HELL'S JOHANN, ANYWAY? I CAN'T GET OUTTA HERE SOON ENOUGH.
HE'S GETTING A CUP OF COFFEE.
STEELKILTS
"WAIT... HE'S WHAT?"

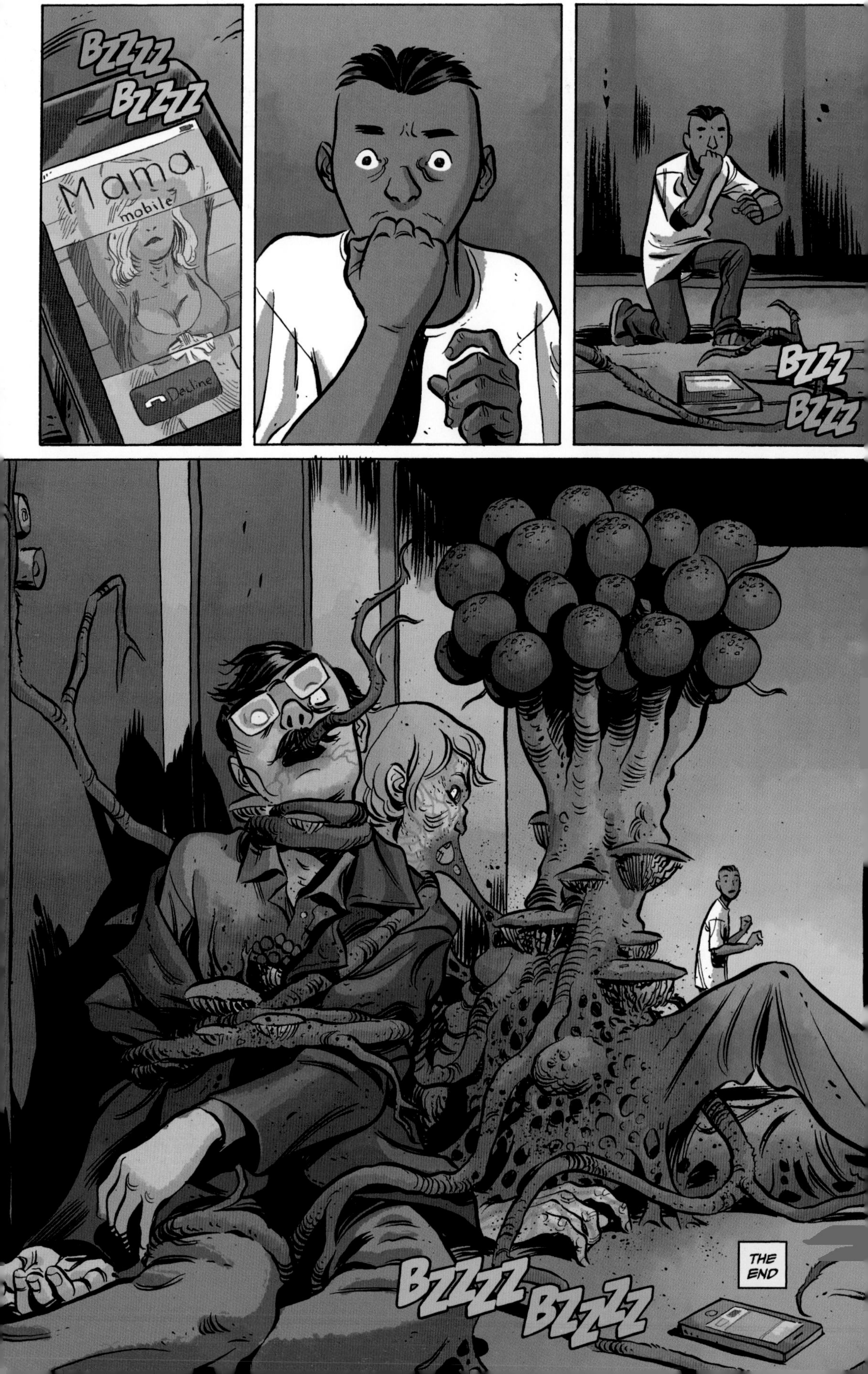
BZZZZ
BZZZZ
Mama
mobile
Decline
BZZZ
BZZZ
BZZZZ
BZZZZ
THE END

B.P.R.D.™

SKETCHBOOK

Notes by Laurence Campbell, Joe Querio, and Tyler Crook

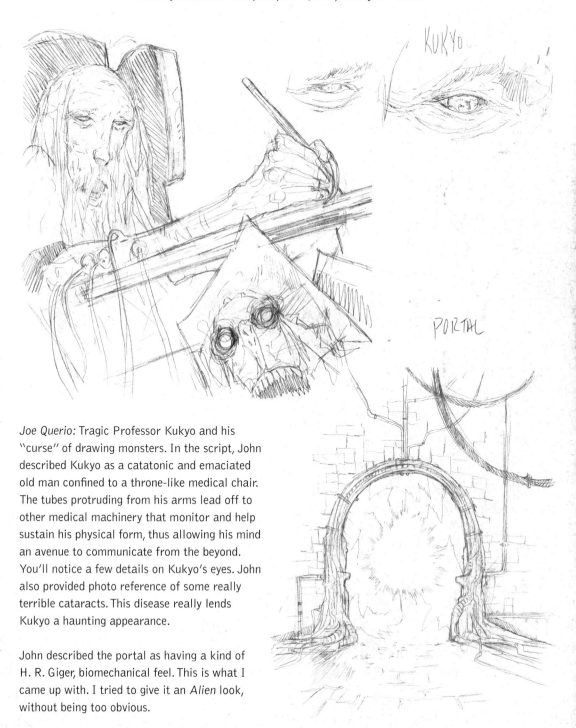

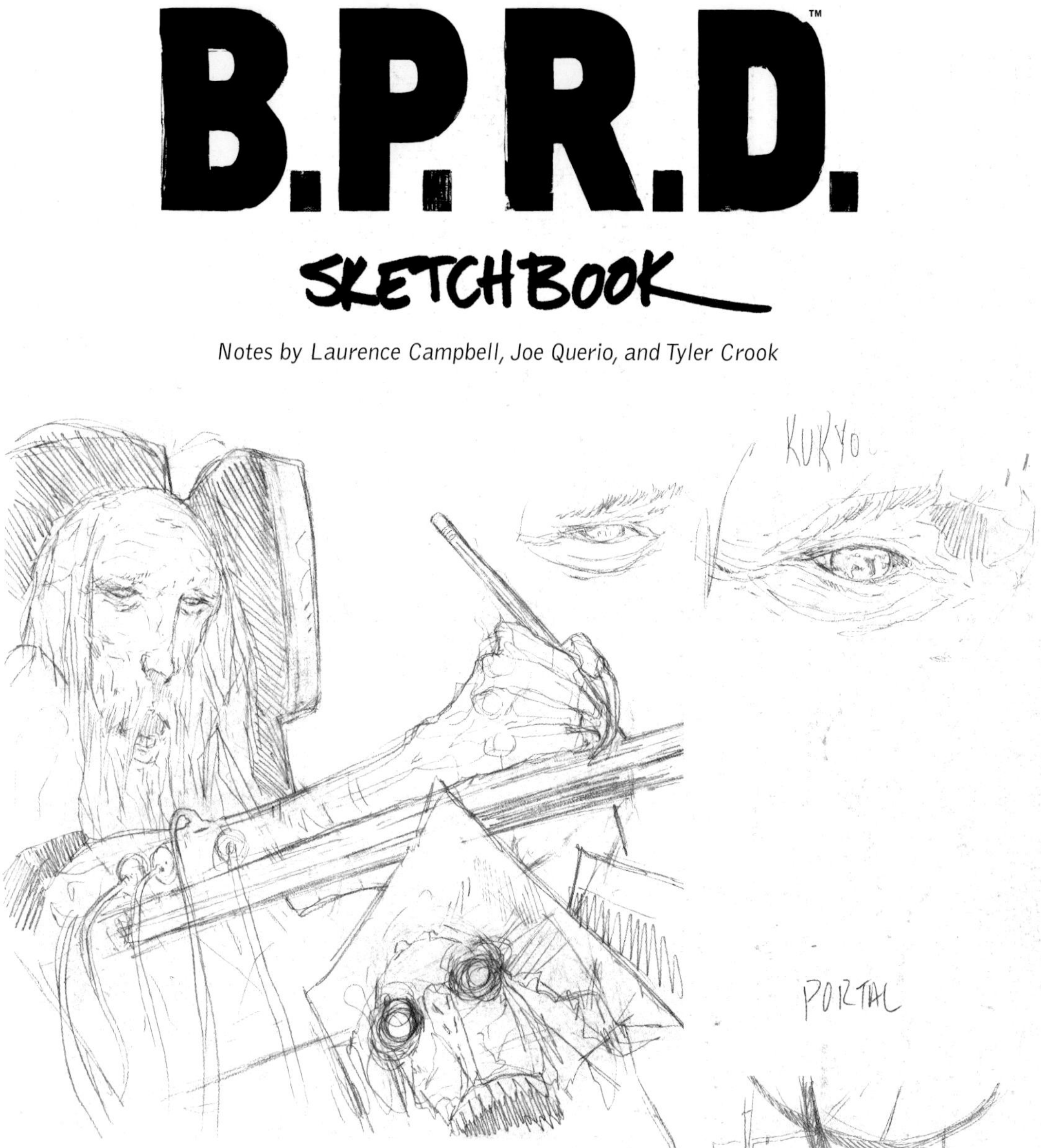
KUKYO

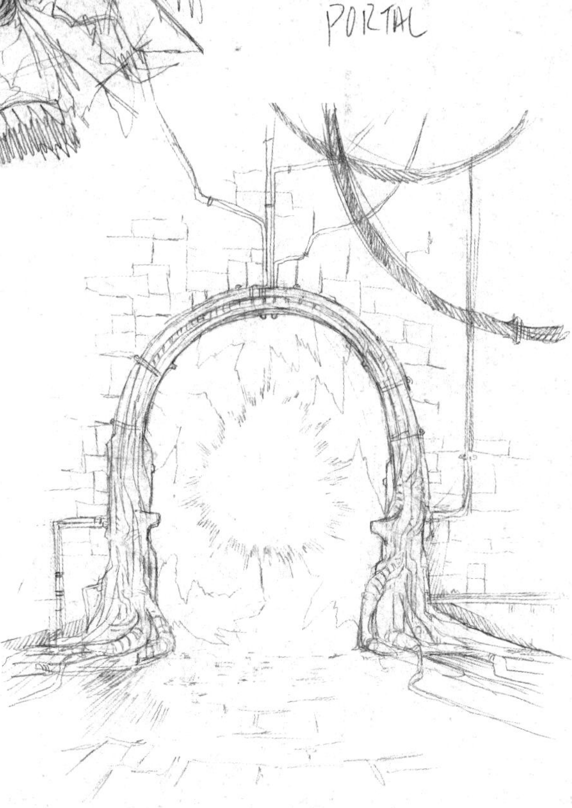
PORTAL

Joe Querio: Tragic Professor Kukyo and his "curse" of drawing monsters. In the script, John described Kukyo as a catatonic and emaciated old man confined to a throne-like medical chair. The tubes protruding from his arms lead off to other medical machinery that monitor and help sustain his physical form, thus allowing his mind an avenue to communicate from the beyond. You'll notice a few details on Kukyo's eyes. John also provided photo reference of some really terrible cataracts. This disease really lends Kukyo a haunting appearance.

John described the portal as having a kind of H. R. Giger, biomechanical feel. This is what I came up with. I tried to give it an *Alien* look, without being too obvious.

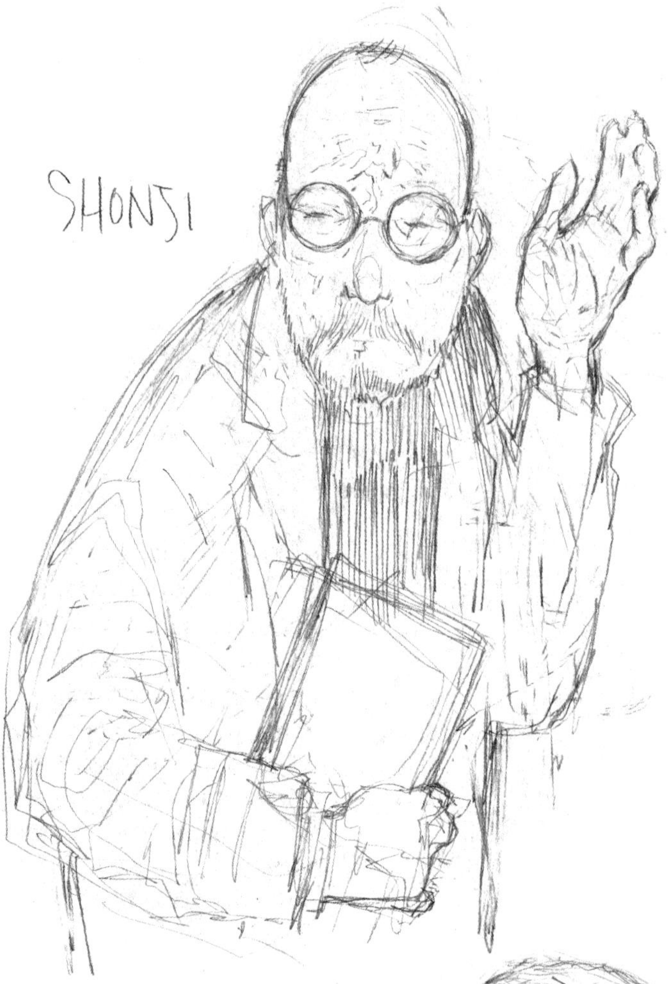
SHONJI

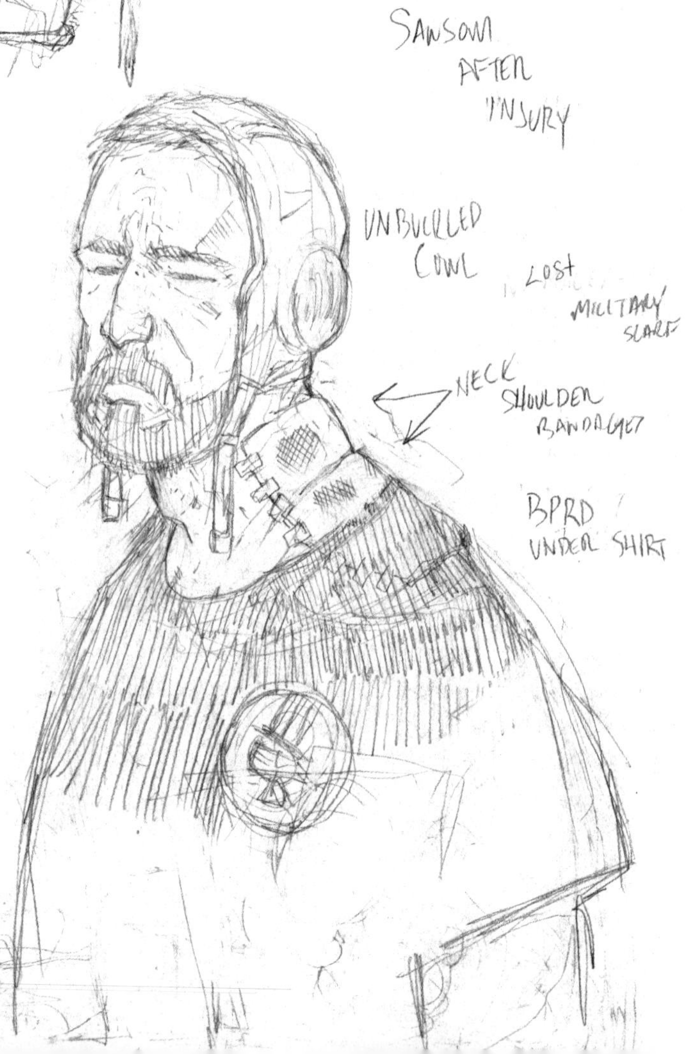
SANSOM
AFTER
INJURY
UNBUCKLED
COWL
LOST
MILITARY
SCARF
NECK
SHOULDER
BANDAGES
BPRD
UNDER SHIRT

JQ: Some new characters here. Well, one, at least. I tried to make Shonji an innocent, unassuming doctor. Not much more to say than that. Sansom was described as being the weathered leader of the team (though I think Johann outranks him). I tried to give Sansom a kind of hard-ass but, at the same time, defeated look. Not too sure if it translates, but that's what I was going for.

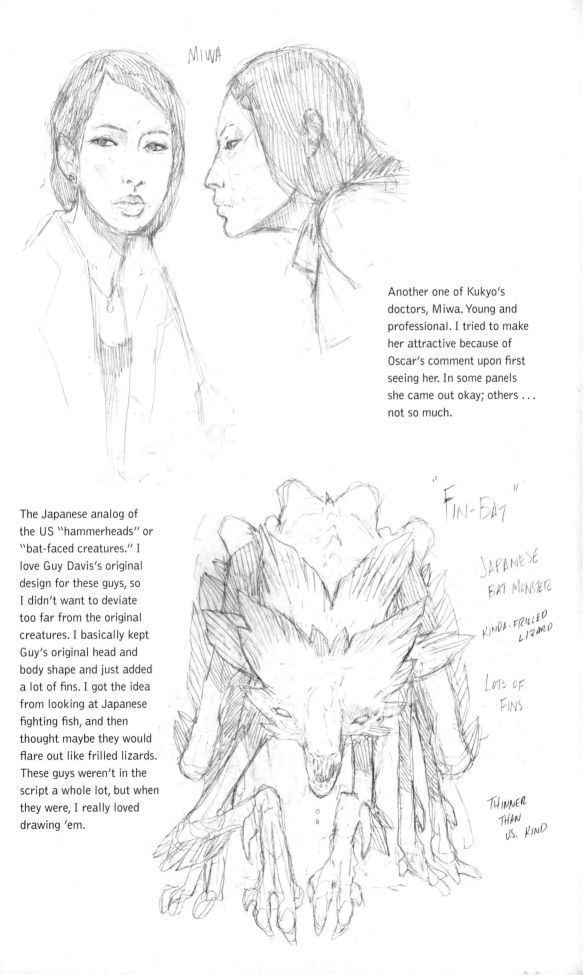

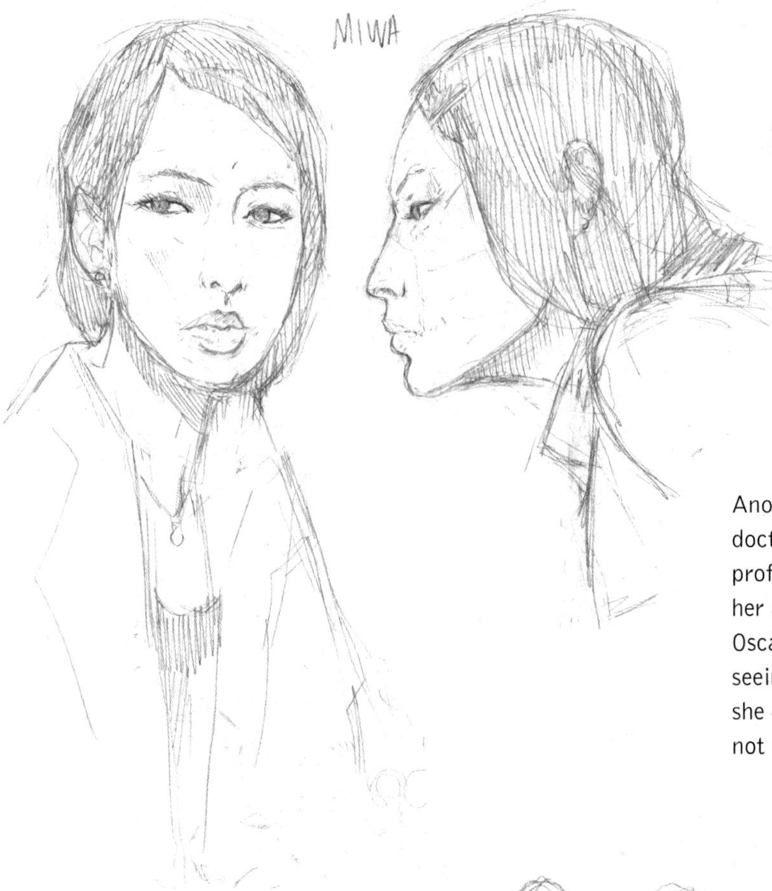
MIWA

Another one of Kukyo's doctors, Miwa. Young and professional. I tried to make her attractive because of Oscar's comment upon first seeing her. In some panels she came out okay; others . . . not so much.

The Japanese analog of the US "hammerheads" or "bat-faced creatures." I love Guy Davis's original design for these guys, so I didn't want to deviate too far from the original creatures. I basically kept Guy's original head and body shape and just added a lot of fins. I got the idea from looking at Japanese fighting fish, and then thought maybe they would flare out like frilled lizards. These guys weren't in the script a whole lot, but when they were, I really loved drawing 'em.

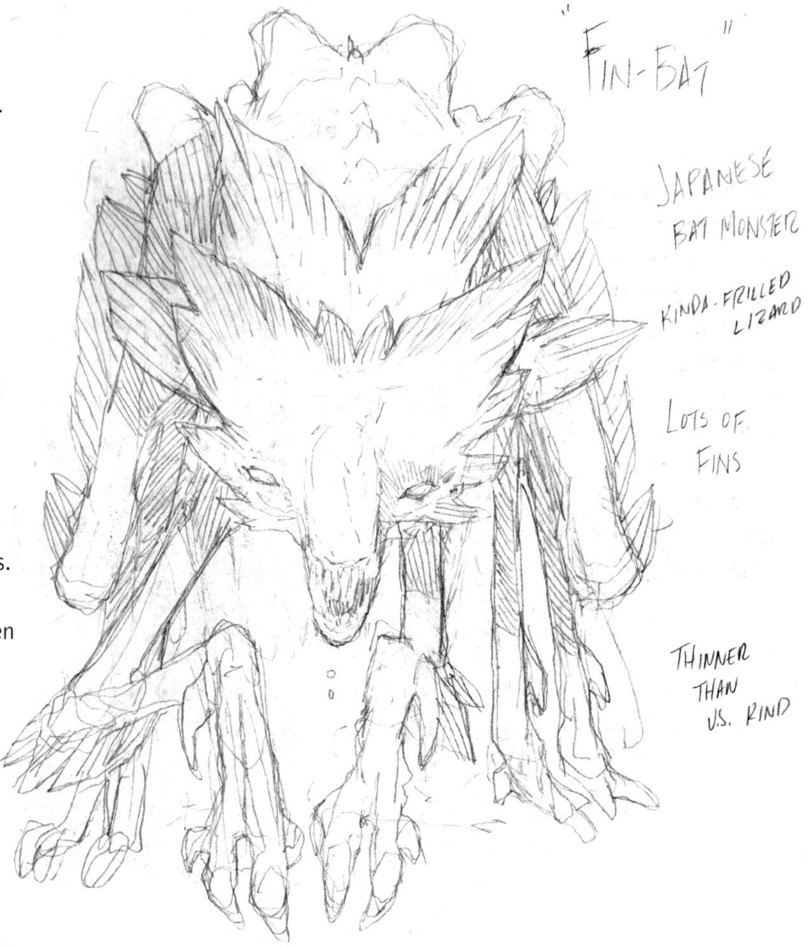
"FIN-BAT"
JAPANESE BAT MONSTER
KINDA-FRILLED LIZARD
LOTS OF FINS
THINNER THAN U.S. KIND

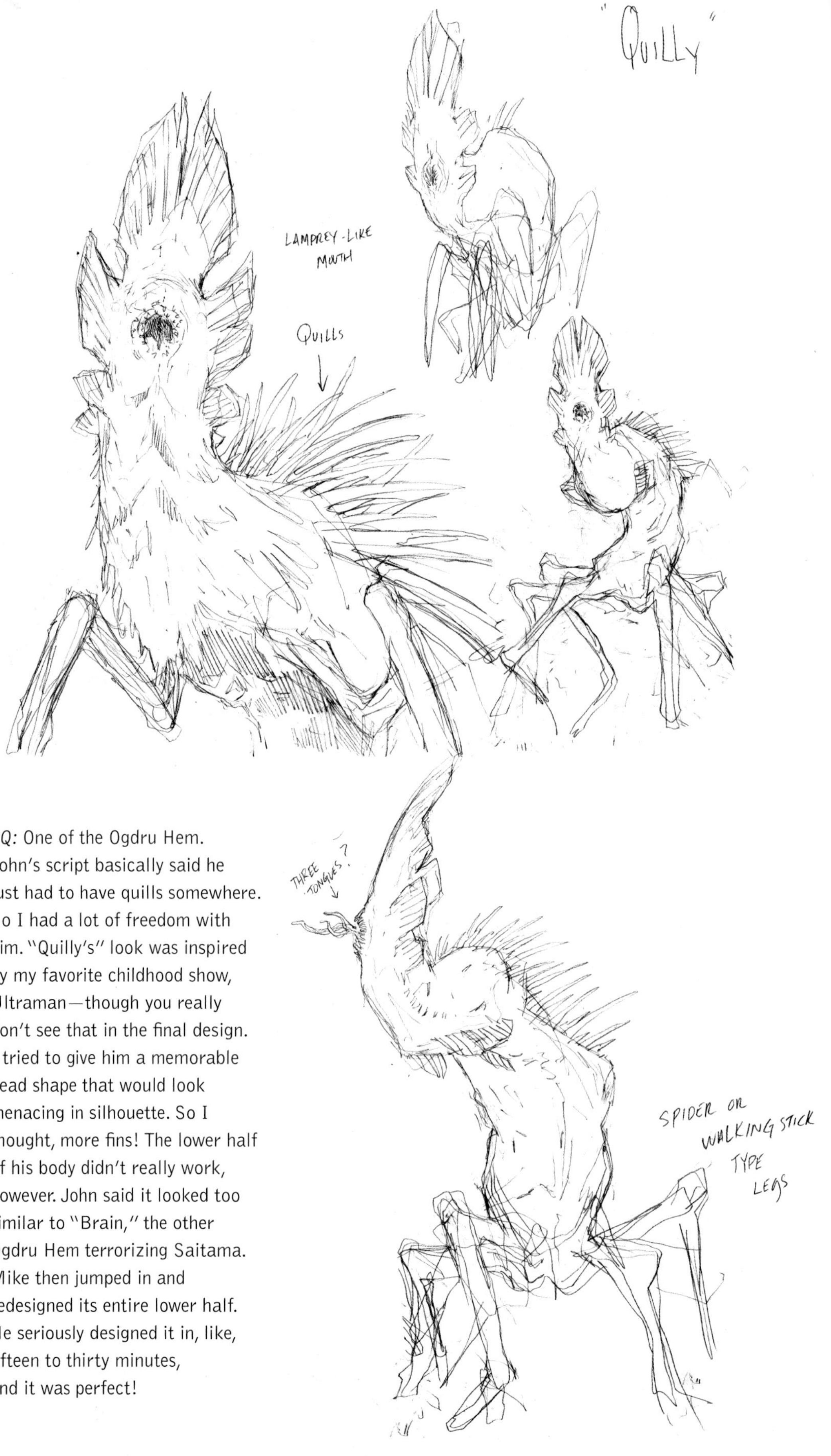
"QUILLY"
LAMPREY-LIKE MOUTH
QUILLS
THREE TONGUES?
SPIDER OR WALKING STICK TYPE LEGS

JQ: One of the Ogdru Hem. John's script basically said he just had to have quills somewhere. So I had a lot of freedom with him. "Quilly's" look was inspired by my favorite childhood show, Ultraman—though you really don't see that in the final design. I tried to give him a memorable head shape that would look menacing in silhouette. So I thought, more fins! The lower half of his body didn't really work, however. John said it looked too similar to "Brain," the other Ogdru Hem terrorizing Saitama. Mike then jumped in and redesigned its entire lower half. He seriously designed it in, like, fifteen to thirty minutes, and it was perfect!

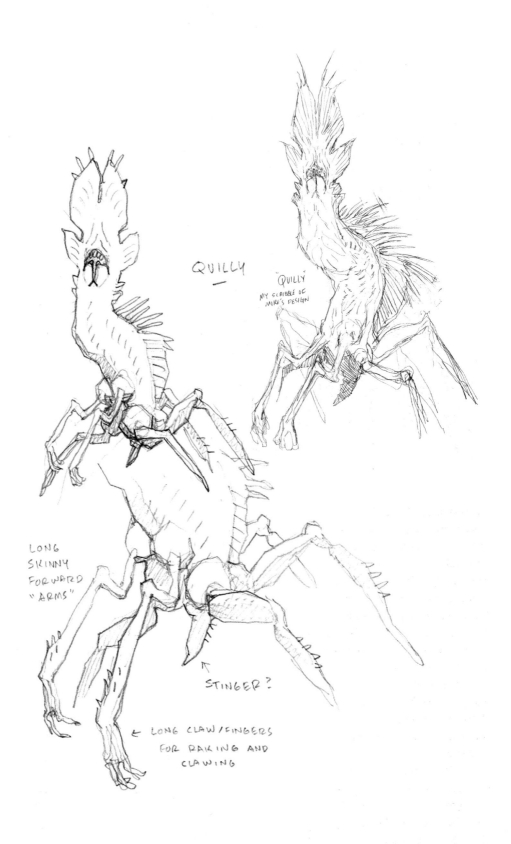

QUILLY

"QUILLY"
MY SCRIBBLE OF
MIKE'S DESIGN

LONG
SKINNY
FORWARD
"ARMS"

STINGER?

← LONG CLAW/FINGERS
FOR RAKING AND
CLAWING

Mike's take on Quilly.

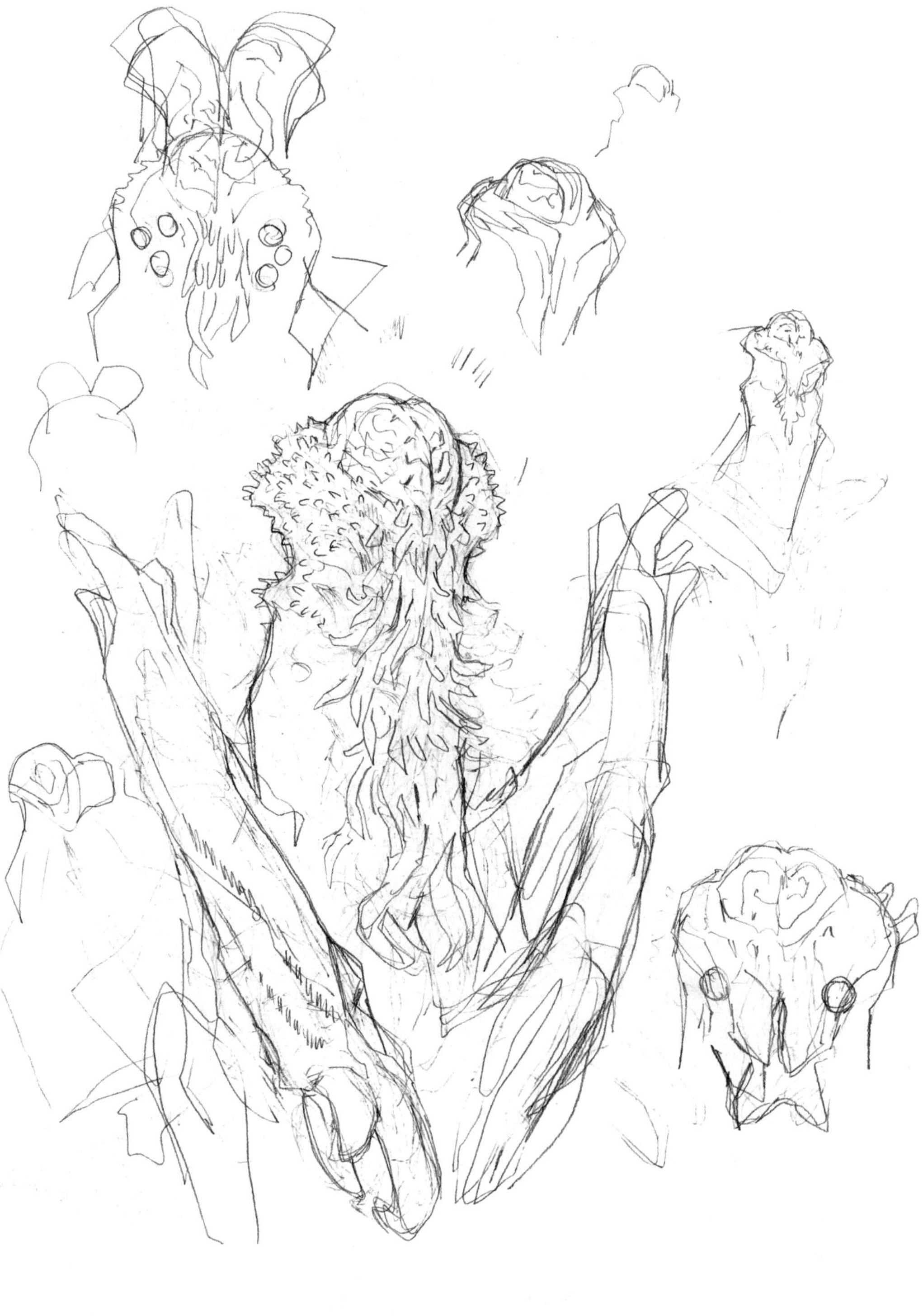

JQ: The other Ogdru Hem, "Brain." This one went through a lot of designs and changes. The next couple of pages show the variations. Another fun monster to design and draw.

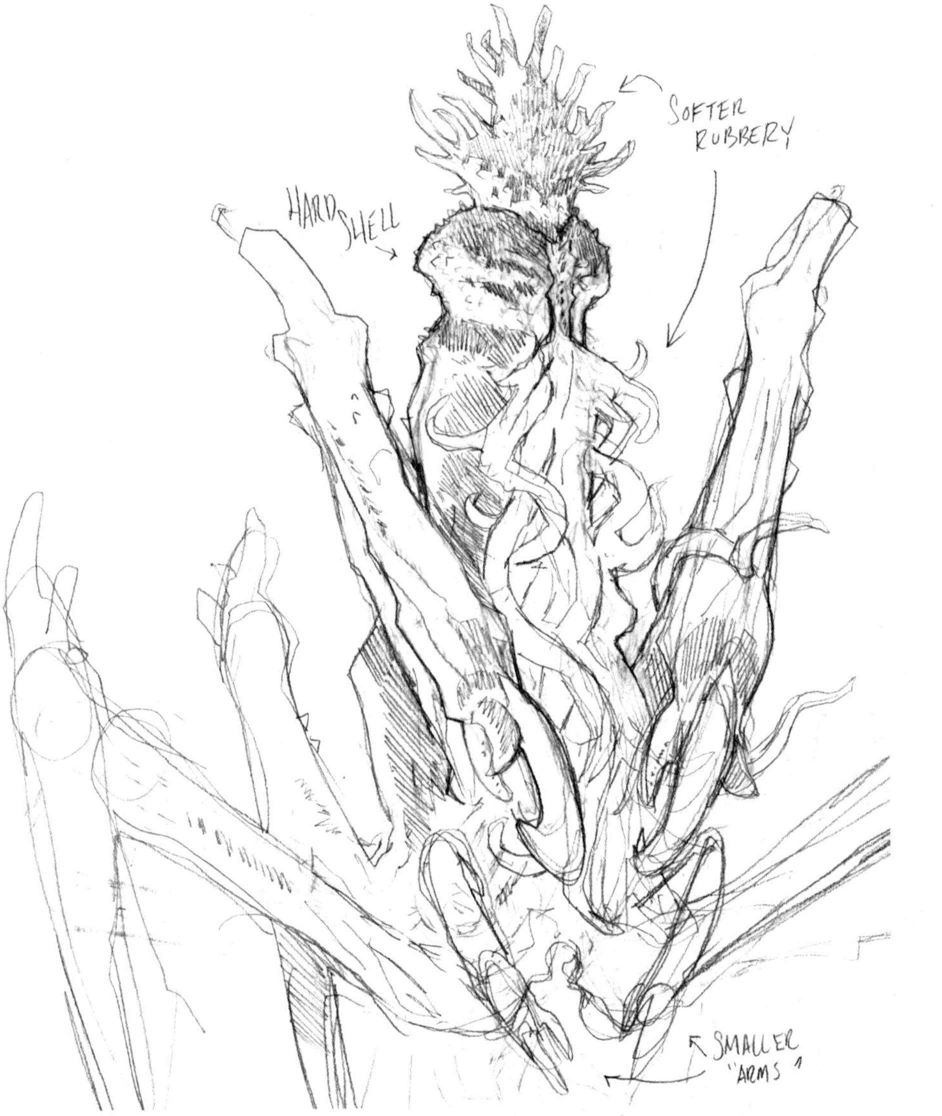
HARD SHELL
SOFTER RUBBERY
SMALLER "ARMS"

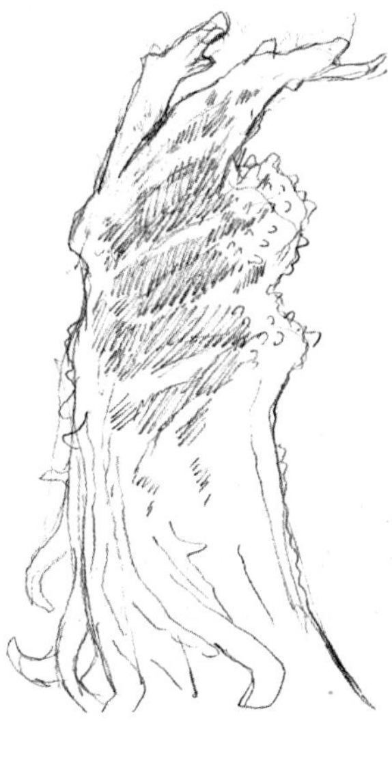

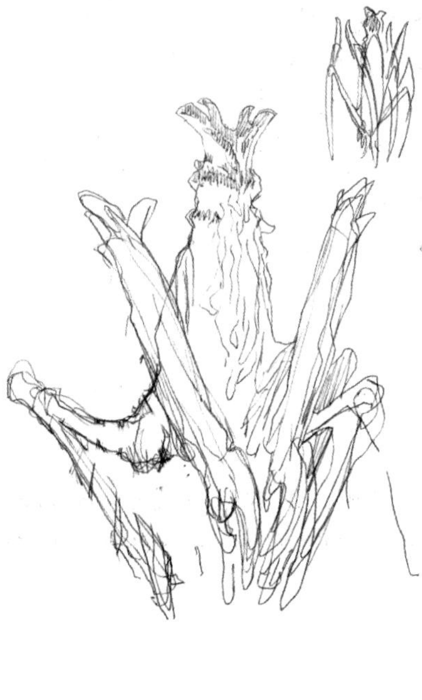

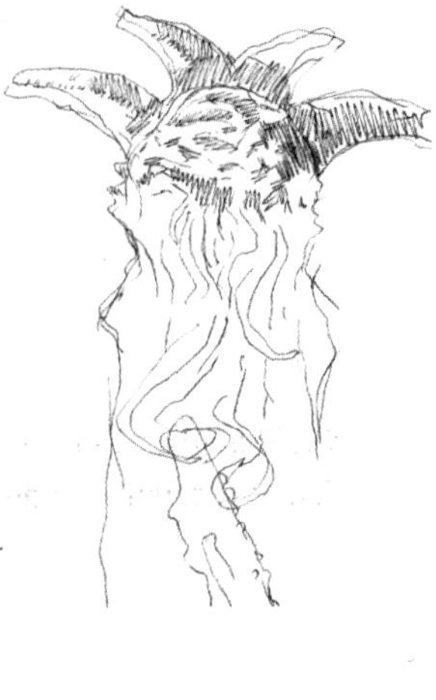

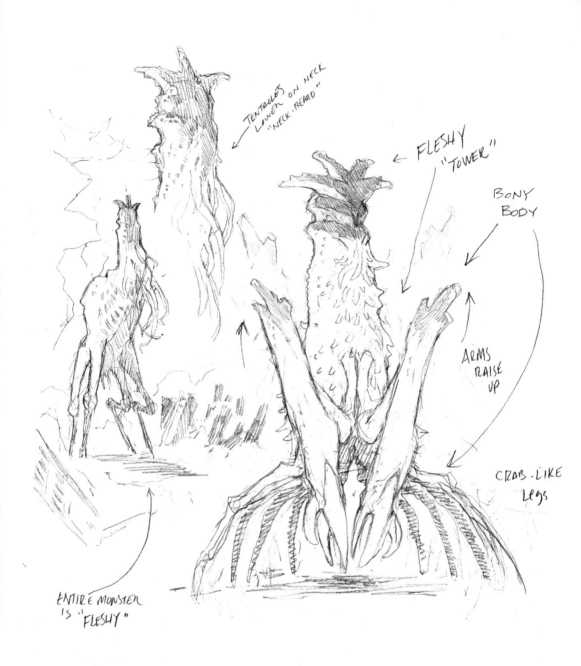

TENTACLES ON NECK
LOWER "NECK-BEARD"

← FLESHY "TOWER"

BONY BODY

ARMS RAISE UP

CRAB-LIKE LEGS

ENTIRE MONSTER IS "FLESHY"

JQ: (Opposite) This guy is one of my favorites. Six astronauts smashed into one living organism. I was beaming with excitement when I read the pages with these hopeless "Challengers of the Unknown," as John described them. John wrote to me, "Just imagine an evil god using a bunch of bodies to make a big doll. He pulls off some pieces, smashes others together, and then there's this thing that can walk, and punch, and it can breathe because of the heads, but otherwise, it's just thrashing around." Seriously, who wouldn't be stoked about getting to design that!

Following page: Final design.

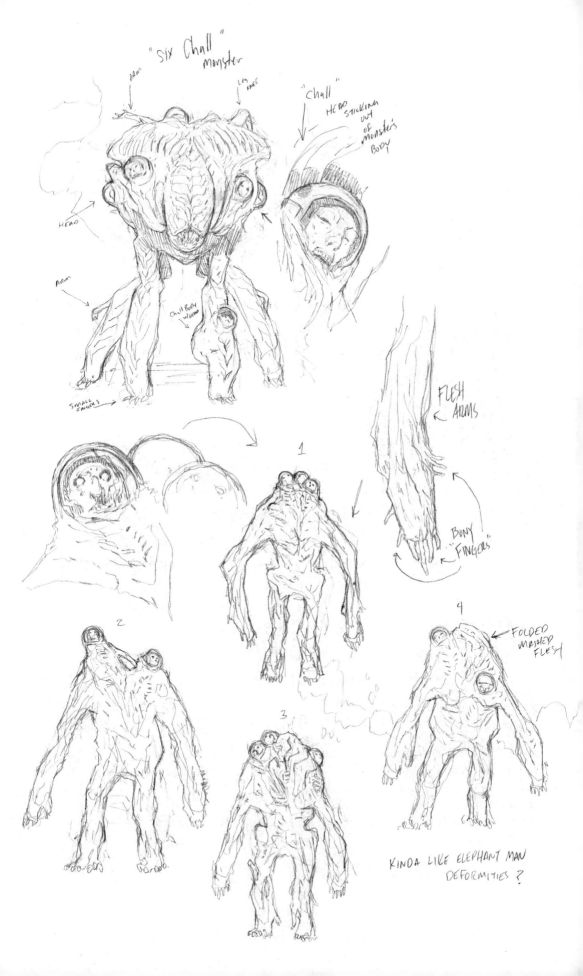

"Six Chall" monster

arm

leg knee

"chall"
HEAD
STICKING
OUT
OF
MONSTER'S
BODY

HEAD

arm

Chall Body w/head

SMALL FINGERS

FLESH ARMS

BONY "FINGERS"

1

2

3

4

FOLDED MASHED FLESH

KINDA LIKE ELEPHANT MAN DEFORMITIES?

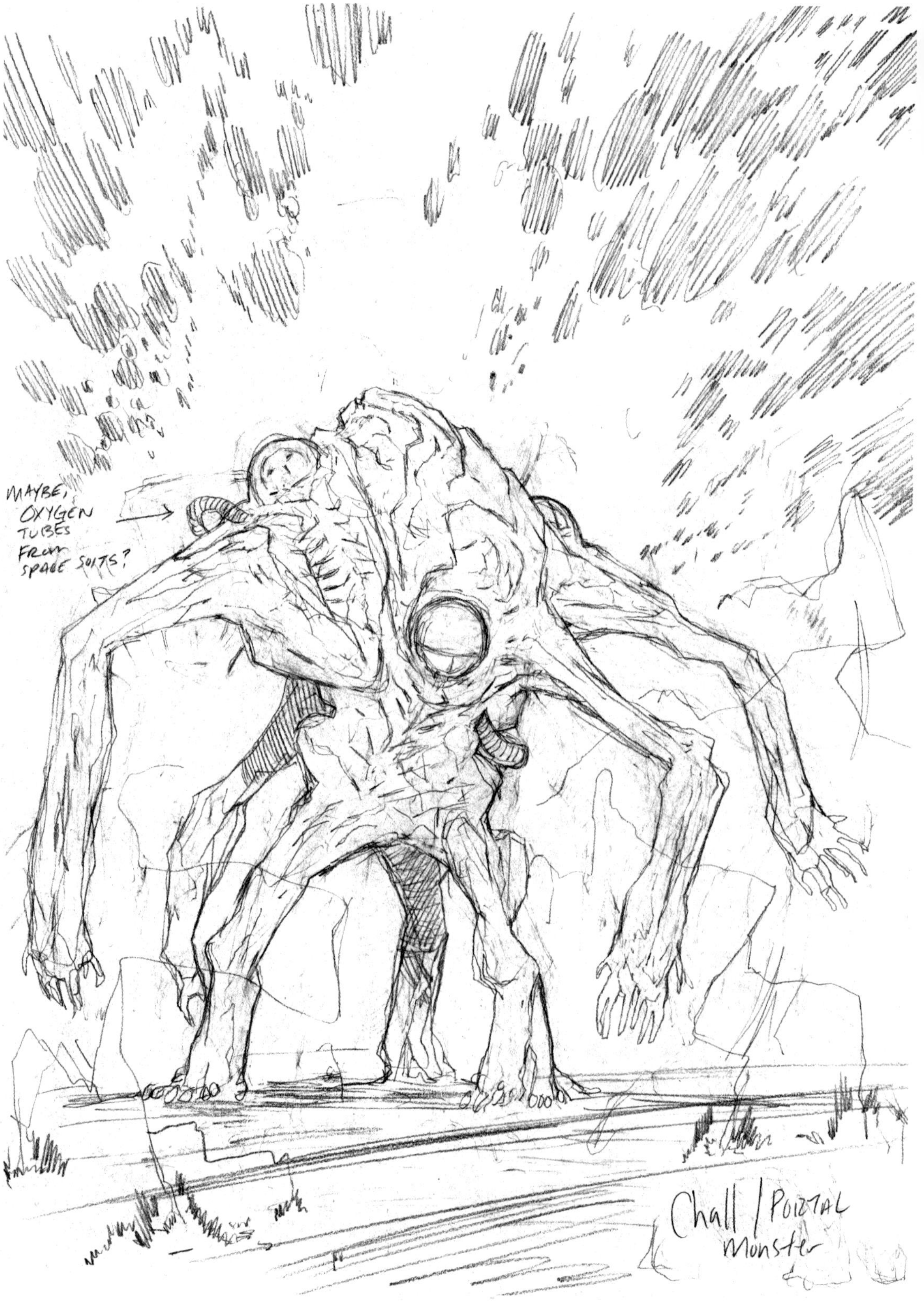
MAYBE, OXYGEN TUBES FROM SPACE SUITS?
Chall / PORTAL monster

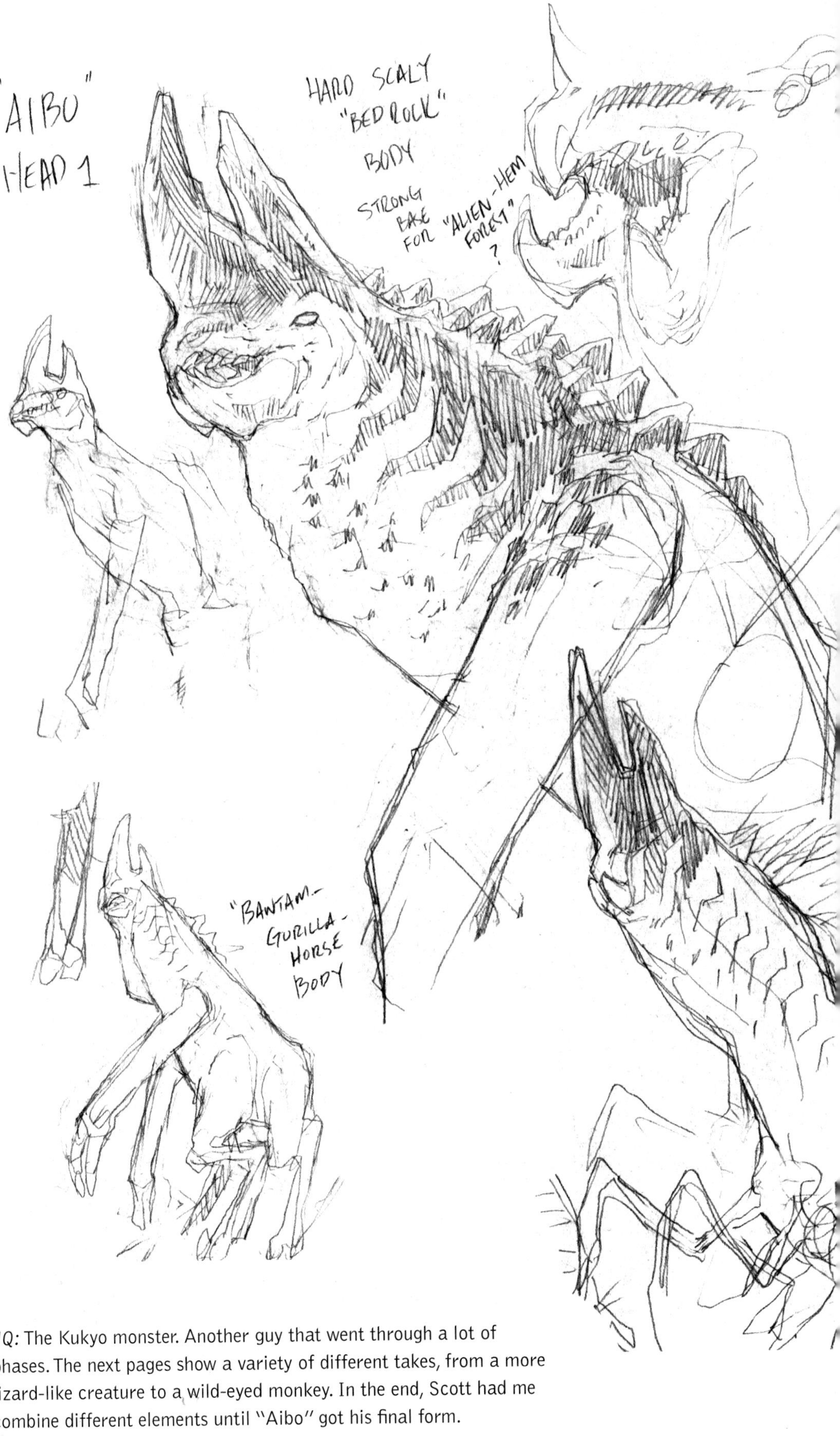
"AIBO"
HEAD 1
HARD SCALY
"BEDROCK"
BODY
STRONG
BASE
FOR "ALIEN-HEM
FOREST"
?
"BANTAM-
GORILLA-
HORSE
BODY

JQ: The Kukyo monster. Another guy that went through a lot of phases. The next pages show a variety of different takes, from a more lizard-like creature to a wild-eyed monkey. In the end, Scott had me combine different elements until "Aibo" got his final form.

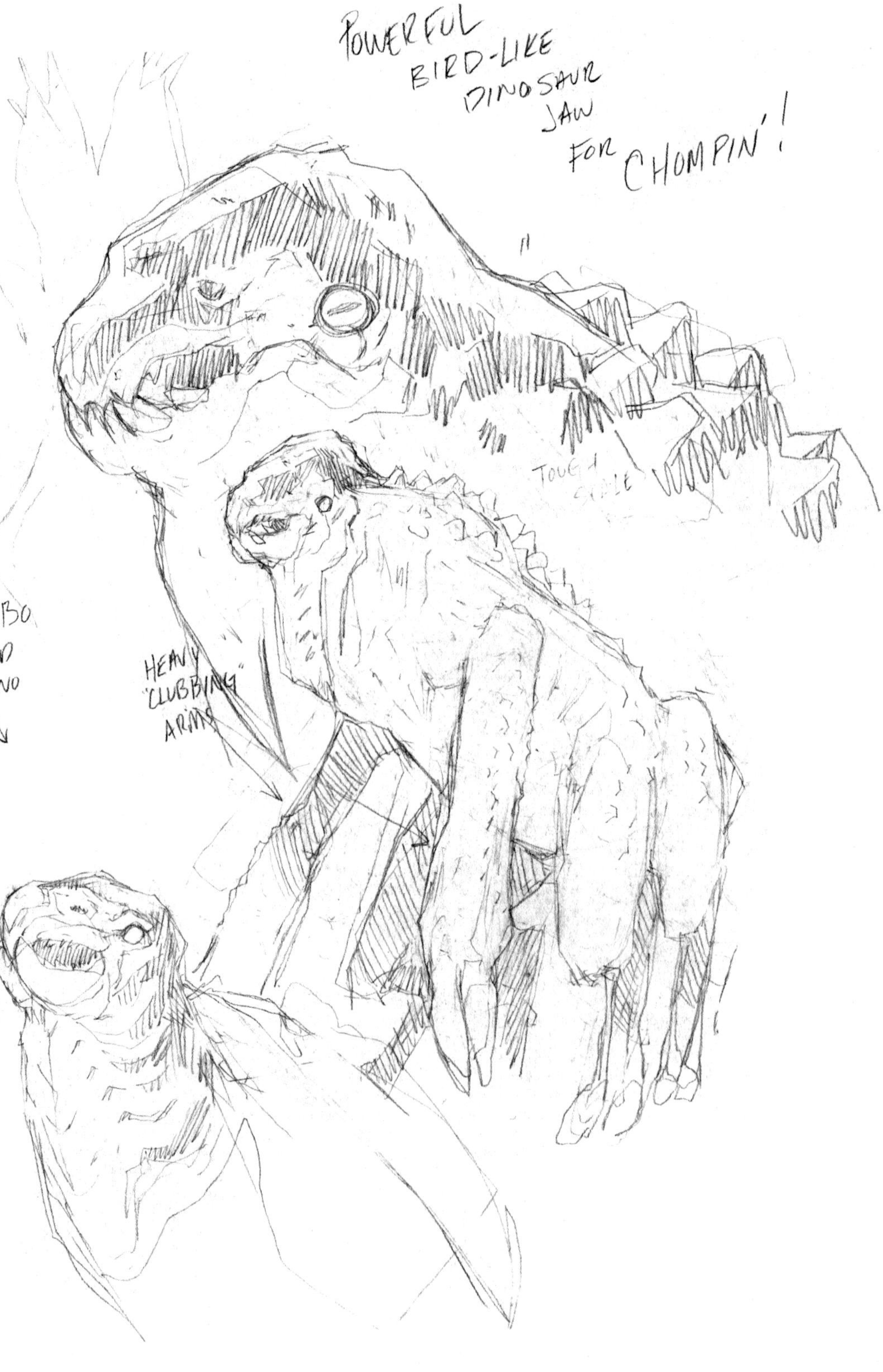
POWERFUL BIRD-LIKE DINOSAUR JAW FOR CHOMPIN'!
TOUGH
AIBO HEAD TWO
HEAVY "CLUBBING" ARMS

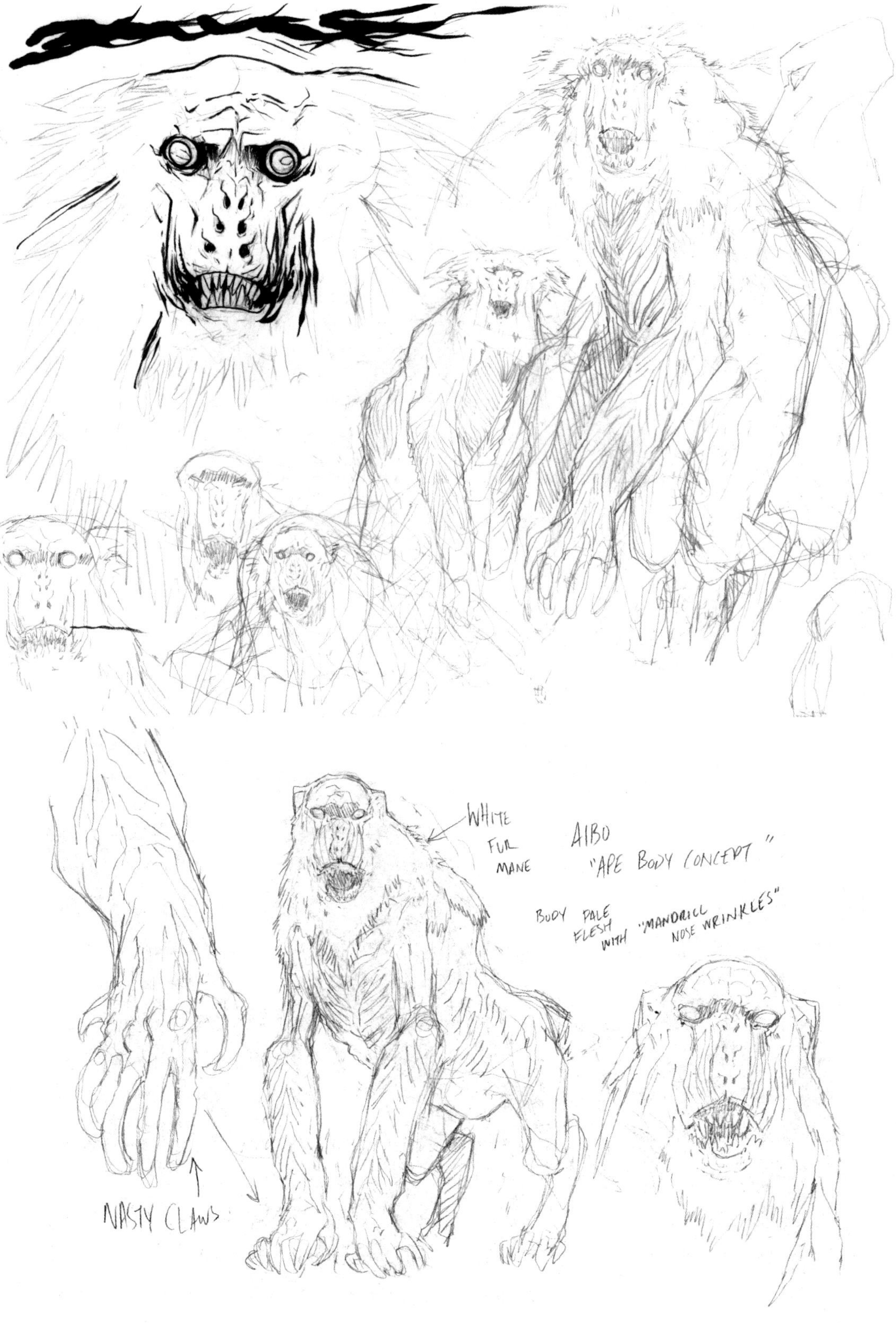
WHITE FUR MANE
AIBO
"APE BODY CONCEPT"
BODY PALE FLESH WITH "MANDRILL NOSE WRINKLES"
NASTY CLAWS

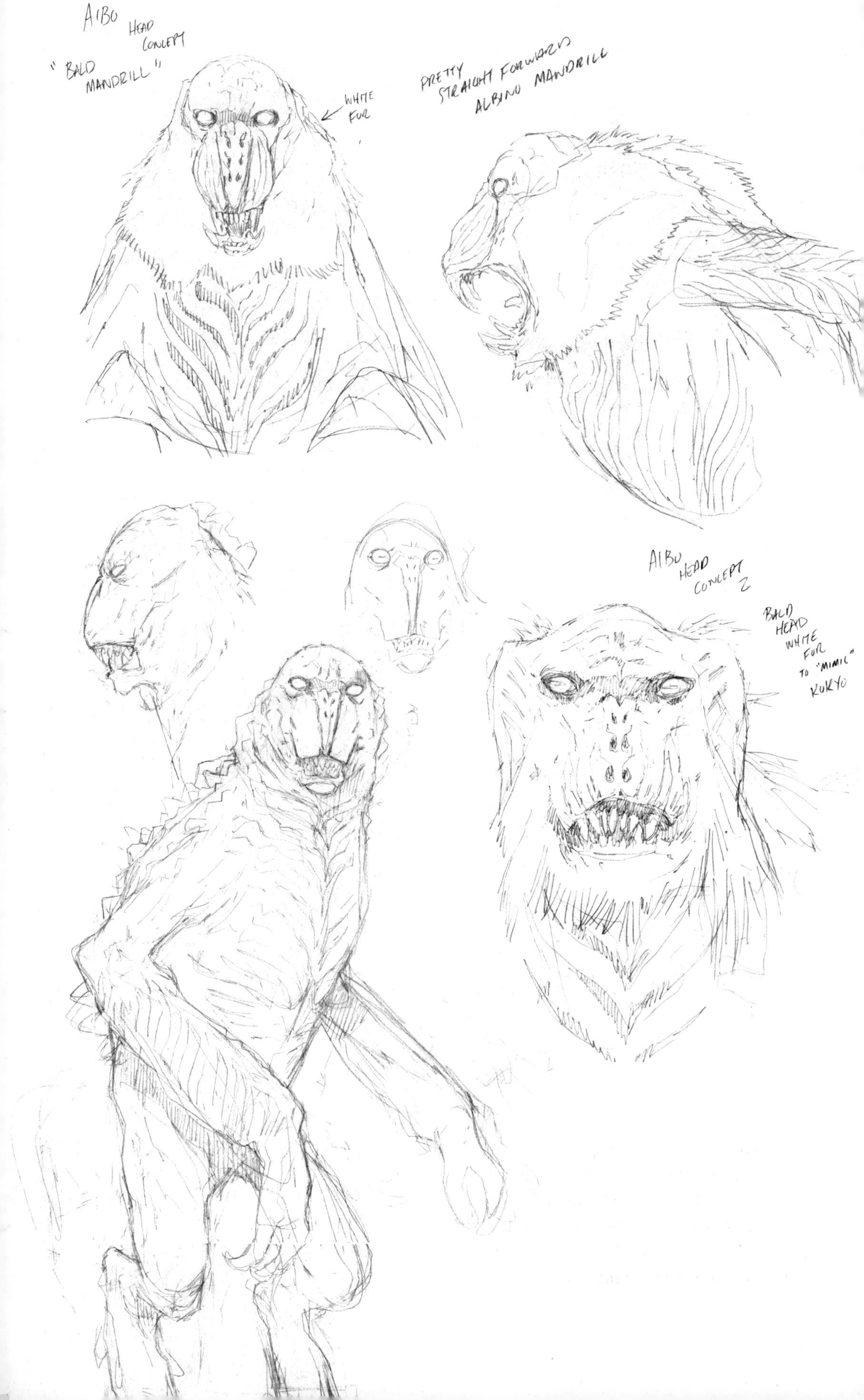
AIBO HEAD CONCEPT
"BALD MANDRILL"
WHITE FUR
PRETTY STRAIGHT FORWARD ALBINO MANDRILL
AIBO HEAD CONCEPT 2
BALD HEAD WHITE FUR TO "MIMIC" KUKYO

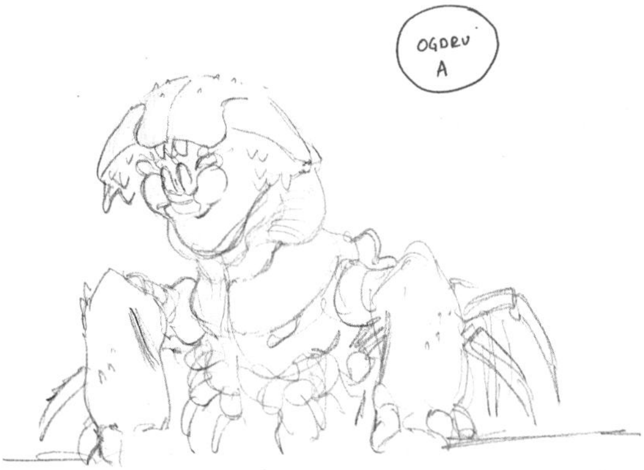
OGDRU
A

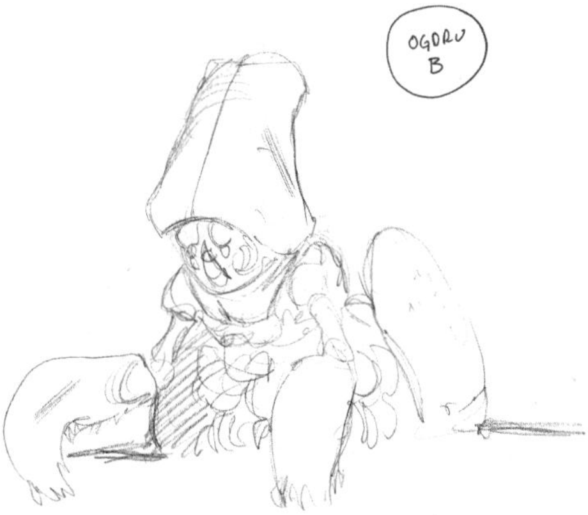
OGDRU
B

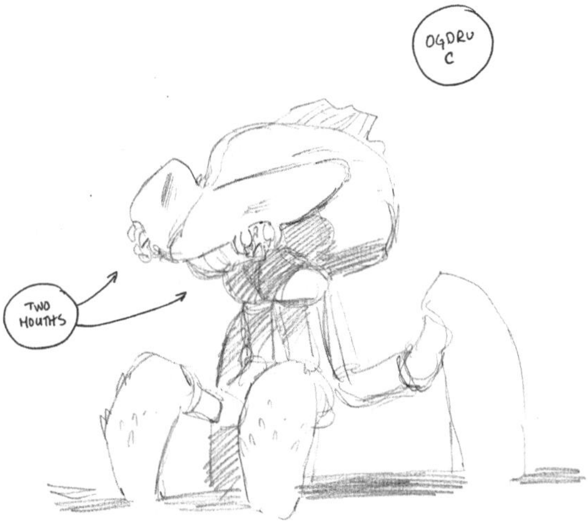
OGDRU
C
TWO MOUTHS

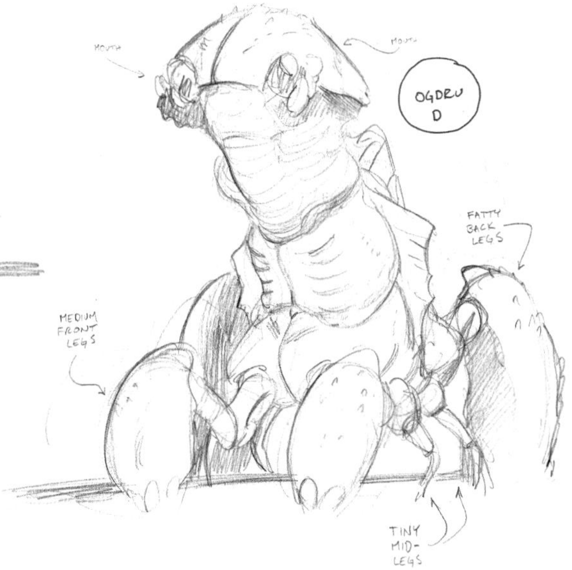
MOUTH
MOUTH
OGDRU
D
FATTY BACK LEGS
MEDIUM FRONT LEGS
TINY MID-LEGS

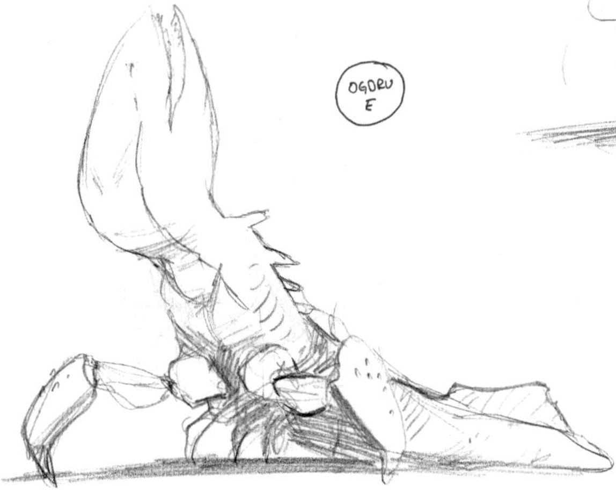
OGDRU
E

Tyler Crook: At this point it's getting harder and harder to come up with new and unique Ogdru designs that still look like they belong to the same family. There is a very specific aesthetic to these things, but that can kind of limit you at the end of the day.

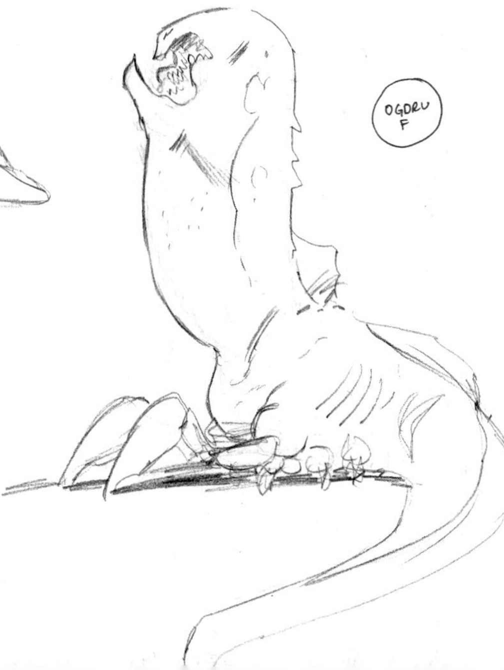
OGDRU
F

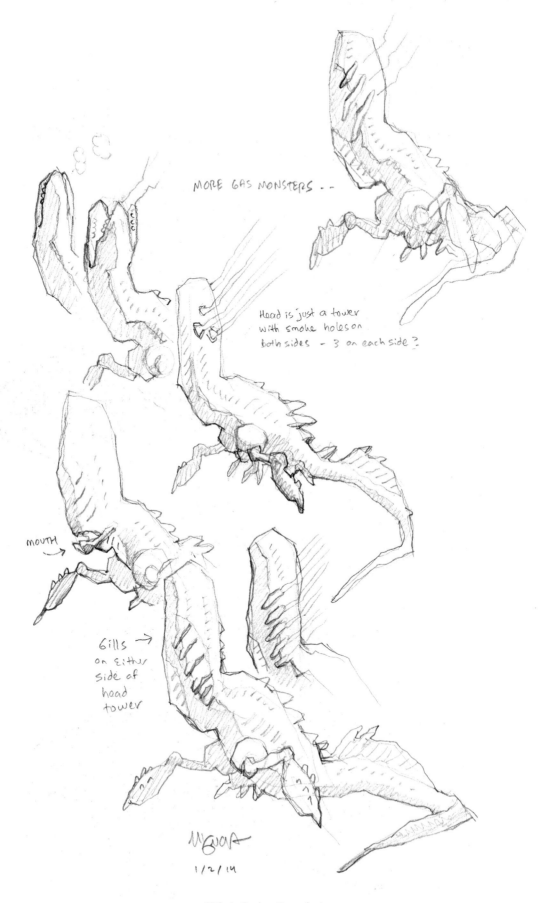

MORE GAS MONSTERS --

Head is just a tower
with smoke holes on
both sides - 3 on each side?

MOUTH →

Gills →
on either
side of
head
tower

1/2/14

Mike's Ogdru Hem design.

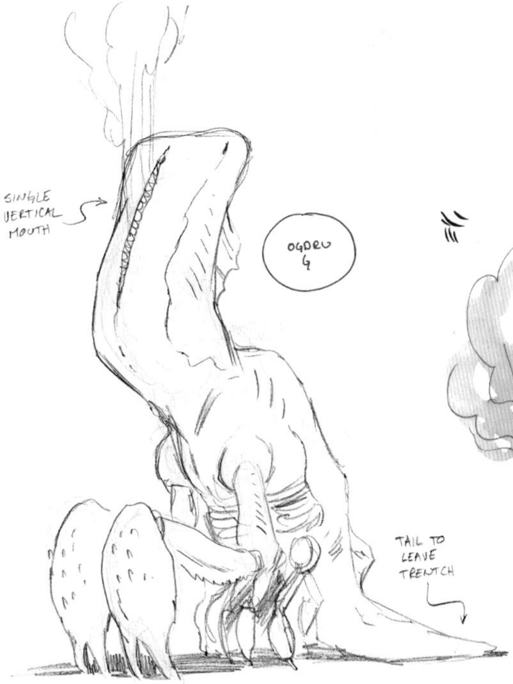
SINGLE VERTICAL MOUTH
OGDRU G
TAIL TO LEAVE TRENTCH

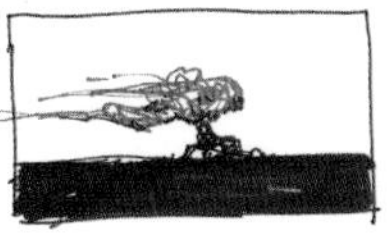

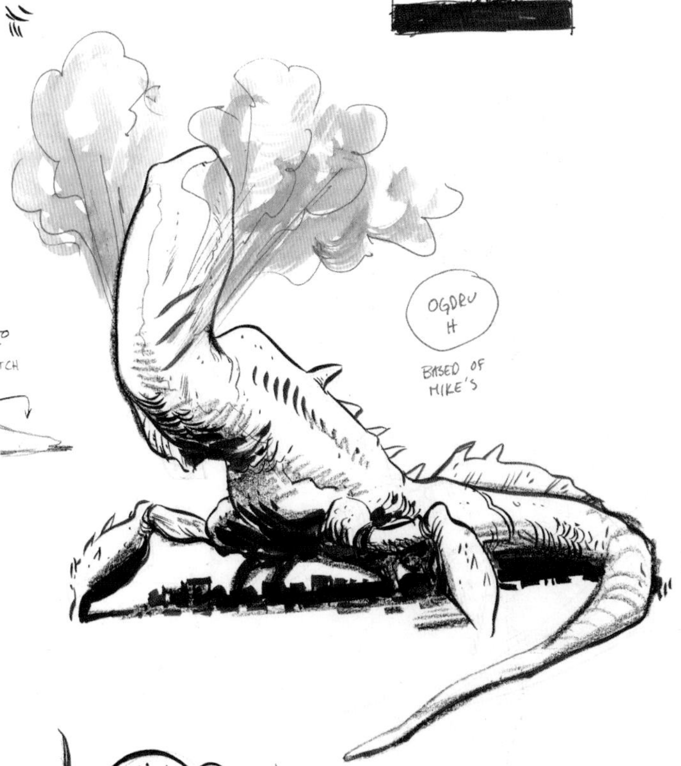
OGDRU H
BASED OF MIKE'S

TC: We finally landed on the guy to the right. He needed to puff out that mutating gas, so we figured these gill things would get the job done. Mike did a pass, and then I did my version of Mike's pass.

This fungus/triffid thing is basically every kind of weird fungus I could find, crammed together.

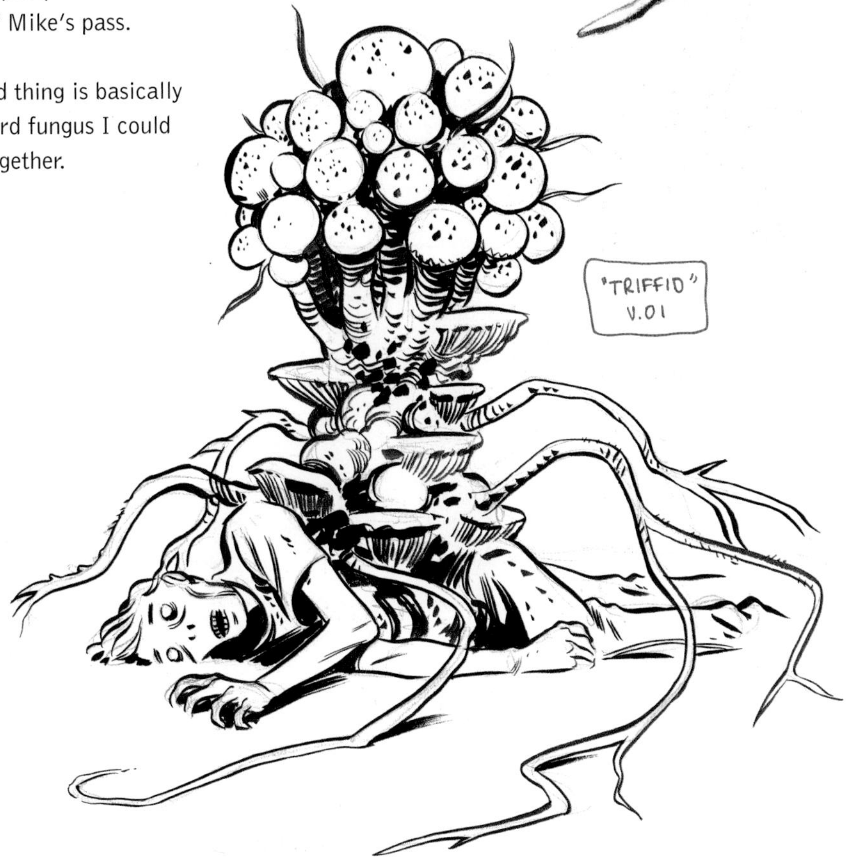
"TRIFFID" V.01

Laurence Campbell: B.P.R.D. #120–#121 cover roughs. Being asked to draw covers for *B.P.R.D.* was a great honor. These issues featured the first appearance of teenage Hellboy, so this was a baptism by fire. After reading the scripts I realized the two-parter featured two objects important to the arc—the dog tags and the wings badge. I came to the decision quickly to try to focus on these objects and use them as the connection between what was happening in the past and the present. #120 A and #121 A were my first ideas. It was then a case of just making sure all the design elements fit together after that.

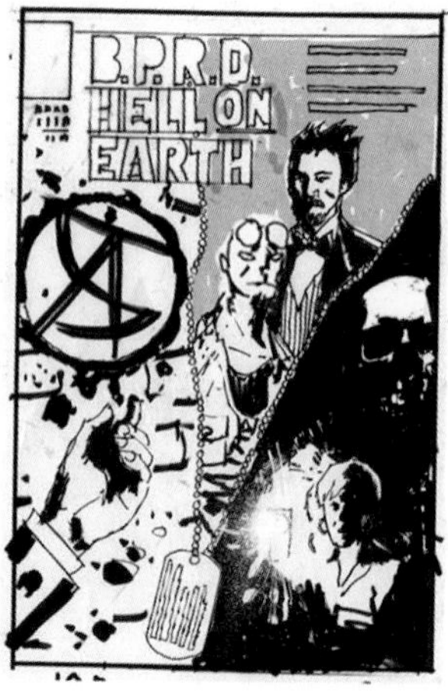

B.P.R.D.
HELL ON
EARTH

120 A •

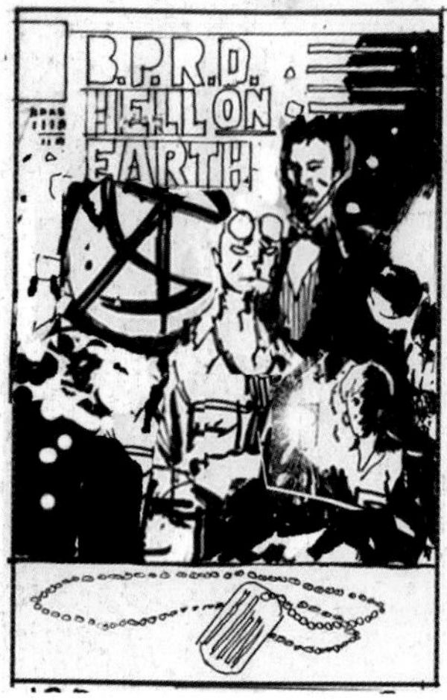

B.P.R.D.
HELL ON
EARTH

120 B

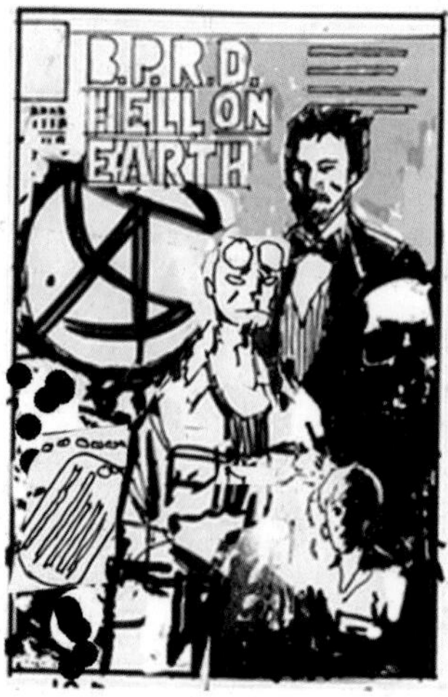

B.P.R.D.
HELL ON
EARTH

120 C

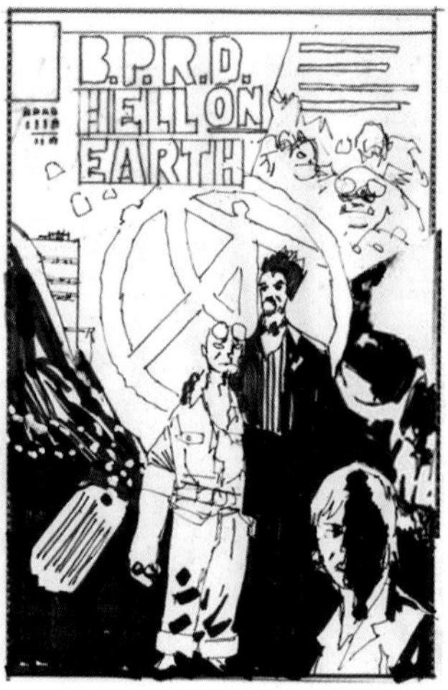

B.P.R.D.
HELL ON
EARTH

120 C

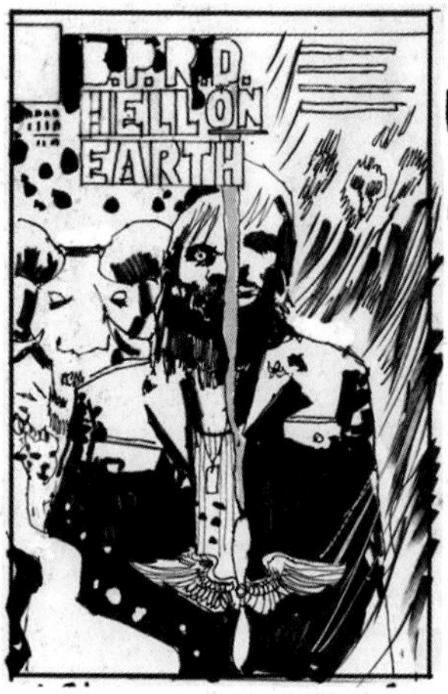

B.P.R.D.
HELL ON
EARTH

121 A •

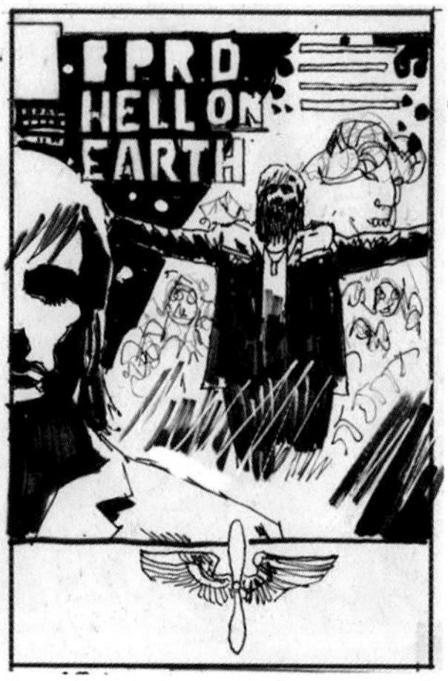

B.P.R.D.
HELL ON
EARTH

121 B

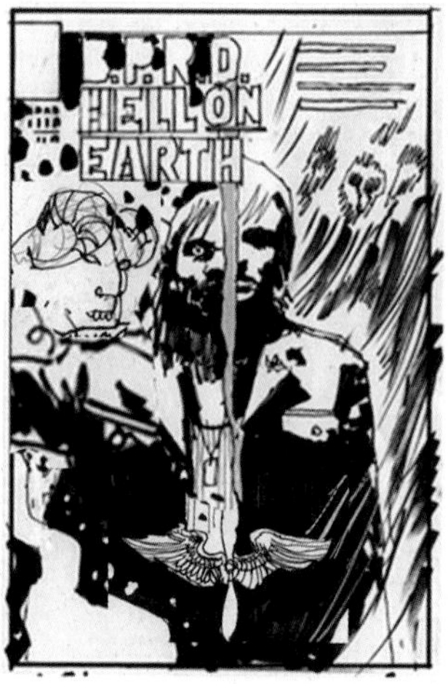

B.P.R.D.
HELL ON
EARTH

121 C

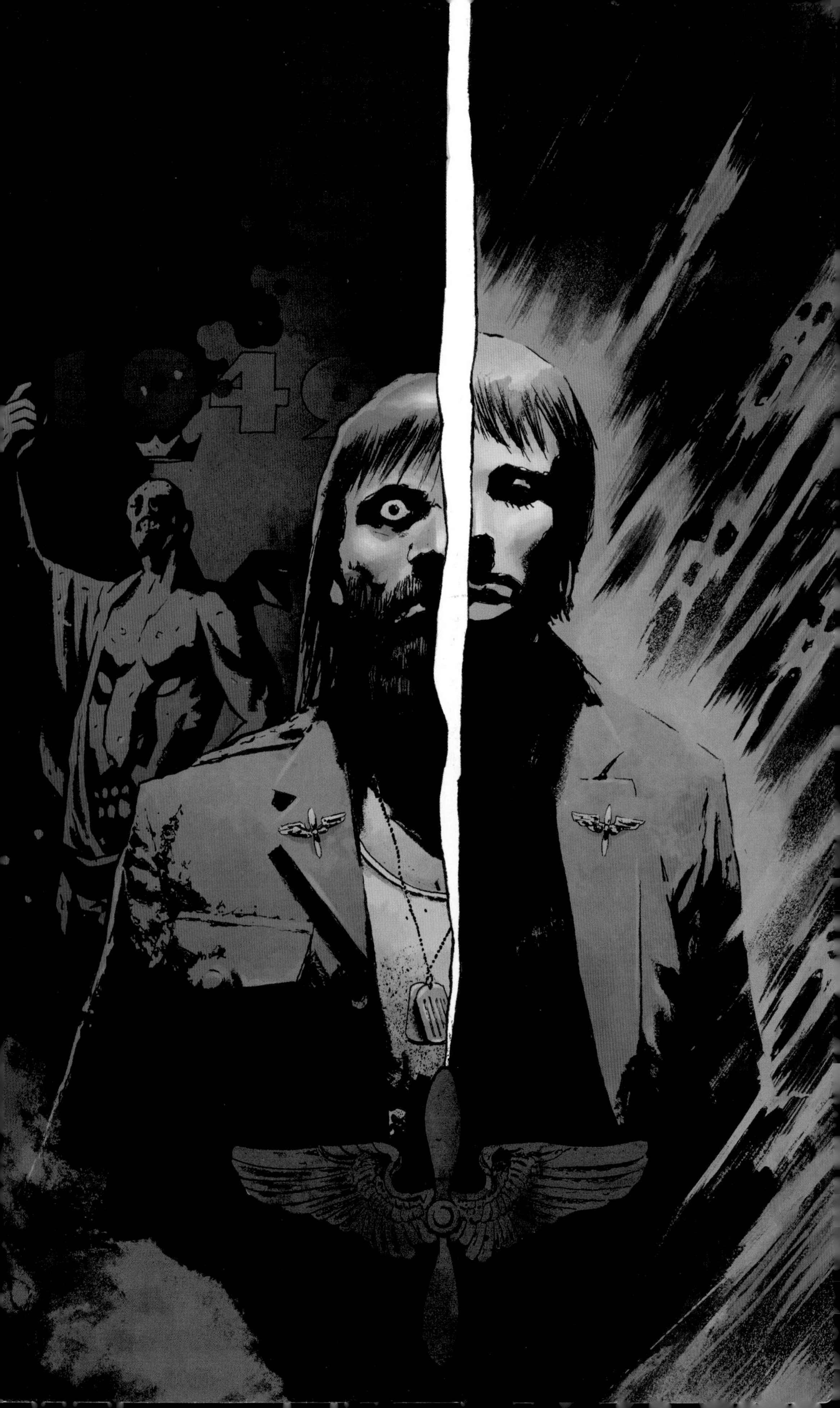

LC: B.P.R.D. #122–#123 cover roughs. The story is set in Japan. I wanted to capture this but in a subtle way. The thought of a red disk similar to what's used on the Japanese flag came pretty quickly; it's a great graphic image. John had given an excellent description of this old guy in a chair with drawings all around him and a gateway behind him. It took some time to connect the gateway to the shape of the red disk, but once I did it flowed very quickly from there. Add "Kirby Krackle" and I was happy.

With the cover for #123, I wanted to give a nod to Godzilla and *kaiju*. We were going to go with version D when Ryan Sook came up with an amazing image for the trade cover. Dark Horse went for another of Ryan's covers for the trade but thought this cover was too good not to use, so I worked with Ryan's rough—which was anything but. To be honest, Ryan did all the heavy lifting on this one.

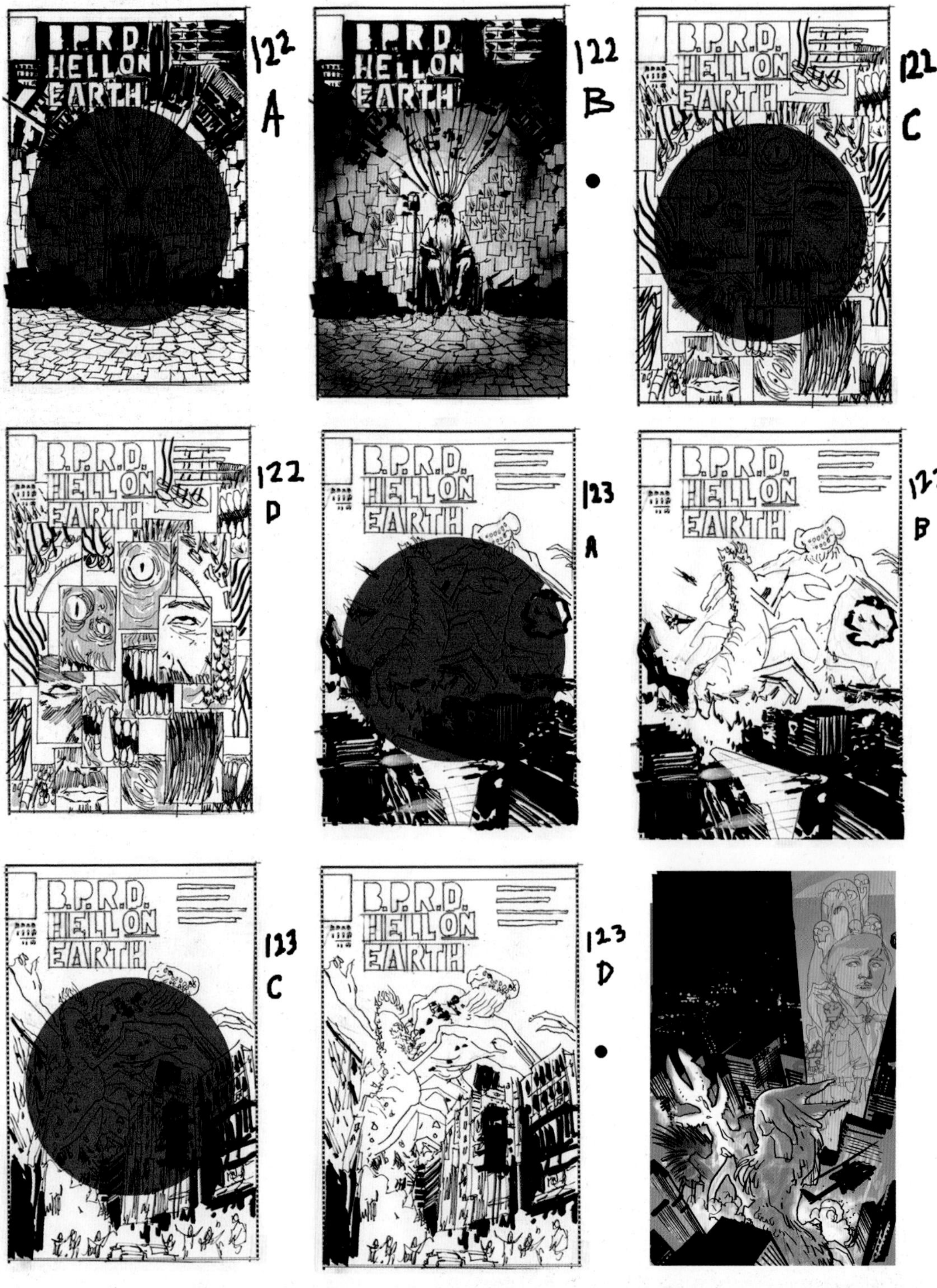
B.P.R.D. HELL ON EARTH
122 A
122 B
122 C
122 D
123 A
123 B
123 C
123 D

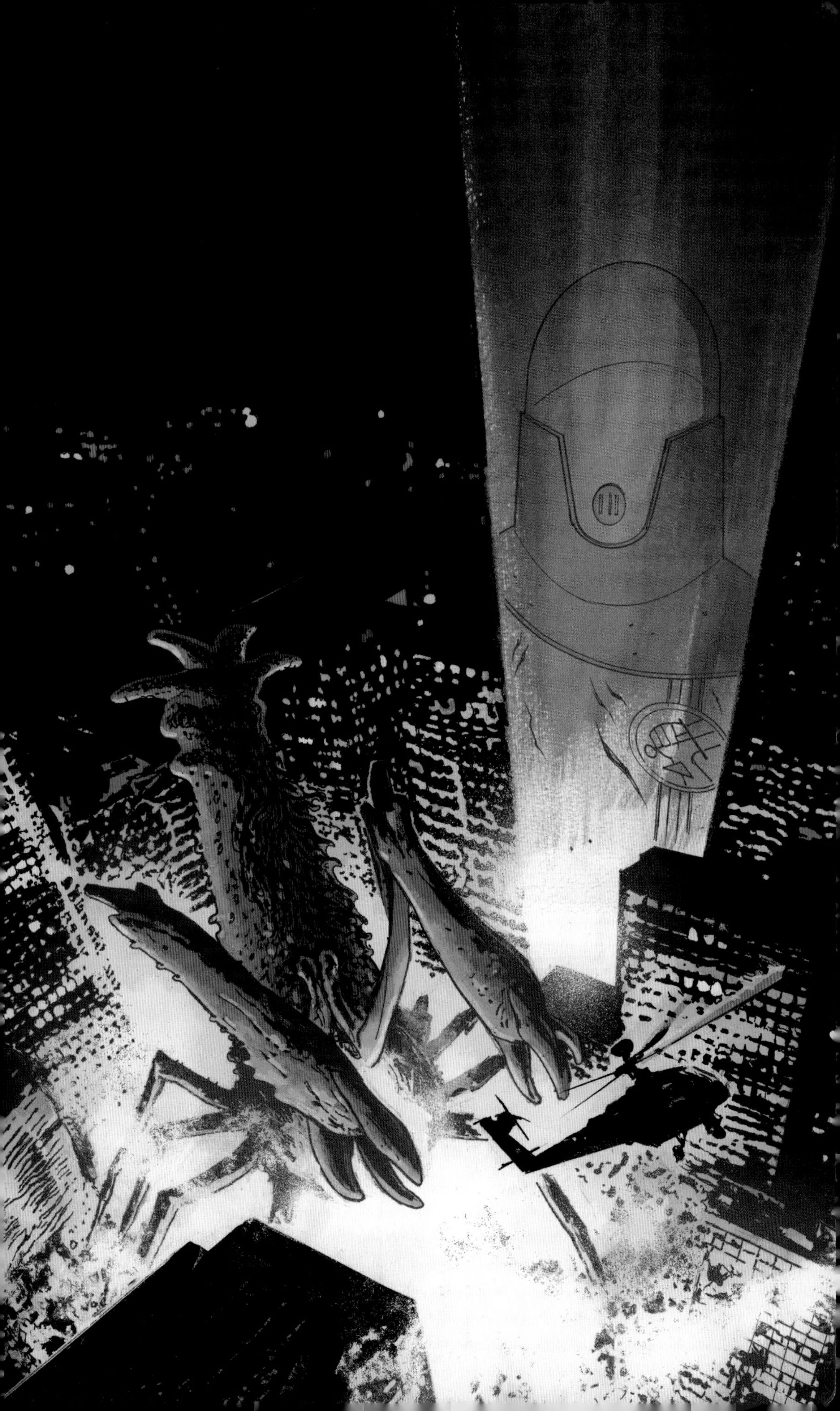

LC: Cover to #124. After reading the script, the final image pretty much came into my head straightaway. Love the idea of two BPRD agents talking over coffee while outside all hell is happening. Probably the easiest cover I've done and probably one of my favorites so far. Wish it was like that all the time.

It also needs to be said that it's always a pleasure working with Dave Stewart on the covers. Frankly, he's the man who pulls it all together and makes it look good.

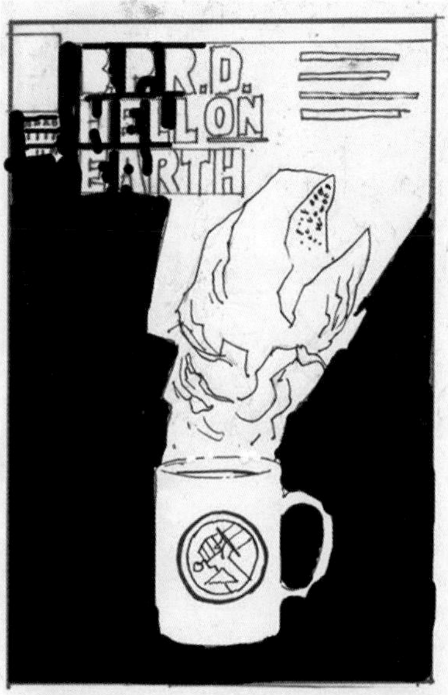
R.D.
LL ON
RTH

A

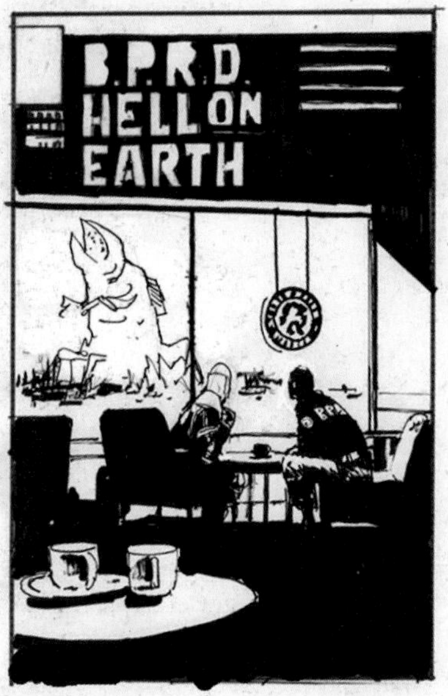
B.P.R.D.
HELL ON
EARTH

B

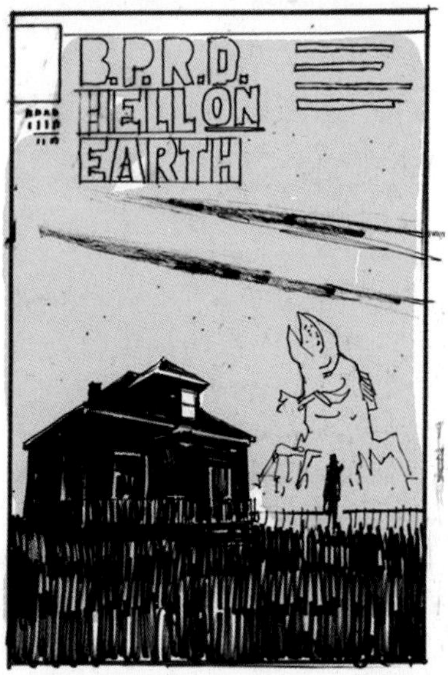
B.P.R.D.
HELL ON
EARTH

C

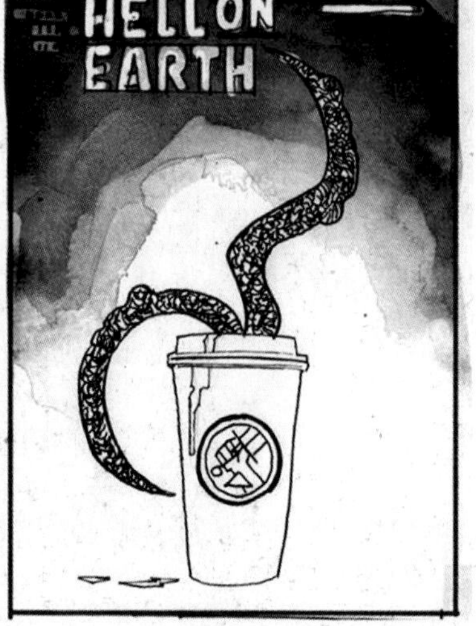
BPRD
HELL ON
EARTH

D

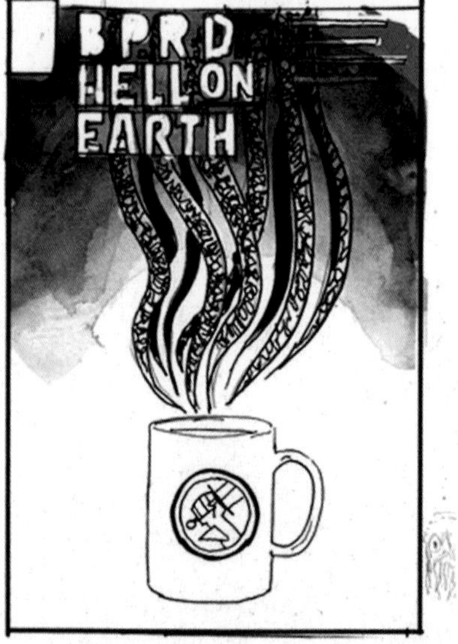
BPRD
HELL ON
EARTH

E

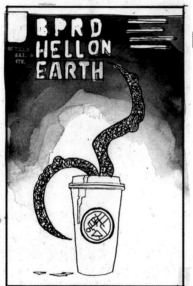

Also by MIKE MIGNOLA

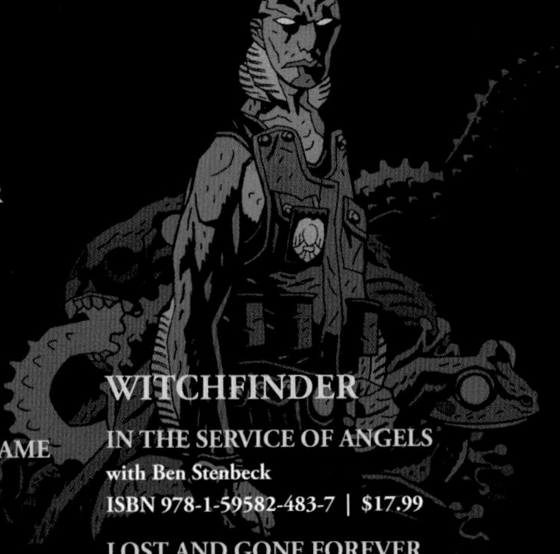

3.P.R.D.

ʾLAGUE OF FROGS
ʾolume 1
ʋith Chris Golden, Guy Davis, and others
ƎC: ISBN 978-1-59582-609-1 | $34.99
ʾPB: ISBN 978-1-59582-675-6 | $19.99

ʾolume 2
ʋith John Arcudi, Davis, and others
ƎC: ISBN 978-1-59582-672-5 | $34.99
ʾPB: ISBN 978-1-59582-676-3 | $24.99

ʾolume 3
ʋith Arcudi and Davis
SBN 978-1-59582-860-6 | $34.99

ʾolume 4
ʋith Arcudi and Davis
SBN 978-1-59582-974-0 | $34.99

1946
ʋith Joshua Dysart and Paul Azaceta
SBN 978-1-59582-191-1 | $17.99

.947
ʋith Dysart, Fábio Moon, and Gabriel Bá
SBN 978-1-59582-478-3 | $17.99

.948
ʋith Arcudi and Max Fiumara
SBN 978-1-61655-183-4 | $17.99

3EING HUMAN
ʋith Scott Allie, Arcudi, Davis, and others
SBN 978-1-59582-756-2 | $17.99

ʌAMPIRE
ʋith Moon and Bá
SBN 978-1-61655-196-4 | $19.99

B.P.R.D. HELL ON EARTH

ɴEW WORLD
ʋith Arcudi and Davis
SBN 978-1-59582-707-4 | $19.99

ɢODS AND MONSTERS
ʋith Arcudi, Davis, and Tyler Crook
SBN 978-1-59582-822-4 | $19.99

RUSSIA
ʋith Arcudi, Crook, and Duncan Fegredo
SBN 978-1-59582-946-7 | $19.9

THE DEVIL'S ENGINE
AND THE LONG DEATH
with Arcudi, Crook, and James Harren
ISBN 978-1-59582-981-8 | $19.99

THE PICKENS COUNTY
HORROR AND OTHERS
with Allie, Jason Latour, Harren,
and Max Fiumara
ISBN 978-1-61655-140-7 | $19.99

THE RETURN OF THE MASTER
with Arcudi and Crook
ISBN 978-1-61655-193-3 | $19.99

A COLD DAY IN HELL
with Arcudi, Peter Snejbjerg, and
Laurence Campbell
ISBN 978-1-61655-199-5 | $19.99

THE REIGN OF THE BLACK FLAME
with Arcudi and Harren
ISBN 978-1-61655-471-2 | $19.99

THE DEVIL'S WINGS
with Arcudi, Campbell, Joe Querio, and Crook
ISBN 978-1-61655-617-4 | $19.99

LAKE OF FIRE
with Arcudi and Crook
ISBN 978-1-61655-402-6 | $19.99

ABE SAPIEN

THE DROWNING
with Jason Shawn Alexander
ISBN 978-1-59582-185-0 | $17.99

THE DEVIL DOES NOT JEST AND
OTHER STORIES
with Arcudi, Harren, and others
ISBN 978-1-59582-925-2 | $17.99

DARK AND TERRIBLE
AND THE NEW RACE OF MAN
with Allie, Arcudi, Sebastián
Fiumara, and Max Fiumara
ISBN 978-1-61655-284-8 | $19.99

THE SHAPE OF THINGS TO COME
with Allie, S. Fiumara, and M. Fiumara
ISBN 978-1-61655-443-9 | $19.99

SACRED PLACES
with Allie, S. Fiumara, and M. Fiumara
ISBN 978-1-61655-515-3 | $19.99

LOBSTER JOHNSON

THE IRON PROMETHEUS
with Jason Armstrong
ISBN 978-1-59307-975-8 | $17.99

THE BURNING HAND
with Arcudi and Tonci Zonjic
ISBN 978-1-61655-031-8 | $17.99

SATAN SMELLS A RAT
with Arcudi, Fiumara, Querio,
Wilfredo Torres, and Kevin Nowlan
ISBN 978-1-61655-203-9 | $18.99

GET THE LOBSTER
with Arcudi and Zonjic
ISBN 978-1-61655-505-4 | $19.99

WITCHFINDER

IN THE SERVICE OF ANGELS
with Ben Stenbeck
ISBN 978-1-59582-483-7 | $17.99

LOST AND GONE FOREVER
with Arcudi and John Severin
ISBN 978-1-59582-794-4 | $17.99

THE MYSTERIES OF UNLAND
with Kim Newman, Maura McHugh,
and Crook
ISBN 978-1-61655-630-3 | $19.99

THE AMAZING SCREW-ON HEAD AND OTHER CURIOUS OBJECTS

ISBN 978-1-59582-501-8 | $17.99

BALTIMORE

THE PLAGUE SHIPS
with Golden and Stenbeck
ISBN 978-1-59582-677-0 | $24.99

THE CURSE BELLS
with Golden and Stenbeck
ISBN 978-1-59582-674-9 | $24.99

A PASSING STRANGER
AND OTHER STORIES
with Golden and Stenbeck
ISBN 978-1-61655-182-7 | $24.99

CHAPEL OF BONES
with Golden and Stenbeck
ISBN 978-1-61655-328-9 | $24.99

THE APOSTLE AND THE WITCH
OF HARJU
with Golden, Stenbeck, and Peter Bergting
ISBN 978-1-61655-618-1 | $24.99

NOVELS

LOBSTER JOHNSON:
THE SATAN FACTORY
with Thomas E. Sniegoski
ISBN 978-1-59582-203-1 | $12.95

JOE GOLEM AND THE
DROWNING CITY
with Golden
ISBN 978-1-59582-971-9 | $99.99

DARK HORSE BOOKS
DarkHorse.com

AVAILABLE AT YOUR LOCAL COMICS SHOP OR BOOKSTORE! • To find a comics shop in your area, call 1-888-266-4226.
For more information or to order direct visit DarkHorse.com or call 1-800-862-0052 Mon.–Fri. 9 AM to 5 PM Pacific Time.
Prices and availability subject to change without notice.

HELLBOY

by MIKE MIGNOLA

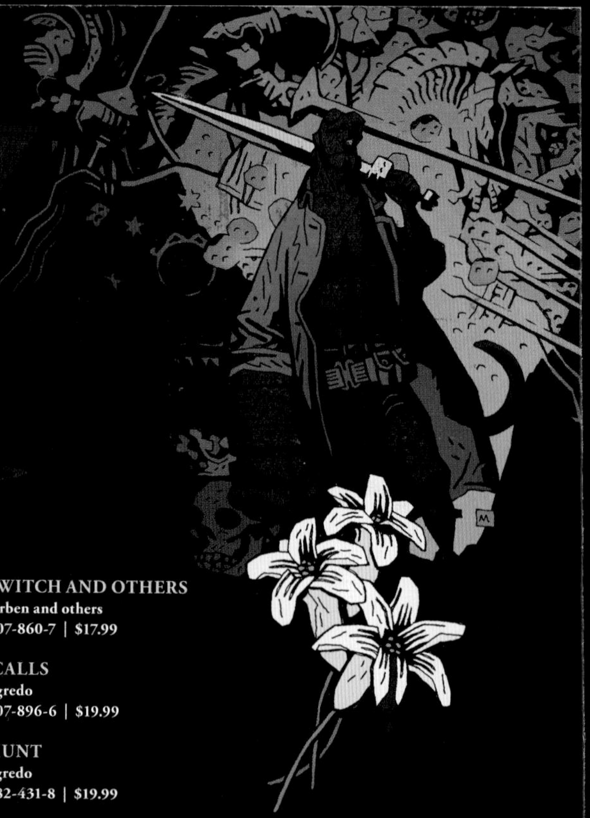